D0403027

PLAYING THE PALACE

PLAYING THE PALACE

A WESTMINSTER COLLECTION

Selected by JAMES NAUGHTIE

First published in 1984 by
MAINSTREAM PUBLISHING COMPANY (EDINBURGH) LTD.
7 Albany Street
Edinburgh EH1 3UG

ISBN 0 906931 73 3

Typeset in 11 point Garamond by Studioscope in conjunction with Mainstream Publishing.
Printed by Forsyth Middleton & Co. Ltd., Kilsyth.

CONTENTS

In memory of my father.

Acknowledgements

MY first debt, and it is enormous, is to the authors who generously gave permission for their work to be included in this collection. They took a risk in doing so: I hope the result is pleasing, and fair. Though politicians' words are public property they have a right to fair treatment as well, and I hope my selections and occasional judgments have not been too harsh. The Press Gallery of the House of Commons is a strange but absorbing and invigorating place and I want now to thank all my colleagues there for their support and comradeship in my work. Some have been particularly close to this book since its rather chaotic beginning (and right up to its frantic end) and my deep gratitude goes to Martin Dowle and Peter Riddell for helping me through at every turn, to Michael White for wise words at the right time, to Bill Russell for the title and to David Bradford, my London editor and an old Westminster hand, for giving me the chance to work there in the first place and encouraging me ever since. To Eric B. Mackay, the editor of *The Scotsman*, I owe a great deal. Below stairs, so to speak, many MPs have been of great assistance in making this selection (some unwittingly) and for their help I offer collective thanks, as well as a preliminary apology to those (some of them distinguished characters) who do not appear in these pages and, perhaps more to the point, to those who do, but in unflattering circumstances. All I can say — and they well know it — is that the Westminster tapestry is rich and glittering and its wide sweep can only be glimpsed, or sensed, in a book like this. If that sounds like an excuse, let me say that this is a personal selection and therefore idiosyncratic and there it is.

Several publishers have kindly given me permission to use material which first appeared in their pages and I am happy to thank them for their co-operation — George Allen and Unwin for passages from *The Glory of Parliament* by Harry Boardman; William Collins Ltd. for entries from *The Diaries of Harold Nicolson*; Victor Gollancz Ltd. for a passage from *Guilty Men* by "Cato"; Hamish Hamilton Ltd. and Jonathan Cape for entries from *The Crossman Diaries* by Richard Crossman (Vols. I and II); David Higham Associates for an extract from *Disraeli in Love* (pub. Collins) by Maurice Edelman, and Robson Books Ltd. for extracts from *Out of Order* by Frank Johnson.

I am grateful too to the editors of *The Scotsman, The Guardian,* the *Daily Telegraph, The Listener,* the *New Statesman* and *The Spectator* for their ready co-operation. The Rt. Hon. Paul Channon, MP, was kind enough to allow me to use passages from his father's diaries (*Chips: The Diaries of Sir Henry Channon*, ed. Robert Rhodes James, Penguin, 1970) and for that I am especially grateful.

Staff at Her Majesty's Stationery Office have been helpful in advising me on the use of *Hansard*. All passages identified as speeches were delivered in the House of Commons, unless otherwise stated, and all nineteenth- and twentieth-century speeches are taken from Hansard's *Parliamentary Debates*, later the House of Commons *Official Report*. As will be obvious, speeches are not reproduced in full but I have edited them in a way which I hope preserves the sense and spirit of the whole. I have not indicated where the start of an extract does not coincide with the start of the original speech, but all subsequent editorial leaps are clearly marked. Earlier speeches, for which records are less reliable, are reproduced in the versions now accepted as the most generally accurate. In speeches and in writing from the gallery I have tried to preserve the style of each extract as it was written, spoken or recorded, even where this results in differences of grammar, punctuation or style among extracts.

Finally, I owe a great debt to my publishers, Bill Campbell and Peter MacKenzie, who have shown more patience than I deserve and a cheerful understanding of the journalist's temperament ("there's always another quarter of an hour . . .") which has made life surprisingly pleasurable of late.

Fortunately I am not responsible for any of the opinions in this collection, save my own. But I confess that any mistakes are mine alone.

J.N.

Introduction

by

JAMES NAUGHTIE

THE Palace of Westminster is a Victorian masterpiece, bold and extravagant in design and, in its day, a physical assertion of great self-confidence in the imperial Parliament. Since the old Queen marked the virtual completion of the familiar building in 1852 that self-confidence has remained, though it has taken many different forms. More than a century of reform in the franchise and the powers of the Commons and the Lords has changed the political game, but the arena has the same capacity to thrill, to terrify, to humble. The social world of politics has gone through a revolution — perhaps several — but the intoxicating quality of Parliamentary life remains. Westminster still casts a spell.

It is not something felt by the politicians alone, though their lifestyle encourages them to believe in the exclusive nature of their experience, but by anyone who watches that Westminster world. Looking down from the reporters' gallery in the House of Commons, listening to speeches and spying the characters, is participating in the Parliamentary theatre. This sense of belonging is a dangerous one, especially for journalists, and it has an attraction that sometimes reduces correspondents to the role of a supporting cast, dancing to order and leaving the stage when required. But it is possible to express the special quality of the place without losing completely a proper sense of distance from those leading players whose performances in the pursuit of power and fame are the stuff of the political theatre. As a balancing act it can be dangerous, but maybe that is why it is so enjoyable.

The purpose of this collection is to try to catch that spirit, with its attractions and its darker side. Why should the great speeches be separated from some of the observer's jottings? Or the reflections of diarists? Or, indeed, the novelists' accounts of Parliamentary life? Anthologies of oratorical masterpieces tend to be dull, perhaps not so much because the speeches do not read well — almost all the best ones do — but because they somehow seem out of context on the written page, taken away from the atmosphere of the Commons or the Lords, cleaned up with antiseptic.

To enjoy some of the best speeches it is worth reading alongside some of the good contemporary writing from the gallery (or indeed from outside Westminster — Samuel Johnson visited the Commons only once, but can't be ignored). Only a backbencher can express the true horror of the tedious side of the Commons, the long nights spent waiting to do the party's duty in the lobbies or to engage in a pointless Parliamentary manoeuvre for a fleeting moment of political advantage, and it takes a Minister to tell just how it feels to experience the weird ritual of the Privy Council in the late twentieth century. That sense of experience is the context in which political speeches are delivered, and shouldn't be forgotten.

No one who has watched even a moderately dramatic scene in the Commons can fail to scent the thrill of the political struggle that drives the performers on: it's at its best when the combat is fiercest, and at its most pompous and self-indulgent when the clash of ideas becomes, from time to time, less important than the dignity of the Parliamentary game.

That is why much of the criticism of the alleged rabble spread over the green leather benches in the Commons is misplaced. Politics is not a bloodless business, and a Parliamentary way of life dictated by gentlemen's rules would be feeble indeed. The rules — and there are many of them — change quickly with events and with personalities, reflecting the mood of the place as much as they dictate it. Certainly there are strong Speakers and weak Speakers, but none can do more than hold the Commons back from its worst excesses and encourage it, fairly gently, to calm down. It's simply not possible to curb its life completely. The theatre thrives on tension among the players and with the audience, and so does national politics.

The tension helps to produce the great performances. Imagine the Don Pacifico debate in 1850, stretching through four long summer nights, in which Gladstone, Disraeli, Bright, Peel, Lord John Russell and Palmerston all spoke — the sense of drama, even in the yellowed pages of old *Hansards*, is gripping. There are, in every Parliamentary session, moments like that (though few which could so effectively captivate the imagination as that fabled debate). The dying moments of a Government; a resignation speech; one of those unexpected announcements of a new conflict, or a death or a disaster; a Ministerial blunder which leaves everyone knowing that the words will haunt the poor figure at the Dispatch Box for years to come. All have their own special place in the Commons' folk memory, embellished and cherished over the years to reinforce its feel for itself.

But how to select it? No one can approach the *Hansard* shelves or the newspaper archives without a sinking feeling of hopelessness. It goes on and on: and relief only comes when you decide reluctantly that any effort to be comprehensive (or, even, fair) is doomed to fail. Then, you can have fun. So this is a declaration: the fact that a reader's favourite speech, or a particularly well-loved character, appears nowhere in these pages is irrelevant to the purpose of this collection. It is neither a historical survey of Parliament (which would take as many years as volumes to produce) nor a carefully judged selection designed to present one view of politics or history or personality. It is just an almost random collection of fine moments, amusing and significant in maybe equal quantities. If it informs, well and good. But its purpose is to enlighten by entertainment, not by the exercise of an editor's didactic hand.

So enthusiasts for Stanley Baldwin, who find that his words have been omitted, or those who thrill to the oratory of Sir Henry Campbell-Bannerman, or even Lord Salisbury, will have to look elsewhere. And anyone who complains about the ever-present Disraeli or Churchill or Gladstone should remember that it is the giants whose footprints are still most clearly visible, and most easily traced. Their efforts, and the performances of others like them, have given the place the character this collection seeks to convey. It was their mastery of the Dispatch Box and the Parliamentary forum that give it its potency, which has survived the efforts of lesser mortals to make it all more predictable and tedious. Imagination and style, in the presentation of politics, have always been the necessary components of success (if not virtue) and without them there would be no point in celebrating it.

But is it just a celebration of the past? In collecting the accounts of great moments and the finest speeches it is impossible to avoid the feeling that this is still a Victorian Parliament, and that therefore its glory is fading. This is no romantic view — a subconscious wish to return to a miserable franchise, socially restricted representation and low standards of public accountability — but a statement of fact. The cumbersome machinery of the Commons, built for two parties and geared up in the heady days of a confident imperial Parliament, is looking antiquated, and is finding it hard to adapt to twentieth-century change. There has always been great dissatisfaction in the ranks, not to mention the public at large, at some aspects of the Parliamentary game, but it is hardly a controversial assertion to suggest that without a fairly rapid overhaul the Commons risks another of the drops in public esteem which it should be politicians' concern to avoid.

As for the Lords, what can you say? There is no legislative assembly anywhere in the rest of the Western world to compare with it and its odd combination of respectability and odium. The one safe statement is that it can't last, but even that seemingly inevitable disappearance has to be balanced against the apparently infinite capacity in Britain for reform in the very last moments of the eleventh hour. Who knows? For the moment it is enough to say that it has long been part of the Parliamentary world and, even since Mr Asquith's reforms took hold, has played its role with some style. Looking at it is like watching the gradual decline of an exotic species, doomed but determined to preserve to the last some of its individuality and its inheritance. There is a fascination about the place which always undermines the ridicule.

So this collection starts with a warning — that it is no history of Parliament, nor is it meant to be — and a fairly confident prediction, that the great words from the Commons and the Lords, and the quirky observations of a few of those who have chronicled them will be, at least, diverting and amusing. No more.

There is a great danger at Westminster of falling weakly under the spell for ever. Most of the politicians represented here have risen above the throng, and have given some leadership to the tribe. But the collection also tries to represent the feelings of some of those who never did have a chance to play leading roles themselves, though they may unwittingly have been agents of fundamental change, and their careers turning points. The perspective of history creates its own characters, and doubtless there are many worthy souls who have slipped away over the years, forgotten to all but the most diligent academic researcher. In a little cluster of highlights that perspective, and some of its manipulations of the scenes as they happened, easily distorts. If, however, some speech or reminiscence prompts a reader to explore further, that is justification enough.

Above all, it is an attempt to convey the sheer excitement that the political world still has. That moment when the House realises a great speech is in the making — or that Fate, as P. G. Wodehouse says, is standing at your shoulder, lead piping in hand — still gives the inimitable *frisson* to any but the most determined cynic. For the enthusiast, willing to be moved from time to time, there is still nothing like it. The Commons can induce fury, despair and deep distress but its people are a community varied enough to provide instant relief. In the end, their weaknesses and their ambitions are always on show — and cannot be concealed indefinitely from the public gaze. So, they are vulnerable and though they can have great triumphs on their chosen stage and can move their audiences near to tears it is always a risky game. There is a fragility in the way of life which gives it a special piquancy. The best way to describe it is not to engage in academic analysis of its character, because it is something to be felt rather than learnt, but to let it emerge itself, from those who find it their favourite stimulant.

So, the scene is set. The players and the critics are in their places, ready to experience the thrill again. They do it because however much their natural cynicism battles against their other instincts, it seldom wins. They like nothing more than the delicious sense of expectation, with its fear as well as its confidence, while they wait with all of us for the curtain to rise.

August, 1984.

1

The Best Club in London?

> "But you have not imparted to me," remarks Veneering, "what you think of my entering the House of Commons."
> "I think," rejoins Mr Twemlow feelingly, "that it is the best club in London."
>
> —Charles Dickens: *Our Mutual Friend*

> Nouns of number or multitude, such as Mob, Parliament, Rabble, House of Commons, Regiment, Court of King's Bench, Den of Thieves, and the like.
>
> —William Cobbett: *English Grammar*

THE Westminster atmosphere, while seductive, also has the tendency to repel — to alarm the stranger with its sense of a shared, and private, experience; its obsession with the dips and jumps in political fortune; above all, its insistence on its own importance. From the reporters' gallery, sceptics have reflected this quality since they were first allowed into the place, and before, when they queued for the public galleries to record the strange scenes below. As well as the observers, standing apart from the scene, the participants have always included compulsive diarists and essayists, though the day of the Man of Letters in politics has all but gone. Anyone who succumbs to the strange hold of the place feels an urge to express it, in personal reminiscence, journalism or even fiction.

So, as an introduction, it is fitting to start with Charles Dickens, who brought the eye of the novelist to the reporter's trade when he sat in the gallery from 1831 and found the experience exhilarating, if frequently depressing. His Parliamentary Sketch from *Sketches by Boz* is as fresh an account of that strange little world as anyone has produced. From the other side of the curtain, looking out to the real world, Julian Critchley, the Conservative MP for Aldershot, has become perhaps the best contemporary chronicler of the frustrations and unexpected excitements of the backbencher's life. His report of life behind the lines catches the droll side of public life, just as James Fenton, the poet, describes with feelings any journalist will recognise the peculiarities of a Parliamentary muddle, in this case the increasingly desperate efforts of the minority Labour Government in 1976 to stay in office with the help of David Steel's band of Liberals and the hastily-concocted proposals for legislative devolution designed to appease the Scottish and Welsh nationalists.

Fenton is one of the best writers to have graced the gallery in recent years, and Frank Johnson is another — here writing about the day the microphones finally invaded the Commons, and brought the hubbub to the public ear for the first time. His sketches in the *Daily Telegraph, Now!* and *The Times* exploited the style which, in its modern form, began with Bernard Levin's columns as Taper in the *Spectator* in the late fifties (here finding himself, like generations of reporters, driven to the very verge of madness by the procedural game). Earlier there was Harry Boardman in *The Guardian*, whose affection for Parliament was matched by an elegant style.

Anthony Trollope, in the Palliser novels, dealt with the nineteenth-century world of politics and here the Duke of Omnium, head of Trollope's own little dynasty, writes to his son to tell him of politics in the House of Commons, a place in which to prosper or to collapse into public ignominy. That cruel side, the club at its most ruthless, has ruined many a man. Henry "Chips" Channon, the sharpest diarist of the world of politics and high society in London in this century, felt that cruelty keenly, and never more than in days when Neville Chamberlain's Premiership was slipping away, with the jeers of many of his former Tory supporters ringing in his ears. The Norway debates were the first turning point of World War II, ending Chamberlain's reign and opening the way for Churchill. Here Channon reflects on the sad side of politics.

The place is a club, but a bear-pit too; an arena where triumph and disaster run together; where its charms can quickly pall. There is also a great sense of continuity, something which irritates observers as much as it delights MPs. Dickens noted, as he settled down to write *Bleak House* in 1851, that whether it was Melbourne, Peel, Derby, Aberdeen or Lord John Russell, cabinets seemed to have a remarkable and alarming similarity. In a complaint which echoes still, he said that Parliament, in the end, never really changed.

***

A PARLIAMENTARY SKETCH

We will try our fortune at the Strangers' gallery, though the nature of the debate encourages very little hope of success. What on earth are you about? Holding up your order as if it were a talisman at whose command the wicket would fly open? Nonsense. Just preserve the order for an autograph, if it be worth keeping at all, and make your appearance at the door with your thumb and forefinger expressively inserted in your waistcoat-pocket. This tall stout man in black is the door-keeper. "Any room?" "Not an inch — two or three dozen gentlemen waiting downstairs on the chance of somebody's going out." Pull out your purse — "Are you *quite* sure there's no room?" "I'll go and look," replies the door-keeper, with a wistful glance at your purse, "but I'm afraid there's not." He returns, and with real feeling assures you that it is morally impossible to get near the gallery. It is of no use waiting. When you are refused admission into the Strangers' gallery at the House of Commons, under such circumstances, you may return home thoroughly satisfied that the place must be remarkably full indeed.

Retracing our steps through the long passage, descending the stairs, and crossing Palace-yard, we halt at a small temporary door-way adjoining the King's entrance to the House of Lords. The order of the serjeant-at-arms will admit you into the Reporters' gallery, from whence you can obtain a tolerably good view of the House. Take care of the stairs, they are none of the best; through this little wicket — there. As soon as your eyes become a little used to the mist of the place, and the glare of the chandeliers below you, you will see that some unimportant personage on the Ministerial side of the House (to your right hand) is speaking, amidst a hum of voices and confusion which would rival Babel, but for the circumstance of its being all in one language.

The "hear, hear", which occasioned that laugh, proceeded from our warlike friend with the moustache; he is sitting on the back seat against the wall, behind the Member who is speaking, looking as ferocious and intellectual as usual. Take one look around you, and retire! The body of the House and the side galleries are full of Members; some, with their legs on the back of the opposite seat; some, with theirs stretched out to their utmost length on the floor; some going out, others coming in; all talking, laughing, lounging, coughing, oh-ing, questioning, or groaning; presenting a conglomeration of noise and confusion, to be met with in no other place in existence, not even excepting Smithfield on a market-day, or a cock-pit in its glory.

But let us not omit to notice Bellamy's kitchen, or, in other words, the refreshment-room, common to both Houses of Parliament, where Ministerialists and Oppositionists, Whigs and Tories, Radicals, Peers, and Destructives, strangers from the gallery, and the more favoured strangers from below the bar, are alike at liberty to resort; where divers honourable members prove their perfect independence by remaining during the whole of a heavy debate, solacing themselves with the creature comforts; and whence they are summoned by whippers-in, when the House is on the point of dividing; either to give their "conscientious votes" on questions of which they are conscientiously innocent of knowing anything whatever, or to find a vent for the playful exuberance of their wine-inspired fancies, in boisterous shouts of "Divide", occasionally varied with a little howling, barking, crowing, or other ebullitions of senatorial pleasantry.

Now, when you have taken your seat in the kitchen, and duly noticed the large fire and roasting-jack at one end of the room — the little table for washing glasses and draining jugs at the other — the clock over the window opposite St. Margaret's Church — the deal tables and wax candles — the damask table-cloths and bare floor — the plate and china on the tables, and the gridiron on the fire; and a few other anomalies peculiar to the place — we will point out to your notice two or three of the people present, whose station or absurdities render them the most worthy of remark.

It is half-past twelve o'clock, and as the division is not expected for an hour or two, a few Members are lounging away the time here in preference to standing at the bar of the House, or sleeping in one of the side galleries. That singularly awkward and ungainly-looking man, in the brownish-white hat, with the straggling black trousers which reach about half-way down the leg of his boots, who is leaning against the meat-screen, apparently deluding himself into the belief that he is thinking about something, is a splendid sample of a Member of the House of Commons concentrating in his own person the wisdom of a constituency. Observe the wig, of a dark hue but indescribable colour, for it is naturally brown, it has acquired a black tint by long service, and if it be naturally black, the same cause has imparted to it a tinge of rusty brown; and remark how very materially the great blinker-like spectacles assist the expression of that most intelligent face. Seriously speaking, did you ever see a countenance so expressive of the most hopeless extreme of heavy dulness, or behold a form so strangely put together? He is no great speaker: but when he *does* address the House, the effect is absolutely irresistible.

The small gentleman with the sharp nose, who has just saluted him, is a Member of Parliament, an ex-Alderman, and a sort of amateur fireman. He, and the celebrated fireman's dog, were observed to be remarkably active at the conflagration of the two Houses of Parliament — they both ran up and down, and in and out, getting under people's feet, and into everybody's way, fully impressed with the belief that they were doing a great deal of good, and barking tremendously. The dog went quietly back to his kennel with the engine, but the gentleman kept up such an incessant noise for some weeks after the occurrence that he became a positive nuisance. As no more parliamentary fires have occurred, however, and as he has consequently had no more opportunities of writing to the newspapers to relate how, by way of preserving pictures he cut them out of their frames, and performed other great national services, he has gradually relapsed into his old state of calmness. . . .

THE BEST CLUB IN LONDON

The two persons who are seated at the table in the corner, at the farther end of the room, have been constant guests here, for many years past; and one of them has feasted within these walls, many a time, with the most brilliant characters of a brilliant period. He has gone up to the other House since then; the greater part of his boon companions have shared Yorick's fate, and his visits to Bellamy's are comparatively few.

If he really be eating his supper now, at what hour can he possibly have dined! A second solid mass of rump-steak has disappeared, and he ate the first in four minutes and three quarters, by the clock over the window. Was there ever such a personification of Falstaff! Mark the air with which he gloats over that Stilton, as he removes the napkin which has been placed beneath his chin to catch the superfluous gravy of the steak, and with what gusto he imbibes the porter which has been fetched, expressly for him, in the pewter pot. Listen to the hoarse sound of that voice, kept down as it is by layers of solids, and deep draughts of rich wine, and tell us if you ever saw such a perfect picture of a regular *gourmand*; and whether he is not exactly the man whom you would pitch upon as having been the partner of Sheridan's parliamentary carouses, the volunteer driver of the hackney-coach that took him home, and the involuntary upsetter of the whole party?

What an amusing contrast between his voice and appearance, and that of the spare, squeaking old man, who sits at the same table, and who, elevating a little cracked bantam sort of voice to its highest pitch, invokes damnation upon his own eyes or somebody else's at the commencement of every sentence he utters. "The Captain," as they call him, is a very old frequenter of Bellamy's; much addicted to stopping "after the House is up" (an inexpiable crime in Jane's eyes), and a complete walking reservoir of spirits and water.

The old Peer — or rather, the old man — for his peerage is of comparatively recent date — has a huge tumbler of hot punch brought him; and the other damns and drinks, and drinks and damns, and smokes. Members arrive every moment in a great bustle to report that "The Chancellor of the Exchequer's up," and get glasses of brandy-and-water to sustain them during the division; people who have ordered supper, countermand it, and prepare to go down-stairs, when suddenly a bell is heard to ring with tremendous violence, and a cry of "Di–vi–sion!" is heard in the passage. This is enough; away rush the members pell-mell. The room is cleared in an instant; the noise rapidly dies away; you hear the creaking of the last boot on the last stair, and are left alone with the leviathan of rump-steaks.

Charles Dickens: Sketches by Boz

***

LIFE BEHIND THE LINES

What are the compensations for a life spent stranded on the back benches? To have been in politics and not tasted office must be rather like a soldier in war who has never heard a shot fired in anger. But there is something to be said for life behind the lines. Junior ministers drive into obscurity in their black Princesses, reappearing once a month at question time in order to read out replies prepared beforehand by some Wykehamist. Occasionally they reply to an adjournment debate held in the small hours. They are excluded from the weekly meetings of the 1922 Committee, that theatre of the absurd which is the political equivalent of an ENSA concert party. I doubt if I could have endured four years as Parliamentary Secretary to the Department of Health and Social Security, stuck in some slum at the Elephant and Castle actually answering my own constituency letters.

I was attracted by office but was never persuaded to take the necessary vows of poverty, chastity and obedience, although I might have been tempted in my extreme youth by the offer of a short spell in the Whips' office, that cheerful freemasonry where I could have learnt to distinguish between those of my colleagues who had 'bottom' (whatever that might mean) and those who had not. It is not possible to understand the nature of that complex and subtle animal the Conservative Party without having been a member of the Broederbond.

But I like to retire early and I would not have made a good whip — someone who agrees with Dr Johnson that anyone who goes to bed before midnight is a scoundrel. Promotion in today's Tory Party depends, to a large extent, upon one of three factors: ideological purity (to be uncertain is uncomfortable, but to be certain is ridiculous), political paternity, or the possesion of what has come to be known as a 'good' MC. I must rid myself of doubt.

Life at Westminster has its risks. I was told when a young man by an elderly Knight of the Shire who looked like Harold Macmillan and bred Sealyhams, that the two occupational hazards of life at the Palace of Varieties were alcohol and adultery. 'The Lords,' he said severely, 'has the cup for adultery.' I have been attracted to both, although middle life, and the misfortunes of others, have served to blunt my appetites. The hurroosh that follows the intermittent revelation of the sexual goings-on of an unlucky MP has convinced me that the only safe pleasure for a parliamentarian is a bag of boiled sweets. The alternative leads to the ultimate humiliation — to be pilloried on moral grounds by our popular press.

Alcohol can improve the quality of front-bench speeches, but not by very much. It can help, too, when the House suspends the ten o'clock rule and business continues into the watches of the night. But its consumption does tend to encourage those MPs of all parties who can neither speak with effect nor be silent with dignity.

But I am straying from my point. What are the compensations for a life spent scrutinising the backs of the heads of members of one's own party for signs of intelligence? There is the library, with its chained copy of *Private Eye*, which scours London for the book of one's choice and provides an unrivalled service. Twenty years ago, when I could take all-night sittings in my stride, I would pass the night in the library, dozing in leather armchairs and browsing fitfully among its shelves. I would like to think that by so doing I was cured of impatience: elderly colleagues in cream silk shirts and dark-blue ties whose sole interest seemed to be in pigs turned out to have rowed across the North Sea single-handed, a wartime exploit which they had turned into a slim volume.

And there are the restaurants. Eating at the Palace of Westminster cannot truthfully be described as a gastronomic experience, but it can be fun. We practise culinary apartheid: at one end of the Members' Dining Room sit the Labour Party, in shirtsleeves and eating black pudding; at the other sit the Tories, whose jackets remain on however hot the weather, eating bloody beef and eggs in aspic. There is a Chief Whip's table, at which I was once invited to dine. Humphry Berkeley used to sit with Barbara Castle, drinking champagne out of pewter mugs and scandalising the old things of both parties. Dinner, and sometimes lunch, can be hilarious, and even interesting, but there is one hazard to avoid at all costs: the MP whose sole topic of conversation is his ward boundaries.

For those who wish to recapture their lost youth, there is the Commons gymnasium where, I am told, you can jump up and down to music, and there is also a rifle range, but I have never been able to find it. And there is a Families' Room where wives can be reunited with their husbands. I have said nothing as yet about constituents, but suffice it to say that we keep in touch. I visit Aldershot once a year, and am met by a brass band at the station. I am in receipt of letters which bob past the Terrace in green glass bottles, down to the mighty sea.

I had the misfortune early on in my political career to blot my copybook by appearing fully clothed in the pages of a men's magazine published by Michael Heseltine. The Chief Whip of the day, picking up the magazine between finger and thumb, asked whether I was hard up. I suppose I was. In the event there was much shaking of grey heads, and my confidential file was taken out and examined. ('Is he a kinsman of that golfin' chappie?') I was found guilty and my file was stamped 'Fit only for the Council of Europe'. I was on my way.

Service in Europe at least means that you meet only the very best sort of foreigners, and then in restaurants. Three times a year a large party of Members of the warrant-officer class flew out to Strasbourg in a chartered aircraft. I put up at the Gutenberg, a family hotel next to the cathedral, which had once been the favourite of officers of the Wehrmacht. I used to imagine them playing Mendelssohn and thinking about killing Hitler. I determined on a new career. I could speak French, had a smattering of German and could read Italian 'in a general sort of way'. I began my first speech to the Assembly by repeating the dictum of Charles V, the Holy Roman Emperor, who said that he spoke French to his wife, Italian to his mistress and German to his horse. I deeply offended the interpreters but, luckily, the scattering octogenarian Belgian stationmasters who made up my audience were asleep, having succumbed to the effects of six-course lunches at the Crocodile.

The Council of Europe, which has a high moral content, rose to the spirit of the times by admitting Liechtenstein to the comity of nations. I attended the opening of the new building (by Giscard). It was all very grand but not a patch on the opening of the Odeon, Swiss Cottage, by Merle Oberon just before the war. If Strasbourg were not enough, exile in Europe included a visit twice a year to Paris, where there is to be found an obscure organisation called the Western European Union, whose faded charms the French government discovers at intervals. The flirtation is intense but brief, and never consummated. Most of the time WEU is ignored, and is permitted to live quietly, doing harm to no one. For seven years I took advantage of them both, writing reports which were never read, sipping Gewürztraminer, and staring gloomily towards the distant blue line of the Vosges.

I have not abandoned travel. I am now a delegate to the North Atlantic Assembly, which attracts a better class of person. Because of its American 'input' of Senators, Congressmen and earnest researchers, we meet in the more congenial cities of southern Europe. I have just returned from Madeira, where we worried about Tomahawks and Pershing IIs and toyed with fresh fish and a good white Dão. An American friend invited me to Reid's for a drink, not in the bar of that great hotel but in the 'control room' which their delegation sets up abroad. We sipped Pepsi among cartons of toothpaste and bottles of kaolin. George V was right: abroad is bloody. If only my photograph had been published in *Country Life*.

Julian Critchley: The Listener, *10 June 1982*

***

LET ME OUT OF HERE

The main thing that worries me about my job is — I am afraid of going mad. For the last week or so I have been suffering from nightmares, all of them about Westminster, and I find it alarming that it is becoming increasingly difficult to tell the difference between what I have dreamt and what I have seen. The philosopher G. J. Warnock, my old tutor, thought that there was a quality in dreams that made them distinguishable from reality. But I don't suppose that Warnock, at the time that he reached this conclusion, had ever seen Norman St John-Stevas floating into the chamber with 200 amendments under his arm; I don't suppose he'd ever sat through one of Robin Maxwell-Hyslop's points of order; and among other Tory back-benchers, I don't suppose he'd studied Michael Brotherton's neck, or Nigel Lawson's face.

Lawson's face is extraordinary. For a start, it dominates the rest of his body in a manner which other faces do not. It has to be displayed, this face, on a more or less horizontal plane. Imagine a man wearing a mask, and imagine that the elastic which holds the mask on has just broken, so that the man (rather than let the mask slip off) has to tilt his head back and balance the mask on his real face. This is the kind of tyranny which Lawson's face exerts over the rest of his body as he cruises along the corridors. Another way of putting it would be to say that Lawson sticks his nose in the air wherever he goes. He doesn't look *down* his nose at you, he looks *along* his nose.

The best place to examine Lawson's face from is therefore the gallery. What you realise is that there are two kinds of tendon concealed somewhere in the ample neck, and that these tendons, because the head is always tilted backwards, draw the corners of his mouth downwards. The result of this anatomical peculiarity is that Lawson's face (such is our natural eagerness to find out the mind's construction from the face) gives an inevitable impression of superiority and self-regard. It's the face of somebody who is intensely conscious of the dignity and pomp of the ceremony in which he is taking part. It is not a front bench face. It's very much below the gangway. In a romantic novel or a Hollywood film with historical pretensions, Lawson's face would belong to the man who throws open the double doors, bangs his staff on the floor and announces the arrival of the duchess. In Beau Brummel's Bath Lawson's face would surmount a natty arrangement of frills and ruffs; there would be a large beauty spot on either cheek; pinches of snuff would regularly make their way up the nostrils; the mouth would be constantly calling on someone to stap Lawson's vitals.

John Peyton's face (it sounds like a television programme — *Peyton's Face*) belongs to a later period. Peyton is a villain from *Bleak House*; he wishes the business of Parliament to turn into something along the lines of Jarndyce and Jarndyce, an interminable legal battle fought in darkened courtrooms, at the end of which all the contestants will be dead or decrepit, penniless or broken with disease. But what gives Peyton his nightmarish quality is not so much his face as his character. He really is a very unpleasant person. That's the only thing he's good at. Whereas most speakers in Parliament tend to get a little confused if attacked, or interrupted in the course of the point they are making, Peyton thrives on insults. I imagine he was born and bred in a briar patch. If he's making his speech as prepared, he's the dullest speaker in the House. The best way to tackle him therefore is to let him have his way. As soon as you give him a chance to depart from his brief, the flick-knife is out. Russell Kerr found this to his cost this week when he attacked what Peyton was saying as empty rhetoric. It turned out to be a quotation from Michael Foot. Not necessarily a quotation appropriately used, of course, but a quotation nevertheless: A trap.

Brotherton's neck (it sounds like a place in Cumberland — "Fire-fighters at Brotherton's Neck have reported extensive damage to hundreds of acres of remote moorland. The fires, which have been raging for the last week, are now said to be under control, although teams of volunteers are on standby to prevent any new flare-ups. Thousands of gallons of much-needed water were poured into the deep crevasses of heather and peat, many of which are expected to continue smouldering until the present dry spell is over"). Brotherton's neck has a quality which renders it unique among the necks in the Commons. The corner of the neck has a penchant for Palatinate purple shirts with white detachable collars. The neck arranges itself over the collar in rich swags of fat. When the owner of the neck becomes incensed — which is often — an astonishing system of capillary tubes draws the purple dye from the shirt up the neck and thereby on to the face. In a matter of seconds, neck, face and shirt can become indistinguishable in pigmentation. Scientists have speculated in vain as to the mechanism whereby this effect is achieved, and as to what survival value, if any, it affords the owner. They can only assume that at some time in the past the Brotherton strain was crossed with that of a chameleon. This would account also for Brotherton's tongue, which can, at a speed too fast for the naked eye to register, dart out across the chamber of the House and snatch the order papers from the hands of astonished Labour back-benchers.

As I look down from the gallery at such scenes, and the eye wanders over Lawson's face, and Peyton's face, and Brotherton's neck, it occurs to me that those who imagine Africa to be a dark continent, those who are afraid that its natives may revert to savagery, those in whom the word "atavism" provokes a shudder, all these are ignoring the threat that exists here in this country. It is said that, as Leader of the House, Foot has severely damaged his reputation as a parliamentarian. It is said that his use of time-table motions is inadmissible, a threat to democracy. Peyton's face referred to Tuesday's proceedings as introducing "dictatorship by consent"—a marvellous concept. Margaret Thatcher has talked about the Iron Curtain being brought down. David Steel has fluffed a carefully prepared line about the guillotine and the French Revolution.

Foot and his team (I suppose Steel imagines Caerwyn Roderick in the role of Saint-Just) see things differently. They say that the cause of the

Tory anger over Labour's refusal to drop any legislation from its programme is part-genuine, yes, since guillotines are indeed a restriction on discussion, but largely the anger of frustration: the Tories are used to ruling, they do not therefore do well in opposition. Labour is much more skilful in opposition. Had *Labour* been running the blocking tactics over this session's legislation, they say, they would have made a much better job of it.

Foot's view is that it is better that Thatcher should *not* take over. So, although he does not claim particularly to like his present job (the previous one was more interesting), and although he is not under any illusions about the power of the Left within the Government, he considers it worth pushing the legislative programme through. The guillotines will enable the Government to bring the session to an end in mid-November, and we shall then get on to the Devolution Bill. Will it have to be guillotined as well? Foot is not saying. Obviously it is much more difficult for him to propose a guillotine on a Bill which introduces such a fundamental constitutional change. However, he does hint that if the vote on the Second Reading is clear enough, there might be some possibility of manoeuvre. In the meantime he can derive some satisfaction from the Tory rage. To be so near and yet so far from government must be frustrating. Yet when I look at what the Opposition have in store, at the faces of those who consider that they rule by right, the Lawsons, the Peytons, the Brothertons and the rest, when I look at the whole bang shoot, I can only say — thank God for the guillotine.

James Fenton: New Statesman, *23 July 1976*

***

ON THE AIR

As the BBC has for days seemingly been reminding us every two and a half minutes, yesterday was the historic first day of the historic permanent broadcasting of the historic House of Commons. Transistor pressed to an ear, and with the day's business about to begin, one heard the BBC commentator, the historic Mr David Holmes, explain that: "Mr Speaker will take the chair. He will start things off with the cry of 'Order, Order!'."

Into the chamber.

Sure enough, the Speaker, Mr George Thomas, was taking the chair. He is a Welsh Methodist, unmarried teetotaller who, so far as is known, is not on drugs either. He is not typical of previous transistor stars.

"Order! Order!" he cried, historically. And, indeed, hysterically: for one could be forgiven for suspecting that someone in the Beeb had told dear old George to speak up for the benefit of the microphones and to put on something of a show for the occasion.

Such advice would not have come from the admirable and stupendously Reithian Mr Holmes. But one feels sure that the corporation is full of trainee-producers named Cindy and Mandy (probably even those who are male are also called Cindy and Mandy) and one of them perhaps asked the occupant of the chair to "camp it up a bit, Speakie darling". Anyway, Mr Thomas yesterday gave his all for the listening millions or hundreds. For example, when Mr Ridsdale, Conservative MP for Harwich, rose on a point of order to complain about slow progress of Question Time that day, the Speaker observed: "It may be my imagination, but I have been under the impression that the supplementary questions have been longer than usual today and I cannot think why."

The subject chosen for the first broadcast was Welsh Questions. This was of course sheer sensationalism on the part of the broadcasting authorities. One has to warn those members of the public who listened that Parliament is not always as exciting as Welsh Questions. Mr Gwynfor Evans, the Welsh Nationalist MP for Carmaerthen, asked a question about Dyfed. Mr Kinnock, the Labour Member for Bedwellty, was worried about Bronglais, which was either a place or an illness. An Under Secretary at the Welsh Office named Mr Jones had an announcement to make about something which had happened at a place which sounded like "Mouldy Fluid". Another Under Secretary at the Welsh Office — who was also named Mr Jones — was for a while annoyed with a Welsh Nationalist named, for the sake of variety, Mr Thomas. In an interview just before the historic day, Mr Michael Foot, the Leader of the House, had said that these broadcasts would mean that newspapers would have to "report better" the proceedings of the House because the public would now be able to "hear how it really happens". Also, one hopes that the broadcast will put an end to the distortion and trivialisation of politics indulged in by MPs. Why don't the politicians report the good things which happen in our society?

How, then, did yesterday's broadcast compare with the unreal thing inside the Chamber? Well, Mr Holmes did wonders at explaining the inexplicable, and the sound was excellent, down to the last rhubarb rhubarb. But disinterest compels one to admit that, whatever miracles this latest phenomenon called the wireless performs in years to come, it will never take the place of the old-fashioned, steam Parliamentary sketchwriter. With our funny old misprints, and unfunny old jokes, we will still be around long after many contemporary politicians have come alive. Only we could tell you, for instance, that throughout yesterday's historic proceedings Mr Russell Kerr, the Labour MP for Feltham, was wearing fluorescent green socks. Perhaps he thought the socks would enable him to be seen better on the radio.

Frank Johnson: Daily Telegraph, *4 April 1978*

THE DOG DAYS

The hot weather is affecting my nerves. Figure to yourself: there I was the other day, sitting with a Member in the tea-room, idly sipping a cup of something that I presume was piped direct from the Thames two yards away. Through the open door we could see the sun on the terrace (the strawberries and cream do not begin until after Whitsun), the pigeons strutting self-importantly about like so many Junior Government Whips, the funnel of a passing ship or two. We could hear the gentle slap of the waves against the stonework, the murmur of voices from outside, the chimes of Big Ben. It was an incredibly peaceful English scene, and sorted well with the scene I had just left — the Chamber. There, some half-dozen Members a side had been dragging themselves to their feet from time to time to deploy all the cut-and-thrust of debate on such grave constitutional questions as the determination of Messrs Harold Wilson, Patrick Gordon Walker, Douglas Jay and Hector Hughes to carry an amendment to the Finance Bill (Page 12, Clause 12, line 33) to leave out the word "and", and the equal determination of the Government that the Opposition should not harm a hair of an and's head.

We spoke, my friend and I, of the only subject anybody at Westminster discusses these days at all: the rigid catalepsy that from Left to Right holds almost undisputed sway within the precincts of the Palace of Westminster. Zombie-like, they go back and forth about their duties, even past praying for death or Mr Macmillan to release them from a travail that the Flying Dutchman and the Wandering Jew, not to mention Sisyphus, would never have dreamed of exchanging for their own. The other day there were forty-seven Tories away from a Division unpaired; nobody paid the slightest attention. (A mere few months ago there would have been a row of such proportions that they would not have needed to take away the statue of Sir William Harcourt that the one of Mr Balfour is to replace; it would have fallen off its pedestal without anybody lifting a finger.) There is no subject in sight, or indeed conceivable, that could cause anybody to get excited or even interested; Mr Profumo's statement about arms for Iraq passed with no more than a perfunctory gibe or two from the Opposition, though this time last year they would have torn the place down around Mr Profumo's sleek ears. Once it was the custom for Members not wishing to attend morning Committees to dream up elaborate excuses; now they have taken to telling the Whips bluntly that they have no intention of turning up, and their names are meekly struck off the lists. If some enterprising lead-swinger should summon up the energy, during the Whitsun recess, to circularise all his fellow-Members with a suggestion that they should none of them come back at all when it was over, the chances are that they would accept the suggestion with joy and unanimity, and that when they put it into effect nobody would notice.

Well, there we were, talking of such matters with many a drowsy pause, when suddenly a bell began to ring; it rang with a loud and ugly clangour, harsh and alarming. I regret to say that I lost my head; assuming that the Palace of Westminster was on fire, I leaped to my feet and, seizing the milk jug, was about to hurl its contents over the Parliamentary Secretary to the Ministry of Pensions and National Insurance (who was sitting at the next table) when I was gently restrained. The bell, I was told, was the Division Bell. Collapsing, all a-quiver, into my seat, I digested this news as my companion went off to register his vote. When he came back, I was careful not to ask him on what he had been voting (I know better than *that*), but he genially volunteered the information that neither he, nor anyone he had met on the day, had any idea. When the figures ticked up on the wall a moment later, I was astonished to see that no fewer than 384 Members had been present, not counting the Tellers, to vote upon an amendment that had been forced to a Division by the Opposition (though the two Conservative sponsors had wished to withdraw it), the effect of which, I later learned, would have been to change the provision for duty payable on club liquor licences so that instead of "five pounds" it would read "five pounds or duty of threepence for every pound's worth of purchases of intoxicating liquor whichever is the less".

As Mr Belloc once asked, what *is* the use of going on like this? How can the time of even 384 grown men and women be justifiably occupied in this way, with the temperature 80 degrees in the shade and the rhododendrons out at Kew? Why do they not go now into recess and not come back until the prorogation? There is an amendment to the Finance Bill which seeks to exempt parking meters from income tax; there is another to omit the word "otherwise" from a passage which admittedly makes no sense as it stands but which will not be affected in the slightest by the omission of the word "otherwise" or for that matter two-thirds of the other words it contains. These amendments will be discussed; they may be voted on; for all I know there may be 484 or even 548 members willing to troop through the lobbies when the bell (oh, my heart! it is thumping still!) goes. What, as I say, is the use?

I do not know; I simply do not know. And what is more to the point, I do not propose to stay and find out. I am going away, and I am not coming back until the Finance Bill has been dealt with, parking meters, otherwise and all. I am going, if you must know, to Elba, where I shall amuse myself by sending picture-postcards of Napoleon to Mr Butler with offensive messages on the back signed "Talleyrand".

Taper: The Spectator, *15 May 1959*

***

THE BEST CLUB IN LONDON

A LETTER TO A NEWCOMER

My Dear Silverbridge,

I am glad that you are in Parliament and am glad also that you should have been returned by the old borough; though I would that you could have reconciled yourself to adhering to the politics of your family. But there is nothing disgraceful in such a change, and I am able to congratulate you as a father should a son and to wish you long life and success as a legislator.

There are one or two things I would ask you to remember;—and firstly this, that as you have voluntarily undertaken certain duties you are bound as an honest man to perform them as scrupulously as though you were paid for doing them. There was no obligation in you to seek the post;—but having sought it and acquired it you cannot neglect the work attached to it without being untrue to the covenant you have made. It is necessary that a young Member of Parliament should bear this in his mind, and especially a Member who has not worked his way up to notoriety outside the House, because to him there will be great facility for idleness and neglect.

And then I would have you always remember the purport for which there is a Parliament elected in this happy and free country. It is not that some men may shine there, that some may acquire power, or that all may plume themselves on being the elect of the nation. It often appears to me that some Members of Parliament so regard their success in life,—as the fellows of our colleges do too often, thinking that their fellowships were awarded for their comfort and not for the furtherance of any object such as education or religion. I have known gentlemen who have felt that in becoming Members of Parliament they had achieved an object for themselves instead of thinking that they had put themselves in the way of achieving something for others. A Member of Parliament should feel himself to be the servant of his country,—and like every other servant, he should serve. If this be distasteful to a man he need not go into Parliament. If the harness gall him he need not wear it. But if he takes the trappings, then he should draw the coach. You are there as the guardian of your fellow-countrymen,—that they may be safe, that they may be prosperous, that they may be well governed and lightly burdened,—above all that they may be free. If you cannot feel this to be your duty, you should not be there at all.

And I would have you remember also that the work of a Member of Parliament can seldom be of that brilliant nature which is of itself charming; and that the young member should think of such brilliancy as being possible to him only at a distance. It should be your first care to sit and listen so that the forms and methods of the House may as it were soak into you gradually. And then you must bear in mind that speaking in the House is but a very small part of a member's work, perhaps that part which he may lay aside altogether with the least strain on his conscience. A good Member of Parliament will be good upstairs in the Committee Rooms, good downstairs to make and to keep a House, good to vote, for his party if it may be nothing better, but for the measures also which he believes to be for the good of his country.

Gradually, if you will give your thoughts to it, and above all your time, the theory of legislation will sink into your mind, and you will find that there will come upon you the ineffable delight of having served your country to the best of your ability.

It is the only pleasure in life which has been enjoyed without alloy by your affectionate father,

'Omnium'.

Anthony Trollope: "The Duke's Children"

***

A CRUEL PLACE

The cataclysmic day has drawn to a welcome close and I am worn out, revolted by the ingratitude of my fellow-men, nauseated by the House of Commons, which I really think ought, though I love it, to be abolished.

When I got there the atmosphere of the House was definitely excited and it intensified as the long hours passed. Herbert Morrison opened the debate with vituperation, and announced that the Opposition would challenge the Government into a division. The PM, angry and worn out, intervened to say that the Government accepted the challenge, and he called upon his friends to rally round and support him. Possibly he was tactless, but I do not quite see what other course he could have followed. We then knew that it was to be war. Samuel Hoare, the pet aversion of the Labour Party, made a boring contribution in defence of the Government, which did not help. The temperature rose, hearts hardened, tempers sharpened, and I came to the conclusion that there is nothing so revolting as the House of Commons on an ugly night. Little Neville seemed heartbroken and shrivelled (as Lady Halifax said) but remained courteous and patient. I sat behind him, hoping to surround him with an aura of affection. From time to time I looked up into Mrs Fitzroy's gallery and several times I caught the eye of poor Mrs Chamberlain, who has hardly left the House for two days: she is a loyal, good woman.... She was in black — black hat — black coat — black gloves — with only a bunch of violets in her coat. She looked infinitely sad as she peered down into the mad arena where the lions were out for her husband's blood.

For hours the issue was in doubt. Duff Cooper made a damaging speech in which he said that he hoped we should get on more actively with the war . . . good advice from someone who has just returned from four months in America. . . .

The whispering in the lobbies was unbearable. Ham Kerr offered to bet that 100 Government supporters would vote against the régime; I scoffed. Mrs Tate offered to bet me £5 that over fifty would do so, but refused to take up the challenge, when I agreed. Lady Astor rushed about, intriguing and enjoying the fray and the smell of blood: she has joined hands with the insurgents, probably because she must always be in the limelight, and also because I think she is seriously rattled by the "Cliveden Set" allegations which were made against her before the war, and now wants to live them down.

At last the atmosphere became so horrible that I decided I must leave for a few minutes — when I came back Alexander was speaking, winding up for the Opposition. The real issue of the debate — Norway — had long since been forgotten: speakers attacked us on any possible ground, and still the doubt was in everbody's mind, would Winston be loyal? He finally rose, and one saw at once that he was in bellicose mood, alive and enjoying himself, relishing the ironical position in which he found himself: i.e. that of defending his enemies, and a cause in which he did not believe. He made a slashing, vigorous speech, a magnificent piece of oratory. I was in the gallery behind him, with Rab, who was, several times, convulsed with laughter. Winston told the story of the Norwegian campaign, justified it, and trounced the Opposition, demolishing Roger Keyes, etc. How much of the fire was real, how much ersatz, we shall never know, but he amused and dazzled everyone with his virtuosity. He taunted the Opposition and accused Shinwell of skulking: a Labour MP — rather the worse for drink — had never heard the word and thought that he had said skunking. There was laughter, but somehow the tension was increased and poor Healy, the new Deputy Sergeant-at-Arms, was quite nervous lest he be called on to eject an unruly member. It was like bedlam.

I asked Roy Wise how many would vote against the Government — and he said that he would, for one: it was the only way to shock us out of our complacency, he said. I told him that he was playing with dynamite: then Charles Taylor ("Cow and Gate" and looks like a calf) came up to me and said: "We are trying to get your Government out tonight." Feeling grew, still we thought we would survive. At last the Speaker called a division, which Winston nearly talked out. I went into the Aye Lobby, which seemed thin for a three line Whip, and we watched the insurgents file out of the Opposition Lobby (Teenie Cazalet could not make up his mind and abstained). "Quislings," we shouted at them, "Rats." "Yes-men," they replied. I saw all the expected ones, and many more — Herbert [Duggan] among them and my heart snapped against him for ever. Then I voted, as usual everyone wondered how many had dared to vote against us: so many threaten to do so, and funk it at the last moment. Anthony

Eden and Jim Thomas in our Lobby looked triumphant, and I saw Winston and his PPS Brendan Bracken there. I went back to the Chamber, and took my seat behind Neville. "We are all right" I heard someone say, and so it seemed as David Margesson came in and went to the right, the winning side of the table, followed by the other tellers. "281 to 200" he read, and the Speaker repeated the figures. There were shouts of "Resign — Resign" . . . and that old ape Josh Wedgwood began to wave his arms about and sing "Rule Britannia". Harold Macmillan, next to him, joined in, but they were howled down. Neville appeared bowled over by the ominous figures, and was the first to rise. He looked grave and thoughtful and sad: as he walked calmly to the door, his supporters rose and cheered him lustily and he disappeared. No crowds tonight to cheer him, as there were before and after Munich — only a solitary little man, who had done his best for England.

What can Neville do now? He can reconstruct his Government: he can resign: but there is no doubt that the Government is seriously jarred and all confidence in it is gone. Hitler will be quick to take advantage of our divided councils.

What changes does that fatal division portend? Neville may survive but not for long: Oh, the cruelty of the pack in pursuit . . . shall I too crash when the Chamberlain edifice crumbles?

I am disgusted by politics and human nature and long to live like Walpole, a semi-social, semi-literary life in a Strawberry Hill (only not Gothic) of my own. Perhaps one day I will.

Chips Channon: Diary, *8 May 1940*

***

COODLE AND DOODLE

England has been in a dreadful state for some weeks. Lord Coodle would go out, Sir Thomas Doodle wouldn't come in, and there being nobody in Great Britain (to speak of) except Coodle and Doodle, there has been no Government. It is a mercy that the hostile meeting between those two great men, which at one time seemed inevitable, did not come off; because if both pistols had taken effect, and Coodle and Doodle had killed each other, it is to be presumed that England must have waited to be governed until young Coodle and young Doodle, now in frocks and long stockings, were grown up. This stupendous national calamity, however, was averted by Lord Coodle's making the timely discovery, that if in the heat of debate he had said that he scorned and despised the whole ignoble career of Sir Thomas Doodle, he had merely meant to say that party differences should never induce him to withhold from it the tribute of his warmest admiration; while it has opportunely turned out, on the other hand, that Sir Thomas Doodle had in his own bosom expressly booked Lord Coodle to go down to posterity as the mirror of virtue and honour. Still England has been some weeks in the dismal strait of having no pilot (as was well observed by Sir Leicester Dedlock) to weather the storm; and the marvellous part of the matter is, that England has not appeared to care very much about it, but has gone on eating and drinking and marrying and giving in marriage, as the old world did in the days before the flood. But Coodle knew the danger, and Doodle knew the danger, and all their followers and hangers-on had the clearest possible perception of the danger. At last Sir Thomas Doodle has not only condescended to come in, but has done it handsomely, bringing in with him all his nephews, all his male cousins, and all his brothers-in-law. So there is hope for the old ship yet.

Doodle has found that he must throw himself upon the country — chiefly in the form of sovereigns and beer. In this metamorphosed state he is available in a good many places simultaneously, and can throw himself upon a considerable portion of the country at one time. Britannia being much occupied in pocketing Doodle in the form of sovereigns, and swallowing Doodle in the form of beer, and in swearing ourselves black in the face that she does neither — plainly to the advancement of her glory and morality — the London season comes to a sudden end, through all the Doodleites and Coodleites dispersing to assist Britannia in those religious exercises.

Charles Dickens: Bleak House

2

Kings and Queens

The use of the Queen, in a dignified capacity, is incalculable.
—Walter Bagehot: *The English Constitution*

At long last I am able to saw a few words of my own. I have never wanted to withhold anything, but until now it has been not constitutionally possible for me to speak.
—Edward VIII: *Abdication Speech 1936*

PARLIAMENT'S relationship with the monarchy is a placid one these days. The extrovert monarchists are few in number and have been tamed and the republicans are largely reconciled to the quiet operation of a formal, constitutional link with Buckingham Palace (and can avoid any direct contact with the Sovereign and her family without much effort). There are still, however, regular outbursts from such inveterate critics as Willie Hamilton, the Labour backbencher who has become part of the institution he abhors: dragged out to comment on every Royal occasion and at every moment of controversy. The Queen's relationship with Parliament is now formal — the dealings of the Privy Council, the giving of the Royal Assent to Bills, the speech from the throne in the Lords at the beginning of each session in the words of the Government — but the present calm has come about through many a storm.

Two examples of Elizabeth I's power — her response to Parliament's criticism in 1566 and the famed "Golden Speech" in 1601 — introduce a few Royal moments. There was not such a dominating relationship again, perhaps, until Victoria's time and the account of Henry W. Lucy, a wonderfully colourful nineteenth-century journalist whose diaries of Parliament are exceptionally vivid, of the succession of Edward VII after her death catches the spirit of that age as it drew to its close. A few years earlier Keir Hardie, after his election to the Commons but before he led his new Labour Party, protested passionately — in a way often echoed since — at the Commons' ritual congratulations to the Duke and Duchess of York (later George V and Queen Mary) on the birth of a son. Since then, one moment stands out — the abdication of Edward VIII before his coronation because of his wish to marry the divorcée Mrs Wallis Simpson. Chips Channon's account of the Commons mood as the abdication crisis reached its climax is the best available, not least because of his own sympathy for the King's predicament.

But over the years the attitude to monarchy has become more relaxed, and the ordinary MP or Minister's view is well expressed in one of Roy Hattersley's short essays, recalling, at the time of the marriage of the Prince of Wales in 1981, how as a Privy Councillor he journeyed to Buckingham Palace carrying a message of congratulations. In the end it has always had a richly comic side to it all.

***

AN ANSWER TO PARLIAMENT

"If the order of your cause had matched the weight of your matter, the one might well have craved reward, and the other much the sooner be satisfied. But when I call to mind how far from dutiful care, yea rather how nigh a traitorous trick this tumbling cast did spring, I muse how men of wit can so hardly use that gift they hold. I marvel not much that bridleless colts do not know their rider's hand whom bit of kingly rein did never snaffle yet. Whether it was fit that so great a cause as this should have had this beginning in such a public place as that, let it be well weighed. Must all evil bodings that might be recited be found little enough to hap to my share? Was it well meant, think you, that those that knew not how fit this matter was to be granted by the prince, would prejudicate their prince in aggravating the matter? So all their arguments headed to my careless care of this my dear realm. . . ."

She was not surprised at the Commons, she said they had small experience and had acted like boys; but that the Lords should have gone along with them she confessed had filled her with wonder. There were some among them who had placed their swords at her disposal when her sister was on the throne, and had invited her to seize the crown; she knew but too well that if she allowed a successor to be named, there would be found men who would approach him or her with the same encouragement to disturb the peace of the realm. If she pleased she could name the persons to whom she alluded. When time and circumstances would allow she would see to the matter of their petition before they asked her; she would be sorry to be forced into doing anything which in reason and justice she was bound to do; and she concluded with a request that her words should not be misinterpreted.

"And you *doctors*, she said — it was her pleasure to ignore their right to a higher title; you I understand make long prayers about this business. One of you dared to say in times past that I and my sister were bastards;

and you must needs be interfering in what does not concern you. Go home and amend your own lives and set an honest example in your families. The Lords in Parliament should have taught you to know your places; but if they have forgotten their duty I will not forget mine. Did I so choose I make the impertinence of the whole set of you an excuse to withdraw my promise to marry; but for the realm's sake I am resolved that I will marry; and I will take a husband that will not be to the taste of some of you. I have not married hitherto out of consideration for you, but it shall be done now, and you who have been so urgent with me will find the effects of it to your cost. Think you the prince who will be my consort will feel himself safe with such as you, who thus dare to thwart and cross your natural queen?"

Queen Elizabeth I: Speech, *5 November 1566*

***

THE GOLDEN SPEECH

"Mr Speaker, we perceive your coming is to present thanks to us. Know I accept them with no less joy than your loves can have desire to offer such a present, and do more esteem it than any treasure or riches; for those we know how to prize, but loyalty, love, and thanks, I account them invaluable. And though God hath raised me high, yet this I account the glory of my crown, that I have reigned with your loves. This makes me that I do not so much rejoice that God hath made me to be a Queen, as to be a Queen over so thankful a people, and to be the means under God to conserve you in safety and to preserve you from danger . . . Of myself I must say this: I never was any greedy, scraping grasper, nor a strict, fast-holding prince, nor yet a waster; my heart was never set upon any worldly goods, but only for my subjects' good. What you do bestow on me, I will not hoard up, but receive it to bestow on you again; yea, my own properties I account yours, to be expended for your good, and your eyes shall see the bestowing of it for your welfare."

—Queen Elizabeth I: Speech, *30 November 1601*

***

A REBEL SPEAKS

"Mr Speaker, on my own behalf and those whom I represent, I am unable to join in this public address. I owe no allegiance to any hereditary ruler — and I will expect those who do to allow me the ordinary courtesies of debate. The Resolution . . . seeks to elevate to an importance which it does not deserve an event of every day occurrence . . . When we are asked as the House of Commons representing the nation to join in these congratulations, then in the interests of the dignity of the House I take leave to protest. . . .

From his childhood onward this boy will be surrounded by sycophants and flatterers by the score — [cries of 'Oh! Oh!'] — and will be taught to believe himself as of a superior creation . . . A line will be drawn between him and the people whom he is to be called upon some day to reign over. In due course, following the precedent which has already been set, he will be sent on a tour round the world, and probably rumours of a morganatic alliance will follow [loud cries of 'Oh! Oh!' and 'Order!' and 'Question!'] — and the end of it all will be that the country will be called upon to pay the bill . . . The Government will not find an opportunity for a vote of condolence with the relatives of those who are lying stiff and stark in a Welsh valley, and, if that cannot be done, the motion before the House ought never to have been proposed either. If it be for rank and title only that time and occasion can be found in this House, then the sooner that truth is known outside the better for the House itself."

Keir Hardie: Speech, *28 June 1894*

***

A QUICK SUCCESSION

There was a swiftness that almost took the breath away in hurrying King Edward VII on to the Throne. It seemed to be done almost in the pause that midway breaks the exclamations, "The Queen is dead! Long live the King!" The majority of members of the House of Commons learned at breakfast this morning that Parliament was summoned for today. To many it was impossible to reach Westminster in time for the opening. The date of the new session being a month ago definitely fixed for February 14, scores, including the Liberal Whip, seized the opportunity to get away to the Riviera. Others were further afield. Nevertheless, when at four o'clock this afternoon the Speaker, with solemn step, walked up the floor of the House, there was a surprisingly large muster upstanding to receive him.

Mr Arthur Balfour, whose well-earned holiday has been broken in upon with excessive bustle, met with a mischance he much laments. Hurrying up from Osborne after the closing scene, he found much work awaiting him in Downing Street. After attending the Privy Council, he looked in at the Treasury for a few minutes to bring up arrears, arriving breathless at the House of Commons to find the swearing-in had already commenced. His opportunity of being the first member after the Speaker to sign the Roll of the First Parliament of King Edward VII had fled.

He had reckoned without the Chaplain of the House. Prayers usually precede the commencement of business. Had the service taken place the Leader of the House would have been in good time to assert his precedence on the Roll. But though, since 1867, the ancient order of Dissolution of Parliament, automatically following on demise of the Crown has been abrogated, its functions lapse until members have taken the oath of allegiance to the new Sovereign. Thus, there being at four o'clock technically no House, there were no prayers, and in the absence of the Premier, Sir M. Hicks-Beach, as Chancellor of the Exchequer, signed the memorable Roll first, Sir H. Campbell-Bannerman, as Leader of the Opposition, coming second.

So closely were things run that up to within ten minutes of the meeting of the House there was dubiety as to the style of the Sovereign to whom allegiance was to be sworn. Under which King, Albert I, or Edward VII? The form of oath was prepared and printed on a dozen forms. A blank was left to fill in the name of the King. From half-past three to ten minutes to four a perturbed figure was observed pacing the inner lobby. It was the Clerk of the Public Bill Office, wondering whether he would have to write in Albert or Edward.

Anxiety relieved by the arrival of a messenger from St James's Palace, he hurried off to complete the formula of the Oath. For members other than Privy Councillors who, gathered in the Banqueting Hall of St James's Palace, heard the King declare for the name Edward, "which has been borne by six of my ancestors", the first news came from the Speaker. Rising from the Chair, Mr Gully called upon members to take the Oath of Allegiance to "His Majesty King Edward VII".

There was a low murmur of pleasure at this announcement. A rumour was current that the Queen, desiring to perpetuate the memory of her ever-loved Consort, had enjoined the Prince of Wales to take the name of Albert when he succeeded to the Monarch's estate. His Majesty's explanation to the Privy Council of the reasons which guided his choice was marked by his familiar tact. He must have been aware of the prevalent popular desire that he should carry on the name not least illustrious amongst the catalogue of kings of England. Possibly he had in his mind his revered mother's desire that the name of Albert should be endowed with Royal state.

"I do not undervalue the name of Albert," the King said in Privy Council, "which I inherit from my ever-to-be-lamented great and wise father, who, by universal consent, is, I think, deservedly, known by the name of Albert the Good, and I desire that his name should stand alone."

Therefore, Lords and Commoners hurriedly assembled at Westminster swore to be faithful, and bear true allegiance to His Majesty King Edward the Seventh, his heirs and successors, according to law. So help them God.

The brief speech addressed to the Privy Council was carefully drawn up in advance, and committed to memory by the King. One of the audience tells me there was in the delivery no sign of formality. When His

Majesty alluded to "the death of my beloved mother the Queen", he faltered and seemed as if he would break down. Recovering himself by gallant effort, he went on to the end, uplifting a note of manly earnestness in his declaration of determination to be a Constitutional Sovereign in the strictest sense of the word.

Henry W. Lucy: The Balfourian Parliament

***

THE END OF A REIGN

The dreadful day dawned coldly, and my limbs were numb and chilled. The telephone began early, and I talked to the Duchess of Kent who told me that all was over. The Duke of Kent returned to the Fort very early. I drove to the House of Commons and noticed that the Royal Standard was still flying.

At 2 p.m. Honor and I left for Parliament as I had secured her a ticket for the fateful day. The House was full, for there has not been an Abdication since 1399, 537 years ago. I thought everyone subdued but surprisingly unmoved, and Lady Astor actually seemed to enjoy herself, jumping about in her frivolous way. Baldwin was greeted with cheers, and sat down on the front bench gravely. At last he went to the bar, bowed twice "A message from the King" and he presented a paper to the Speaker who proceeded to read it out. At the words "renounce the Throne" his voice broke, and there were stifled sobs in the House. It was a short document, more moving by implication than by phrase, to the effect that the King could no longer remain on the Throne. The Speaker was tearful, but very few others were though Geoffrey Lloyd was in tears, and so I thought, was David Margesson. . . . Then Baldwin rose, and in half an hour told us the tale of his meetings with the King and their protracted discussions. He was a little muddled, there were many notes scattered on the Dispatch Box, but a few points, spoken simply, emerged, as Mr Baldwin paid His Majesty tribute after tribute. That the King throughout had behaved in a constitutional and upright manner, and that the Cabinet was dead against morganatic marriage, which was only suggested by the King on 1 December, long after the original marriage scheme had been broached. Mr Baldwin admits that he had little time to consider this second proposal (and to my mind he committed a crime in not allowing it). He said the Cabinet would not agree, nor would the Dominions, but surely he could have persuaded them. Winston Churchill sat doubled up throughout the speech. One other fact came out and of this I was always sure, that at no time did the King really hesitate, it was always a choice between marriage and abdication. At last Mr Baldwin sat down, and the Speaker adjourned the House until 6 p.m. I found Honor, put her in the car, and am now writing these lines. It is 5.42 and the House empty, the Chamber has witnessed yet again a scene that will always live in history. As I walked to my locker and fetched this diary, Lady Astor sang out to me, "People who have been licking Mrs Simpson's boots ought to be shot." I was too tired to retort and pretended I did not hear.

It is not known when the King will leave, nor how, but probably he will go tomorrow; what a heart-rending farewell. . . .

"The King is gone, Long Live the King." We woke in the reign of Edward VIII and went to bed in that of George VI. Honor and I were at the House of Commons by eleven o'clock, and as she stood for a time in the queue waiting to go to the Strangers Gallery, I talked with Mikey and David Lyon who were waiting to hear their sister made Queen of England. They were simple, charming and bored as ever. When the Bill came it was passed into Law with the minimum of time. Lord Halifax who moved it, and Lord Onslow who was on the Woolsack, are both Honor's uncles, and I realised how vested and what a close corporation the aristocracy of England still is. Then the Royal Commission was sent for, and the Lords Onslow, Denman and one other, filed out of the Chamber, and returned in full robes and wigs. Black Rod was sent to summon the Speaker, who, followed by his Commons, appeared at the bar. The Clerk read the Royal Commission. The three Lords bowed, and doffed their hats. The Bill was read. The King was still King Edward. The Clerk bowed "Le Roi le veult" and Edward, the beautiful boy King with his gaiety and honesty, his American accent and nervous twitching, his flair and glamour, was part of history. It was 1.52.

We went sadly home, and in the street we heard a woman selling newspapers saying, "The Church held a pistol to his head". In the evening we dined at the Stanleys' cheerless, characterless house, and at ten o'clock turned on the wireless to hear "His Royal Highness, Prince Edward" speak his farewell words in his unmistakeable slightly Long Island voice. It was a manly, sincere farewell, saying that he could not carry on the responsibilities of Kingship without the support of the woman he loved. There was a stillness in the Stanleys' room. I wept, and I murmured a prayer for he who had once been King Edward VIII.

Chips Channon: Diary, *10-11 December 1936*

***

DRESSING UP FOR THE QUEEN

Just before Parliament rose for the summer recess, both Commons and Lords presented the Queen with a Loyal Address which congratulated Her Majesty in suitably archaic language on the marriage of her "dearly beloved son, the Prince of Wales — etc. etc. etc.", as another monarch (the King of Siam) would have said, at least according to Oscar Hammerstein II. With initial reluctance and eventual enthusiasm, I took part in the event. Anyone who has any feeling for either history or England finds it difficult to resist an antiquarian excitement at the prospect of climbing inside the time machine of royal ceremonial. The bearers of last month's formal, but affectionate, message were greeted on their arrival at Buckingham Palace by a piper whose presence was clearly a relic of Queen Victoria's Highland obsession. From then on the clock moved backwards until I felt like a page out of a textbook of Tudor history — or an extra from *The Six Wives of Henry VIII.*

My Privy Councillor's oath prevents me from describing all that took place. Indeed, it probably prohibits me from using the Privy Councillor's oath as the reason for not describing all that took place. So abiding, as I must, by its secrecy clause (the existence of which I neither confirm nor deny), I am unable to reveal that the Lord Chancellor shamelessly hammed up his part in the proceedings. Nor can I give a full account of the way that fragments of gold embroidery fell from the Speaker's robes. Anxious, as always, to ingratiate myself with authority, I picked up the gleaming desiderata and handed them back to their temporary owner. As I did so, I felt that my role had changed. The peasant from the wild North Country who goes to court, sees the Queen and recovers the gold that has fallen from the wise man's raiment is clearly a character from Hans Christian Andersen.

If the word "peasant" implies a life deeply rooted in the soil, it may not be the most technically precise description of my origins — although, during the war, my father did briefly rent an allotment. However, the more accurate phrase "industrial proletariat" (which, now that I have thought of it, I propose to insinuate into *Who's Who*) does not fit into a fairytale, and in the middle of all those City of London aldermen in their red robes and bearskin caps, with the gentlemen ushers ushing away like mad, and ladies-in-waiting about all over the place, a fairy story it was. And I, for reasons that my Privy Council oath in no way prevents me from explaining, had the momentary feeling of a mendicant at court. The reason concerned my shirt.

I make no proletarian claims concerning my shirts in general. Indeed, I admit extravagance in every particular — capital cost, frequency of maintenance and speed of turnover. The problem on the day of the Loyal Address was specific. It first appeared that (as a result of summer holidays at the laundry) two weeks' supply languished in some Kentish Town depot. Then hope was revived by news that a van had arrived at the Horseferry Road shop. But, instead of containing boxes of carefully ironed cotton Oxford and Bengal stripes, complete with little cardboard bow-ties to keep the collars straight, it was filled with coat-hangers from which were suspended crumpled pieces of cloth. The presser had missed his flight back from Tahiti or some such holiday resort.

There will be those who say that I should have slipped into a heavy brown check or the little white sleeveless number with the crocodile on the breast pocket. My argument with them will have to await my years of political re-education in the jungles of Barnsley or the time when the cultural revolutionaries require me to contemplate past sins in a Lambeth cowshed.

I could have carefully pulled on a bright blue confection with dazzling white collar and cuffs. But, apart from being out of fashion, my Jermyn Street rhapsody on an original theme by Everton Football Club had a small tear that would have easily survived a normal day's wear but which might well have extended itself across the front of the shirt if provoked by violent movement; like, for instance, a low bow. Since I was preparing for the only day in my life when a low bow might have been required of me, wearing a shirt which would fall apart at the moment of obeisance seemed at best perverse and at worst treasonable.

So I got the ironing-board out. I have no social or sexist objections to ironing. I send my partner (as Councillor Valerie Wise would call her) out to work as an indication of my enthusiasm for equal opportunities. And although she has not (unlike Councillor Wise herself) signed over all the property to the better half of the partnership, I try to accept some share of domestic duties. This highly moral attitude is reinforced by my actual enjoyment of ironing. Smoothing out the wrinkles and making straight what previously was crooked seems to me a rewarding way to spend a Sunday morning. With a little Rodgers and Hart on the gramophone and the smell of Sunday dinner coming round the door, it is possible to think great thoughts while flattening the final crease out of a sleeve or into a trouser leg.

Indeed, I have been accused in the past of being an ironing obsessive. I possess a travelling iron which I take wherever I go. And I pride myself on my hotel bedroom technique — folded towel on the dressing-table to provide a suitable surface, clean handkerchief soaked in water to protect the wool, knob turned round to "v.hot" and the Hattersley auto-valet service is in action.

I even own that special mark of ironing class, a sleeve-board. When Sarah Wilson — my agnostic equivalent of a god-daughter — was a child, she mistook it for "an ironing thing made for little girls". If she had asked me for the diningroom table to make into a "Wendy house", I would have found it difficult to deny her request. But I put the sleeve-board on a high shelf, well out of her reach.

I have loyally maintained my affection for ironing through every vicissitude. Humiliating phone calls to hotel receptionists, asking for a quick check on the room to which I will soon return, "to make sure that the iron is switched off', have done nothing to cool my ardour for applying hot pressure to bent lapels and crushed pocket flaps. The briefcase that marked my first ministerial promotion is scarred for life with a horseshoe-shaped scorch mark. But my search for suitable portable surfaces on which to make the whole world flat continues.

I did not become an ironer, or have ironing thrust upon me. I was born to it. If I am not very careful, I will draw psychological conclusions about my enthusiasm. They concern the Levellers and the pursuit of equality.

Despite all that, I could not resist wondering if any of the other men at the auspicious Buckingham Palace gathering had done any ironing that day. The Speaker wore beneath his velvet suit a riot of ruffles which, if they were prepared by mortal hand, must have been the work of a team of professionals. There was no way of knowing what state shirt (or, indeed, if any shirt at all) was concealed by the Archbishop of York's stock and clerical collar. Loyalty prevented my mind dwelling on either the Duke of Edinburgh's or the Prince of Wales' laundry. But I did speculate a little about the Lord Chamberlain. As Chief Scout, he must often have started fires by rubbing two twigs together and tied securely pieces of rope of unequal thickness. But I was unable to envisage him doing his good deed for the day, stooped over some old lady's ironing-board.

I drew no conclusions from my musing, except the obvious one that ironing is, for better or worse, a wholly working-class occupation. But then, so is bricklaying, and Sir Winston Churchill boasted of that as an achievement as well as a hobby. Perhaps I should include "ironing" in *Who's Who* when I change the entry to include a reference to my industrial proletarian origins. Of course, I could not tell the truth and put my pastime as *ironing exceedingly well*. Thinking of that in Buckingham Palace, I looked down at my shirtfront and felt with pride that, thanks to my own efforts, I was the smoothest man there.

Roy Hatterlsey: The Listener, *27 August 1981*

3

Some Leading Players

What is merit? The opinion one man entertains of another.
—Lord Palmerston

PARLIAMENTARY fashions change quickly, giving political moments of fame and popularity or consigning them in a flash to the ranks of the outsiders, the failures. But there are figures whose stature is apparently permanent, and who escape the wearing process of that ebb and flow of popular esteem. They are giants, recognised by contemporaries and successors as masters of the place in some way, and their traces remain long after they are gone. Their words, associated with the great events, have become Parliamentary history. Some appear elsewhere, but here are a few of these leading players — revealed in speeches to the Commons, and in some descriptions from the reporters' gallery. Starting with Oliver Cromwell is natural: his battles with Parliament cast a long shadow. Here he dismisses the Commons, which sought to limit his power and to increase its own authority. Cromwell's lengthy complaint at Parliament's meddling with his power ended with the issue that disturbed him most, control of the Army.

***

THE PROTECTOR

"There is another Necessity, which you have put upon us, and we have not sought. I appeal to God, Angels and Men, — if I shall 'now' raise money according to the Article in the Government, whether I am not compelled to do it! Which 'Government' had the power to call you hither; and did: — and instead of seasonably providing for the Army, you have laboured to overthrow the Government, and the Army is now upon Free-quarter! And you would never so much as let me hear a title from you concerning it. Where is the fault? Has it not been as if you had a purpose to put this extremity upon us and the Nation? I hope this was not in your minds. I am not willing to judge so: — but such is the state into which we are reduced. By the designs of some in the Army who are now in custody, it was designed to get as many of them as possible, — through discontent for want of money, the Army being in a barren country, near thirty weeks behind in pay, and upon other specious pretences, — to march for England out of Scotland; and, in discontent, to seize their General there [*General Monk*], a faithful and honest man, that so another [*General Overton*] might head the Army. And all this opportunity taken from your delays. Whether will this be a thing of feigned Necessity? What could it signify, but 'The Army are in discontent already; and we will make them live upon stones; we will make them cast-off their governors and discipline?' What can be said to this? I list not to unsaddle myself, and put the fault upon your backs. Whether it hath been for the good of England, whilst men have been talking of this thing or the other, and pretending liberty and many good words, — whether it has been as it should have been? I am confident you cannot think it has. The Nation will not think so. And if the worst should be made of things, I know not what the Cornish men nor the Lincolnshire men may think, or other Counties; but I believe they will all think *they are not safe.* A temporary suspension of 'caring for the greatest liberties and privileges' (if it were so, which is denied) would not have been of such damage as the not providing against Free-quarter hath run the Nation upon. And if it be my 'liberty' to walk abroad in the fields, or to take a journey, yet it is not my wisdom to do so when my house is on fire!

I have troubled you with a long Speech; and I believe it may not have the same resentment with all that it hath with some. But because that is unknown to me, I shall leave it to God; — and conclude with this: That I think myself bound, as in my duty to God, and to the People of these Nations for their safety and good in every respect, — I think it my duty to tell you that it is not for the profit of these Nations, nor for common and public good, for you to continue here any longer. And therefore I do declare unto you, That I do dissolve this Parliament."

Oliver Cromwell, Speech, *22 January 1655*

***

In 1788 Warren Hastings, the former Governor General of India, faced impeachment and it was during the hearings that Richard Brinsley Sheridan — playwright and actor as well as politician — established his lasting reputation as one of the great orators. He began his most celebrated speech in Westminster Hall on June 3 and days later was still going strong. His peroration was hailed by Edmund Burke as unmatched by "every kind of eloquence that had been heard in ancient or modern times".

IMPEACH!

"Other tyrants of whom we read, such as a Nero, or a Caligula, were urged to their crimes by the impetuosity of passion. High rank disqualified them from advice, and perhaps equally prevented reflection. But in the prisoner we have a man born in a state of mediocrity; bred to mercantile life; used to system; and accustomed to regularity; who was accountable to his masters, and therefore was compelled to think and to deliberate on every part of his conduct. It is this cool deliberation, I say, which renders his crimes more horrible, and his character more atrocious.

When, my Lords, the Boards of Directors received the advices which Mr Hastings thought proper to transmit, though unfurnished with any other materials to form their judgment, they expressed very strongly their doubts, and properly ordered an inquiry into the circumstances of the alleged disaffection of the begums, declaring it, at the same time, to be a debt which was due to the honour and justice of the British nation. This inquiry, however, Mr Hastings thought it absolutely necessary to elude. He stated to the council, in answer, 'that it would revive those animosities that subsisted between the begums and the nabob [Asoph Dowlah], which had then subsided. If the former were inclined to appeal to a foreign jurisdiction, they were the best judges of their own feeling, and should be left to make their own complaint.' All this, however, my Lords, is nothing to the magnificent paragraph which concludes this communication.

'Besides,' says he, 'I hope it will not be a departure from official language to say, that the *majesty of justice* ought not to be approached without solicitation. She ought not to descend to inflame or provoke, but to withhold her judgment until she is called on to determine.' What is still more astonishing is, that Sir John Macpherson, who, though a man of sense and honour, is rather Oriental in his imagination, and not learned in the sublime and beautiful from the immortal leader of this prosecution, was caught by this bold, bambastic quibble, and joined in the same words, 'That the *majesty of justice* ought not to be approached without solicitation.' But, my Lords, do you, the judges of this land, and the expounders of its rightful laws — do you approve of this mockery and call it the character of justice, which takes the *form of right* to excite wrong? No, my Lords, justice is not this halt and miserable object; it is not the ineffective bawble of an Indian pagod; it is not the portentous phantom of despair; it is not like any fabled monster, formed in the eclipse of reason, and found in some unhallowed grove of superstitious darkness and political dismay! No, my Lords. In the happy reverse of all this, I turn from the disgusting caricature to the real image! *Justice* I have now before me august and pure! The abstract idea of all that would be perfect in the spirits and the aspirings of men! — where the mind rises; where the heart expands; where the countenance is ever placid and benign; where her favourite attitude is to stoop to the unfortunate; to hear their cry and to help them; to rescue and relieve, to succour and save; majestic, from its mercy; venerable, from its utility; uplifted, without pride; firm, without obduracy; beneficient in each preference; lovely, though in her frown!

On that justice I rely: deliberate and sure, abstracted from all party purpose and political speculation; not on words, but on facts. You, my Lords, who hear me, I conjure, by those rights which it is your best privilege to preserve; by that fame which it is your best pleasure to inherit; by all those feelings which refer to the first term in the series of existence, the original compact of our nature, our controlling rank in the creation. This is the call on all to administer to truth and equity, as they would satisfy the laws and satisfy themselves, with the most exalted bliss possible or conceivable for our nature; the self-approving consciousness of virtue, when the condemnation we look for will be one of the most ample mercies accomplished for mankind since the creation of the world! My Lords, I have done."

Richard Brinsley Sheridan: Speech, *June 1788*

***

Of the speeches of William Pitt the Elder, Earl of Chatham, only bits and pieces remain. But, as compensation, there are accounts by Samuel Johnson of what he believed Pitt to have said, though no doubt the Doctor's superior command of the language has created for Pitt a reputation as an orator which otherwise he might never have had. Here he is, aged thirty-three, responding to an attack by Horatio Walpole — the Prime Minister's brother — who accused him of producing "formidable sounds and lofty declarations" in an oratorial style moulded by youth and inexperience rather than good sense. Dr Johnson reported in *The Gentleman's Magazine* that this was Pitt's reply.

YOUTH DEFENDS ITSELF

"Sir, — The atrocious crime of being a young man, with which the honourable gentleman has with such spirit and decency charged upon me, I shall neither attempt to palliate nor deny, but content myself with wishing that I may be one of those whose follies may cease with their youth, and not of the number who are ignorant in spite of experience. Whether youth can be imputed to any man as a reproach, I will not, sir, assume the province of determining, but surely age may become justly contemptible, if the opportunities which it brings have passed away without improvement, and vice appears to prevail when the passions have subsided. The wretch that, after having seen the consequences of a thousand errors, continues still to blunder, and whose age has only added obstinacy to stupidity, is surely the object of either abhorrence or contempt, and deserves not that his grey head should secure him from insults. Much more, sir, is he to be abhorred who, as he advanced in age has receded from virtue, and becomes more wicked with less temptation; who prostitutes himself for money which he cannot enjoy and spends the remains of his life in the ruin of his country.

But youth, sir, is not my only crime. I have been accused of acting a theatrical part. A theatrical part may either imply some peculiarities of gesture, or a dissimulation of my real sentiments, and an adoption of the opinions and language of another man. In the first sense, sir, the charge is too trifling to be confuted, and deserves only to be mentioned that it may be despised. I am at liberty, like every other man, to use my own language; and though I may perhaps have some ambition to please this gentleman I shall not lay myself under any restraint, nor very solicitously copy his diction, or his mien, however matured by age or modelled by experience.

If any man shall, by charging me with theatrical behaviour, imply that I utter any sentiments but my own I shall treat him as a calumniator and a villain, nor shall any protection shelter him from the treatment which he deserves. I shall on such an occasion, without scruple, trample upon all those forms with which wealth and dignity intrench themselves, nor shall anything but age restrain my resentment; age, which always brings one privilege, that of being insolent and supercilious without punishment."

Samuel Johnson: The Gentleman's Magazine, *September 1741*

***

The Younger Pitt, Prime Minister at twenty-four, can be more accurately reported. There was no doubt about his power on his feet in the Chamber. Here, in 1792, the Prime Minister supports a motion to end the slave trade.

AN ATTACK ON THE BARBARIANS

"There was a time, Sir, when the very practice of the slave trade prevailed among us. Slaves, as we may read in Henry's *History of Great Britain*, were formerly an established article in our exports. 'Great numbers,' he says, 'were exported like cattle from the British coast, and were to be seen exposed for sale in the Roman market.' But is the slavery in Africa which is now called on to furnish the alleged proofs that Africa labours under a natural incapacity for civilization; that Providence never intended her to rise above a state of barbarism; that Providence has irrecoverably doomed her to be only a nursery for slaves for us free and civilized Europeans. Allow of this principle as applied to Africa, and I should be glad to know why it might not also have been applied to ancient and uncivilized Britain? Why might not some Roman Senator, reasoning on the principles of some Hon. Gentleman, and pointing to British barbarians, have predicted, with equal boldness, 'There is a people that will never rise to civilization; there is a people destined never to be free'? We, Sir, have long since emerged from barbarism; we have almost forgotten that we were once barbarians. There is, indeed, one thing wanting to complete the contrast and to clear us altogether from the imputation of acting even to this hour as barbarians; for we continue even to this hour a barbarous traffic in slaves.

Sir, I trust we shall no longer continue this commerce, to the destruction of every improvement on that wide continent; and shall not consider ourselves as conferring too great a boon in restoring its inhabitants to the rank of human beings. I trust we shall not think ourselves too liberal, if, by abolishing the slave trade, we give them the same common chance of civilization with other parts of the world; and that we shall allow to Africa the opportunity — the hope — the prospect of attaining to the same blessings which we ourselves, through the favourable dispensations of Divine Providence, have been permitted, at a much more early period, to enjoy. If we listen to the voice of reason and duty, and pursue this night the line of conduct which they prescribe, some of us may live to see a reverse of that picture from which we now turn our eyes with shame and regret. We may live to behold the natives of Africa engaged in the calm occupations of industry, in the pursuits of a just and legitimate commerce. We may behold the beams of science and philosophy breaking in upon their land, which, as some happy period in still later times, may blaze with full lustre; and joining their influence to that of pure religion, may illuminate and invigorate the most distant extremities of that immense continent. Then may we hope that even Africa, though last of all the quarters of the globe, shall enjoy at length, in the evening of her days, those blessings which have descended so plentifully upon us in a much earlier period of the world. Then also will Europe, participating in her improvement and prosperity, receive an ample recompense for the tardy kindness, if kindness it can be called, of no longer hindering that continent from extricating herself out of the darkness which, in other more fortunate regions, has been so much more speedily dispelled. *'Nos . . . primus equis Oriens afflavit anhelis; Illic sera rubens accendit lumina Vesper'.*"

William Pitt: Speech, *2 April 1792*

***

Pitt's rival, Charles James Fox, was a performer of at least equal power, and their verbal duels over the war with France were passionate affairs. In May 1796 Fox moved a motion criticising the Government's conduct of the war.

AN EVIL WAR?

"No minister who commenced and carried on a war ever made an advantageous peace; but if the present ministers expect to prove an exception to this rule, they should show that they are seriously convinced of their past errors; they should renounce the principles on which they have acted, before they can hope to put an end, with safety and honour, to a war which they have conducted with so much rancour and with so little success.

We have, Sir, completely failed in all the objects for which the war was commenced. Holland is lost, the King of France exiled, and the aggrandisement and power of the French republic is more alarming than ever. Of our allies, the King of Prussia, who was the first to treat with the French, has sustained the least injury; the King of Spain has been forced to make peace in order to save his dominions; and the King of Sardinia is now in the same predicament, compelled, for his own safety, to accept such terms as the directory may choose to grant. The fate of this monarch, whose good faith was so loudly extolled in a late debate, who was termed the very pattern of fidelity, most forcibly and unequivocally demonstrates that in proportion as every ally of this country, in the present contest, has been a pattern of fidelity, he has also been an example of misfortune. The Empress of Russia has indeed suffered nothing. It is impossible not to see that her only object in the alliance was to plunder Poland, in which she has been collaterally supported by England. This is a mortal blow to another professed object of the war, the balance of power. Will any man believe that the avowed object of the partition, the destruction of Jacobinism in Poland, was the real cause of dividing that unfortunate country? And will any man contend that England and France united might not have prevented that transaction, and by that means preserved the balance of power in Europe? But Poland was abandoned to its fate, suffered to be sacrificed, annihilated, destroyed, for the sake of those absurd and vicious principles which govern the policy of ministers, and which have involved us in the present war. These principles must now be deserted. If the country is to be saved, we must retrace our steps; that is the only course which presents any hope of an effectual cure for the evil."

Charles James Fox: Speech, *10 May 1796*

***

Of all Sir Robert Peel's speeches in the Commons, the most dramatic was certainly his defence, in 1846, of the repeal of the Corn Laws — the issue which led to the downfall of his Government, and split the Conservative Party asunder. This is the end of the speech.

REPEAL

"Sir, if I look to the prerogative of the Crown, if I look to the position of the Church, if I look to the influence of the aristocracy, I cannot charge myself with having taken any course inconsistent with Conservative principles, calculated to endanger the privileges of any branch of the Legislature, or any institutions of the country. My earnest wish has been, during my tenure of power, to impress the people of this country with a belief that the Legislature was animated by a sincere desire to frame its legislation upon the principles of equity and justice. I have a strong belief that the greatest object, which we or any other Government can contemplate, should be to elevate the condition of that class of the people with whom we are brought into no direct relationship by the exercise of the elective franchise. I wish to convince them that our object has been to apportion taxation, that we shall relieve industry and labour from any undue burden, and transfer it, so far as is consistent with the public good, to those who are better enabled to bear it. I look to the present peace of this country; I look to the absence of all disturbance; to the non-existence of any commitment for a seditious offence; I look to the calm that prevails in the public mind; I look to the absence of all disaffection; I look to the increased and growing public confidence on account of the course you have taken in relieving trade from restrictions and industry from unjust burdens: and where there was dissatisfaction, I see contentment; where there was turbulence, I see there is peace; where there was disloyalty, I see there is loyalty: I see a disposition to confide in you, and not to agitate questions that are at the foundations of your institutions. Deprive me of power tomorrow, you can never deprive me of the consciousness that I have exercised the powers committed to me from no corrupt or interested motives, from no desire to gratify ambition, or attain any personal object; that I have laboured to maintain peace abroad consistently with the national honour and defending every public right, to increase the confidence of the great body of the people in the justice of your decisions, and by the means of equal law to dispense with all coercive powers, to maintain loyalty to the Throne and attachment to the Constitution, from a conviction of the benefit that will accrue to the great body of the people."

Sir Robert Peel: Speech, *15 May 1846*

***

One of the radicals who had led the Anti-Corn Law League was John Bright, whose fiery style was one of the great features of the Commons. His oposition to the Crimean War was instant — and, initially, unpopular. Here he addresses Lord Palmerston, the Prime Minister, and states his case.

A SOLEMN APPEAL

"There is one subject upon which I should like to put a question to the noble Lord at the head of the Government. I shall not say one word here about the state of the army in the Crimea, or one word about its numbers or its condition. Every Member of this House, every inhabitant of this country, has been sufficiently harrowed with details regarding it. To my solemn belief, thousands — nay, scores of thousands of persons — have retired to rest night after night whose slumbers have been disturbed or whose dreams have been based upon the sufferings and agonies of our soldiers in the Crimea. I should like to ask the noble Lord at the head of the Government — although I am not sure if he will feel that he can or ought to answer the question — whether the noble Lord the Member for London has power, after discussions have commenced, and as soon as there shall be established good grounds for believing that the negotiations for peace will prove successful, to enter into any armistice? [Shouts of 'No! No!']

I know not, Sir, who it is that says 'No, no', but I should like to see any man get up and say that the destruction of 200,000 human lives lost on all sides during the course of this unhappy conflict is not a sufficient sacrifice. You are not pretending to conquer territory — you are not pretending to hold fortified or unfortified towns; you have offered terms of peace which, as I understand them, I do not say are not moderate; and breathes there a man in this House or in this country whose appetite for blood is so insatiable that, even when terms of peace have been offered and accepted, he pines for that assault in which of Russian, Turk, or French and English, as sure as one man dies, 20,000 corpses will strew the streets of Sebastopol? I say I should like to ask the noble Lord — and I am sure that he will feel, and that this House will feel, that I am speaking in no unfriendly manner towards the Government of which he is at the head — I should like to know, and I venture to hope that it is so, if the noble Lord the Member for London has power, at the earliest stage of these proceedings at Vienna, at which it can properly be done — and I should think that it might properly be done at a very early stage — to adopt a course by which all further waste of human life may be put an end to, and further animosity between three great nations be, as far as possible, prevented?

I appeal to the noble Lord at the head of the Government and to this House; I am not now complaining of the war — I am not now complaining of the terms of peace, nor, indeed, of anything that has been done — but I wish to suggest to this House what, I believe, thousands and tens of thousands of the most educated and of the most Christian portion of the people of this country are feeling upon this subject, although, indeed, in the midst of a certain clamour in the country, they do not give public expression to their feelings. Your country is not in an advantageous state at this moment; from one end of the kingdom to the other there is a general collapse of industry. Those Members of this House not intimately acquainted with the trade and commerce of the country do not fully comprehend our position as to the diminution of employment and the lessening of wages. An increase in the cost of living is finding its way to the homes and hearts of a vast number of the labouring population.

At the same time there is growing up — and, notwithstanding what some Hon. Members of this House may think of me, no man regrets it more than I do — a bitter and angry feeling against that class which has for a long period conducted the public affairs of this country. I like political changes when such changes are made as the result, not of passion, but of deliberation and reason. Changes so made are safe, but changes made under the influence of violent exaggeration or of the violent passions of public meetings, are not changes usually approved by this House or advantageous to the country. I cannot but notice, in speaking to gentlemen who sit on either side of this House, or in speaking to any one I meet between this House and any of those localities we frequent when this House is up — I cannot, I say, but notice that an uneasy feeling exists as to the news which may arrive by the very next mail from the East. I do not suppose that your troops are to be beaten in actual conflict with the foe, or that they will be driven into the sea; but I am certain that many homes in England in which there now exists a fond hope that the distant one may return — many such homes may be rendered desolate when the next mail shall arrive. The Angel of Death has been abroad throughout the land; you may almost hear the beatings of his wings. There is no one, as when the first-born were slain of old, to sprinkle with blood the lintel and the two sideposts of our doors, that he may spare and pass on; he takes his victims from the castle of the noble, the mansion of the wealthy, and the cottage of the poor and the lowly, and it is on behalf of all these classes that I make this solemn appeal."

John Bright: Speech, 7 *June 1855*

***

Benjamin Disraeli — whom Michael Foot has called "the good Tory" — has had a lasting appeal for Parliamentarians, perhaps because of the startling combination of political resolution and skill and his exotic style. As Lord Beaconsfield he went to the Congress of Berlin in 1878 and when he returned to address the Lords the scene was described by Henry W. Lucy.

A TRIUMPH

It was charming to see how Lord Beaconsfield, back from Berlin, bringing "Peace with Honour", entered just now, as if nothing particular were the matter, and as if the last thing in the world he expected was to find the House of Lords crowded from the floor to the roof of the canopy over the Throne. In the same unpretentious and unexpected manner he had, a few minutes earlier, quitted the dull-looking house at the bottom of Downing Street. Whilst the thoughts of all the world were centred at Westminster, and whilst some thousands of hero-worshippers were thronging the gates of Palace Yard, the hero of the day was quietly walking down Parliament Street bent upon recommencing his Parliamentary duties interrupted by a trip to Berlin. He had not even done the day the honour of specially dressing for it. When Gladstone is about to make a great speech in the House of Commons, somebody — surely not himself — brushes him up, "tidies" him, and puts a flower in a buttonhole of his coat. Beaconsfield did not do all his dressing in the far-off days when he wore ringlets and twirled a gold-headed cane, dexterously attached to his wrist by a silken tassel. Even now strangers may occasionally meet in the neighbourhood of Parliament Street a notable figure making its way through the throng. They note how frail and weary the body seems, how bent the shoulders, how sunken the cheeks, how leaden-hued the lineaments. But they also note the dauntless spirit which still affects a jaunty carriage, and makes-believe that progress is slowly made only because there is no hurry. They further observe with admiration the careful newness of the accessories of the figure — the shapely coat of the lightest material, the negligent but elegant neckcloth, the pearl-grey gloves guiltless of wrinkle, and the glossy hat.

These things are, however, only for commonplace occasions. Today, which marks a crowning stage in a memorable career, let us put on the old coat, the second-best hat, and the dingy-brown trousers of long ago. Let us, also, walk down Parliament Street instead of driving in a coach and four, and let us take by surprise the crowd which has its back turned to us, and is eagerly scanning the interior of the stately equipages which drive into the Yard in quick succession.

A crowd in Palace Yard! A surging multitude by the railings! Beaconsfield was never more surprised in his life. What could be the matter? Had some one in authority been pulling up park railings, and was this ovation intended for the champions of the popular right? Had Gladstone been reducing some taxes, or freeing the Church, or emancipating the land, and was this the grateful throng come to sing paens in his honour? Beaconsfield could not imagine; but he walked slowly on unnoticed, and crossing on the right-hand side, as if he were making for the quietness and peace of the cloisters of Westminster Abbey, he turned sharply off to the left when he neared the gates of Old Palace Yard. Then with a sudden rush and a ringing cheer the surprised crowd closed round him, and threatened to carry him off his feet.

And so they bore him into the Houses of Parliament, whither his colleagues of the Commons had already arrived, breathless after the rush across the lobby. Here another surprise awaited him. Instead of the empty benches over which the sound of Big Ben chiming five o'clock usually booms, here was the Chamber thronged in every part. At the far end, piled head over head, were the strangers in the gallery, and on either side, packed equally close, were many familiar faces, often turned upon him in "another place". This he saw, entering from behind the Throne, and while making his way through a multitude of Privy Councillors in whom there was the wisdom to be early in their places in the space before the Throne. Except one kept vacant for him, a hurried glance round the benches showed not a single empty seat, whilst from the galleries that run round the Chamber bright eyes looked down and rained influence upon a Premier who is not only a politician but a courtier.

It is a summer day, and all the hues of a flower-garden are blended in the soft lights of the rainbow which the beauty and rank of the Empire form, and through which, after the storm of the Congress, the sun shines down on the Prime Minister. Royalty is not lacking to the stateliness of the historic scene. If the Premier were to look up he would see in the gallery straight before him the Princess of Wales, fairest among the fair. But he does not look up. He has got over the surprise that awaited him outside, and is satisfied with the glance around which he took when first seating himself on the Ministerial bench. Thereafter he relapsed into his immobile manner, with arms crossed and head held down, the observed of all observers, himself observing none.

A profound silence, broken only by the rustling of fans in the gallery, fell upon the assembly. The Premier had fortunately timed his entry so that all the private business was disposed of, and no consideration of such topics as Vivisection or the Scotch Roads and Bridges Bill lowered the dignity of the occasion. There was nothing to do but to listen to the eagerly anticipated statement. At this moment an unseen hand flung back one of the painted windows near the roof, and a great beam of white light flashed across the solemn gloom of the Chamber, bringing into sudden brilliancy the white law of the Bishops, and falling upon the rainbow hues of the group at the lower end of the gallery, just below the Princess of Wales. Salisbury entered, and was greeted with cheers from his friends. As if Beaconsfield were only waiting for the arrival of his companion in the journey to Berlin, he now rose, and, advancing to the table, was received with renewed cheers.

Henry W. Lucy: A Diary of Two Parliaments

***

In this century Winston Churchill's place as *the* master of the Commons has hardly been challenged. It is a reputation established by the wartime speeches (allowing MPs to forget some less distinguished performances in the past) and they still have their old power on the printed page. This is Churchill's first address to the Commons as Prime Minister in May 1940, looking ahead to the coming conflict and seeking to inspire MPs — and a nation — downcast at nine months of failure under Neville Chamberlain since the declaration of war.

TO VICTORY

"On Friday evening last I received His Majesty's Commission to form a new Administration. It was the evident wish and will of Parliament and the nation that this should be conceived on the broadest possible basis and that it should include all parties, both those who supported the late Government and also the parties of the Opposition. I have completed the most important part of this task. A War Cabinet has been formed of five Members, representing, with the Opposition Liberals, the unity of the nation. The three party Leaders have agreed to serve, either in the War Cabinet or in high executive office. The three Fighting Services have been filled. It was necessary that this should be done in one single day, on account of the extreme urgency and rigour of events. A number of other positions, key positions, were filled yesterday, and I am submitting a further list to His Majesty tonight. I hope to complete the appointment of the principal Ministers during tomorrow. The appointment of the other Ministers usually takes a little longer, but I trust that, when Parliament meets again, this part of my task will be completed, and that the administration will be complete in all respects. . . .

In this crisis I hope I may be pardoned if I do not address the House at any length today, I hope that any of my friends and colleagues, or former colleagues, who are affected by the political reconstruction, will make allowance, all allowance, for any lack of ceremony with which it has been necessary to act. I would say to the House, as I said to those who have joined this Government: 'I have nothing to offer but blood, toil, tears and sweat'.

We have before us an ordeal of the most grievous kind. We have before us many, many long months of struggle and of suffering. You ask, what is our policy? I will say: it is to wage war, by sea, land and air, with all our might and with all the strength that God can give us; to wage war against a monstrous tyranny, never surpassed in the dark, lamentable catalogue of human crime. That is our policy. You ask, what is our aim? I can answer in one word: it is victory, victory at all costs, victory in spite of all terror, victory, however long and hard the road may be; for without victory, there is no survival. Let that be realised; no survival for the British Empire, no survival for all that the British Empire has stood for, no survival for the urge and impulse of the ages, that mankind will move forward towards its goal. But I take up my task with buoyancy and hope. I feel sure that our cause will not be suffered to fail among men. At this time I feel entitled to claim the aid of all, and I say, Come then, let us go forward together with our united strength."

Winston Churchill: Speech, *13 May 1940*

***

The scene was described for the *Manchester Guardian* by Harry Boardman.

BLOOD, TOIL, TEARS AND SWEAT

The new Government met the House of Commons today and received a vote of confidence that was unanimous except for the opposition of Mr Maxton and Mr Campbell Stephen. These two parachutists, dropping from cloud-cuckoo-land, insisted on dividing the House. The division thus resulted in 381 votes being cast for the Government and none against because, of course, Mr Maxton and Mr Campbell Stephen had to act as "tellers" for the cloud-cuckoo-land party, and the other member of it, Mr McGovern, was last heard of setting out for a holiday in Holland, last week.

When the division was called it was queer to see Conservatives, Labour men, Liberals, Simonites, National Labour, all massing at the entrances to the "Aye" Division Lobby. As a too-eloquent Welsh member said, trying to express everybody's puzzlement, "It is very difficult to reorientate oneself to what has happened." Corinthian and true.

There was Mr Churchill sitting opposite the Treasury Box, hands on knee. Mr Chamberlain was on his right, Mr Attlee and Mr Alexander on his left. Sir Archibald Sinclair was further down the bench, while behind the Speaker's chair, peering into the chamber like lost angels outside paradise, were some of the ministers who have gone. Mr Herbert Morrison took the corner seat above the gangway, while below the gangway, three seats up, was Sir Samuel Hoare, in the very place from which he made his speech of resignation as Foreign Secretary.

A solid phalanx of Labour second strings confronted the Government on the Opposition front bench. Very obviously they, like their Welsh colleague, were struggling to "reorientate" themselves to a world in which Mr Attlee, Mr Alexander and Mr Herbert Morrison sat opposite them.

Mr Churchill had an inspiring cheer when he entered the Chamber, but Mr Chamberlain, when he came in a moment later, was cheered even more loudly by the Conservatives, some of whom stood up to greet the late Prime Minister.

The House was grave, graver than on the September Sunday morning when war was declared. But that does not mean it was depressed. Far from it. It was exalted as well as grave. At last it has seen the peril that impends over us in all its fearful menace, and the vision has raised it to an invincible temper. Now has it become a Grand Committee of National Safety, willing to back Mr Churchill and his colleagues to the utmost limit.

Mr Churchill was the calmest man in the Chamber. Calm in crisis was his great ancestor's quality. He himself has described his mode of address in the House of Commons as "formal conversation". That exactly describes his words today. He even had his hands in his pockets at times. And yet there was solemnity enough in his words.

To his new colleagues he could offer nothing but "blood, toil, tears, and sweat". This echo of Garibaldi prepared the way for the further warning that the country has before it a most grievous ordeal and many long months of struggle and suffering. To those who asked for the Government's policy he answered: "It is to wage war by sea, land, and air, war with all our minds and with all our strength that God gives us; to wage war against a monstrous tyranny never surpassed in the dark and lamentable catalogue of human crimes."

As the cheers were echoing round the Chamber Mr Churchill put the second question, "What is our aim?" To which he replied, "Victory at all costs and in spite of all terrors; victory, however long and hard the road may be, for without victory there is no survival." There were again resounding cheers for this pithy yet eloquent definition of the new Government's purposes. Then we heard Mr Churchill concluding on a note of buoyancy and hope, because "our cause cannot be suffered to fail among men".

Of the speeches that followed one rose most surely to the height of this moment of destiny. It was Mr Lloyd George's. He called it "a critical and terrible moment — a graver moment of jeopardy than has confronted a British Minister for all time". This from the man who saw us so near defeat in 1917. "We all, from the bottom of our hearts, wish him well. The friends of freedom and of human right throughout the world will wish him God-speed." Lincoln could not have bettered his brief speech.

Harry Boardman: Manchester Guardian, *14 May 1940*

Boardman, whose reporting exhibited a great affection for the Commons as well as a sharp eye for the failings of mortal politicians, worked at Westminster from 1929 until his death in 1958. He was noted as a fastidious correspondent, a studious man of great knowledge, and he never used a typewriter. This is his account of the appointment as Prime Minister of another of the giants, Harold Macmillan, after the fall of Anthony Eden.

SUPERMAC

It was a mercy that doubts about the succession were so quickly put to rest. The political misfortune of the country being Prime Ministerless for any length of time was obvious, but by the evidence on all hands people were suffering, even for this short time, a suspense that is only a justifiable infliction on Derby Day.

So conscious of this were people in authority in institutions, clubs, and the like, that the appointment of Mr Macmillan was being proclaimed at half-past two over numberless loudspeakers. The majority had made up their minds that it must be either Mr Macmillan or Mr Butler, or, rather, if attention is to be paid to "form" as it weighed in the popular mind, Mr Butler or Mr Macmillan. The choice of Mr Macmillan in preference to the supposed favourite was determined by considerations all of which cannot be known to the public.

If this Government had to continue in being, and the test was to be pure intellectual capacity, the choice would have fallen on Mr Butler, but brains cannot be the sole test. Strength of character, political acumen and judgment are as important considerations. In these Mr Butler does not suffer in comparison with Mr Macmillan. Where he did compare unfavourably with the new Prime Minister is in the mysterious emanations of character that make a personality.

No one would describe Mr Macmillan as a winning personality, but he has an air. He does not think it out of place to bring a little artistry to the business of the House of Commons. Again, as one might expect from one owing so much to a great firm of publishers, he falls easily into literary allusiveness. He knows, too, that slang can be occasionally effective, though he has no doubt never ceased to repent that unpremeditated exclamation: "There ain't gonna be no war."

This dashing side of him has its amiable appeal, but it must not be exaggerated. A sense of humour, it has been said, is only possible in serious men, and Mr Macmillan is as deeply serious in his approach to public affairs as Mr Butler or anyone else. There is Scottish blood in him.

In his earlier years, when office seemed remote, he took it upon himself to instruct the Tory Party about a new ordering of our industrial and economic system on Tory democratic lines. This he did in several books that were not altogether innocent of collectivist tendencies. He was toying, you might say, with "Butskellism" before Mr Butler or Mr Gaitskell. What commends him as much as anything to many in his party is that he is of a frank and open mind, not tempted to clutch at half-truth, that life-belt of so many politicians.

Harry Boardman: Manchester Guardian, *11 January 1957*

4

"Upstairs": The House of Lords

"I am dead: dead, but in the Elysian fields."
—Benjamin Disraeli, asked if he would miss the excitements of the Commons on becoming the Earl of Beaconsfield

A severe though not unfriendly critic of our institutions said that the cure for admiring the House of Lords was to go and look at it.
—Walter Bagehot: *The English Constitution*

FROM the Commons it is always "upstairs", the place you go when your political life is drawing gently to its close. No matter that many have prospered in the Upper House, nor that it has a reputation (only partly deserved) for civilised and informed debate, it is still regarded as a sort of half-way house between the real world of politics and oblivion. The Lords is the only House in a Western democracy which works on the understanding that more than half its members do not turn up to vote. The hereditary Peers, the Bishops and the Life Peers lead a strange life, caught between their duty as a revising chamber and the constant threats of abolition which have been ringing in their ears for decades. It is a place for Heath-Robinson politics, produced by an intricate machine whose complexities seem unnecessary, if delightfully Byzantine. In the Parliamentary world it has its own strange atmosphere. Disraeli, who fulfilled his ambition of prospering in both Houses, wrote in his political novel *Coningsby* of the peerage and its place of work.

***

MAINTAINED BY MANNERS?

"I have always understood," said Coningsby, "that our peerage was the finest in Europe."

"From themselves," said Millbank, "and the heralds they pay to paint their carriages. But I go to facts. When Henry VII called his first

Parliament, there were only twenty-nine temporal peers to be found, and even some of them took their seats illegally, for they had been attainted. Of those twenty-nine not five remain, and they, as the Howards for instance, are not Norman nobility. We owe the English peerage to three sources: the spoilation of the Church; the open and flagrant sale of its honours by the elder Stuarts; and the boroughmongering of our own times. Those are the three main sources of the existing peerage of England, and in my opinion disgraceful ones. But I must apologise for my frankness in thus speaking to an aristocrat."

"Oh, by no means, sir, I like discussion. Your son and myself at Eton have had some encounters of this kind before. But if your view of the case be correct," added Coningsby, smiling, "you cannot at any rate accuse our present peers of Norman manners."

"Yes, I do; they adopted Norman manners while they usurped Norman titles. They have neither the right of the Normans, nor do they fulfil the duty of the Normans: they did not conquer the land, and they do not defend it."

"And where will you find your natural aristocracy?" asked Coningsby.

"Among those men whom a nation recognises as the most eminent for virtue, talents, and property, and, if you please, birth and standing in the land. They guide opinions; and, therefore, they govern. I am no leveller; I look upon an artificial equality as equally pernicious with a factitious aristocracy; both depressing the energies, and checking the enterprise of a nation. I like man to be free, really free: free in his industry as well as his body. What is the use of Habeas Corpus, if a man may not use his hands when he is out of prison?"

"But it appears to me you have, in a great measure, this natural aristocracy in England."

"Ah, to be sure! If we had not, where should we be? It is the counter-acting power that saves us, the disturbing cause in the calculations of short-sighted selfishness. I say it now, and I have said it a hundred times, the House of Commons is a more aristocratic body than the House of Lords. The fact is, a great peer would be a greater man now in the House of Commons than in the House of Lords. Nobody wants a second chamber, except a few disreputable individuals. It is a valuable institution for any member of it who has no distinction, neither character, talents, nor estate. But a peer, who possesses all or any of these great qualifications, would find himself an immeasurably more important personage in what, by way of jest, they call the Lower House."

"Is not the revising wisdom of a senate a salutary check on the precipitation of a popular assembly?"

"Why should a popular assembly, elected by the flower of a nation, be precipitate? If precipitate, what senate could stay an assembly so chosen? No, no, no! The thing has been tried over and over again; the idea of restraining the powerful by the weak is an absurdity; the question is settled. If we wanted a fresh illustration, we need only look to the present state of our own House of Lords. It originates nothing; it has, in fact, announced itself as a mere Court of Registration of the decrees of your House of Commons; and if by any chance it ventures to alter some miserable detail in a clause of a bill that excites public interest, what a clatter through the country, at Conservative banquets got up by the rural attorneys, about the power, authority, and independence of the House of Lords; nine times nine, and one cheer more! No, sir, you may make aristocracies by laws; you can only maintain them by manners. The manners of England preserve it from its laws. And they have substituted for our formal aristocracy an essential aristocracy; the government of those who are distinguished by their fellow-citizens."

"But then it would appear," said Coningsby, "that the remedial action of our manners has removed all the political and social evils of which you complain?"

"They have created a power that may remove them; a power that has the capacity to remove them. But in a great measure they still exist, and must exist yet, I fear, for a long time. The growth of our civilisation has ever been as slow as our oaks; but this tardy development is preferable to the temporary expansion of the gourd."

"The future seems to me sometimes a dark cloud."

"Not to me," said Mr Millbank. "I am sanguine; I am the Disciple of Progress."

Benjamin Disraeli: Coningsby

***

Among the many peculiarities of the Lords, now long passed out of use, is the right of a Peer to be tried by his fellows, under the magnificent ceiling of Augustus Pugin's great chamber, with the Peers and the judges clustered on the scarlet benches. Chips Channon described the trial, on a charge of manslaughter, of Lord de Clifford — the last of its kind to take place.

AN ACQUITTAL

House of Commons all day and it seems interminable. Am I to sit and smoke and drink myself to death in the smoking-room, thus making myself better-known and, perhaps liked? Or shall I burrow in the library for the next five years and re-become what I once was, well educated and well read? Most of today I spent reading Lamartine.

But I am forgetting the trial. At 10 a.m. Alfred Beit fetched me and we drove to the Royal Gallery in the House of Lords to attend the much-discussed trial of young Lord de Clifford. The Hall resembled a Venetian canvas, gilt and red. There were places assigned for the Peeresses, others for Ambassadors, for strangers, for Members of the House, for witnesses, etc. At 11 o'clock the Lord Chancellor, red-robed, bewigged, entered and was followed by the Peers; about 105 of them in glorious robes and cocked hats. But I noticed that the more venerable peers, including Desborough, Scarborough, Londonderry, etc., were not in their robes, whereas others such as Donegal, Faringdon, etc., were resplendent in red. Some documents were read, old fashioned Norman documents sounding like Froissart. Then young de Clifford was brought in . . . tall, good-looking and sufficiently distinguished; he was wearing morning clothes. He was charged and pleaded "not guilty" in an audible voice. The trial then proceeded; it was like Iolanthe. The policemen who were witnesses wore new uniforms; and they were followed by two pretty girls who testified. As one gave her name and address I saw one old Peer raise his robes, fish out a pencil and, no doubt, note down her address. I went to the trial thoroughly believing in de Clifford's guilt, as did many others, considering him a déclassé night-club Peer, and a semi-drunkard. Within a quarter of an hour, so clear and concise is British justice, everyone was convinced of his innocence.

When the verdict was announced, it was a unanimous one — a complete acquittal. There was no case against de Clifford, scarcely a shred of evidence, and he is a teetotaller. It has now been divulged that the man who was killed had four motoring offences against him, some for driving when intoxicated. These were not mentioned at the trial.

It was a glorious sight, and perhaps one that will never be seen again.

Chips Cannon: Diary, *12 December 1934*

***

For two generations now Lords reform has seldom been out of politicians' minds, since Asquith's Parliament Act of 1911 began to curb the power of the Upper House. The Labour Government of 1966-70 proposed another Parliament bill, destined to fall, to reform the chamber. Richard Crossman, the Leader of the House of Commons, described in his diary the Queen's Speech in which it was announced.

A LITLE *FRISSON*

In due course Frank Longford and I stroll through the anteroom of the Lords and there we are suddenly in the Royal Gallery — usually a huge empty corridor with the vast picture of the battle of Waterloo on the one side and that of the battle of Trafalgar on the other. Now there are boxes on each side, packed with people who've been standing there for hours.

They've done this just to see the Queen emerge from the Robing Room and walk with her procession behind her into the House of Lords. Then they won't see anything more until she has read the Queen's Speech and walked back down the Royal Gallery again. That's all that this distinguished crowd of waiting people will see. Gradually the boxes begin to fill up and the space where we are standing fills up with chaps wearing swords. Frank and I are told we should be stationed behind the Lord Chancellor on the stairs leading down to the Norman Porch, where the Queen enters. These stairs are also packed with troops on both sides and when we stand there it is very difficult not to get knocked by the trooper behind you when he presents swords, which he seems to be doing on and off for twenty minutes or so. Above us in the Royal Gallery are Field-Marshal Montgomery and Eddie getting ready for their function, surrounded by Air Marshals and Generals. But I am down on one of the lower stairs and suddenly looking up I see a bloated caricature, whose eyes you can hardly see because he is covered by a helmet with white plumes flying at the edge. It is Frank Bowles, walking very gingerly down the stairs so as not to trip over his golden spurs because if he did he could never get up. And then I see Frank Beswick looking almost as idiotic in his costume of Captain of the Gentlemen-at-Arms. In all this fancy dress Frank Longford and I stand out because we're the only people in ordinary civilian clothes — yes, my morning coat felt quite ordinary in that assembly. We are able to stroll about and talk to our friends and quite to enjoy ourselves.

What do I think? I think it's like the *Prisoner of Zenda* but not nearly as smart or well done as it would be at Hollywood. It's more what a real Ruritania would look like — far more comic, more untidy, more homely, less grand. The only grand things I saw were the Crown dazzling with jewels on its cushion and the Queen herself, with the royal princes and princesses. However, even there one could see that Snowdon's top hat had fallen off before he could get out of his car. The older royals are the best — particularly the Dowager Duchess of Kent, but not the goofy Duke of Gloucester, looking terrible with his very dull wife. Well, they come piling in one after another, the Cap of Maintenance comes, the Sword comes, the Crown comes and then down comes the Lord Chancellor in his magnificent robes and stands just in front of Frank and me — I on the right and Frank on the left. And suddenly I notice that the lace under his chin is trembling. The whole Lord Chancellor — though he adores these ceremonies, he tells me, because he always wanted to be a great actor — is trembling. Is it emotion or fear or tension? I don't know, but for more than half an hour he stands there trembling before the Queen arrives. And, of course, we never get more than a glimpse of her because as she arrives we have to turn and march smartly ahead of her up the stairs whereupon she turns left into the Robing Room while we form up and wait inside the Royal Gallery and then in due course process in front of her into the House of Lords.

On this state occasion the House of Lords is really magnificent — all the Law Lords, the Bishops, then the diplomats and their ladies with all their jewels, and behind them lines and lines of peers and peeresses, and above all of them the gallery and enormous arc lights for the televising of the Queen.

I come in at the right-hand door and stand just by the throne next to the Lord Chancellor and the Duke of Norfolk. And I have to watch her reading the appalling Speech for which I am responsible. It is certainly not designed for reading aloud in the House of Lords. Next time I must take some trouble to get a speech that sounds good when it's read aloud because this one sounds difficult and Harold Wilson's sentences about inflation are impossible to enunciate. But I did notice that when she read the sentence about curbing the power of the Lords she made a little pause and read it with just a *frisson* and the whole House had just a *frisson* too.

Richard Crossman: Diary, *October 1967*

***

Crossman again, this time on the Second Reading of the Reform Bill. He described the first rumblings of dissatisfaction that were to destroy his scheme for a nominated Upper House.

A BATTLE IS JOINED

I had cut out about a fifth of our final draft and, looking back, I delivered it too fast and too self-confidently. My greatest mistake was that when I was interrupted, which was a great deal, I replied cleverly, intellectually, superiorly, and the more I was questioned from behind the more clearly I showed what fools they were to put things to me in that way. So, though the back benchers didn't dislike me, by the end I had done nothing whatsoever to persuade them. My speech was followed by Dingle Foot, Enoch Powell and Willie Hamilton. I heard those three before I had to leave. The second and third speeches were ribald and dangerous, with Powell fanatically proving the case that no change could be made, Hamilton fanatically proving the case that the whole House of Lords must be abolished. Then came Maurice Edelman, mostly about placemen, portraying Harold like another Robert Walpole, and then David Marquand, whose speech I really recommend as by far the most revealing.

It was this, when I read it later, that made me suddenly realise something I had completely failed to anticipate. I had always known we would have great difficulty with our scheme and that it would be extremely difficult to get people in the House of Commons to accept it, and we knew that the point about remuneration and nomination had not been understood at the Party meeting. What I hadn't realised was the inferiority complex, the deep suspicion that if at the other end of the passage on those red carpets we set up a nominated House of Lords with a real, nice, tidy, neat job at £2,000 a year, it would be far more attractive to be a peer than to be a commoner, sitting on the green benches. MPs cannot tolerate the idea of giving the Lords a sensible job in the best club in the world. There really is something in this.

I felt this very strongly when I went along to the Lords and sat on the steps of the Throne and had a drink with Eddie in their bar, a magnificent room, a club room. There were Beattie Plummer and Patricia Llewelyn-Davies and Ted Heath talking to St Aldwyn, Eddie, Malcolm Shepherd and me. It was frankly a far more civilized, clubby atmosphere. I must admit that though people laugh and say "Lord Crossman of Banbury" there is a great deal of truth in it because I would be wholly at home in the reformed House of Lords I have been creating, and I think back benchers have a point when they feel that we on the front bench are creating a better hole for ourselves.

Richard Crossman: Diary, *19 November 1968*

***

It is of course a place dominated by conservative instincts, and Conservative Peers. But in 1984 there was a shock, recorded by Godfrey Barker in the *Daily Telegraph* — the inbuilt Conservative majority was an illusion. What next?

A MOMENT OF DISBELIEF

The Government solemnly told the House of Lords yesterday that it has lost its overall majority there.

"My lords, as of April 28, 1,097 peers were in receipt of a writ of summons. Of these, only 462 were Government peers, or 42.1 per cent of the total," intoned Lord Denham, Chief Whip.

What? Mrs Thatcher has an overall majority of 141 in the Commons and none in the Lords?

The news appeared to unhinge their lordships. Derision, guffaws, noble ho-hos and cackles rocked the crimson Opposition benches.

Lord Denham gazed impassively back at the split in the aisles.

He did, let's face it, have a credibility problem. Not just you, me and Mr Roy Hattersley have swallowed that cliché that the Lords is stuffed with last-gasp loyalty to the Conservative Party. But *tempus fugit* (Virgil).

Lord Wilson's been at work. The place is now replete with Ron

Brigginshaws and Hugh Scanlons and the horny sons of toil.

Just to explain his anguish another way, Bertie rattled off that if you took the 281 Lords who attended half or more the sessions in 1982-83, 122 of them, or 43.4 per cent, supported the Government.

Disbelief still racked the faces opposite. "Of 353 peers who attended one-third or more, 147 were Government peers, or 42.6 per cent. Of 754 who attended at least once, 344 backed us, or 45.6 per cent," he rammed it home further.

If you sampled 27,226 peers' attendances in 1982-83, only 11,816 were by Tory peers (43.4 per cent) of the 100 most frequent peers, 43.355 per cent were Conservative.

If you went through life peers and first creations only, Labour had a Lords majority of 9 over the Conservatives. Labour and the Alliance together had a Lords majority of 55.

"Ow ow ow! Pull the other one," roared the Lords at the news that they are now a hung Parliament (official).

This is far from idle invention, of course. Mrs T has so far been defeated 57 times in the Lords since 1979 (fewer than five in the Commons) and she well knows that on the Rates Bill, the Police Bill and the Trade Union Bill, she has no assurance at all she can get everything through.

"It's a fallacy to believe that all peers are Conservative until proven innocent," rhubarbed Lord Denham piously.

So it's fact. Rather less plausible was the urbane fantasy of Lord (Jo) Grimond, one of nature's peers, that there is considerable public debate about who really represents the majority of the electors.

"The Government do not — they were elected at the General Election without an overall majority of votes," he drawled loudly.

"Surely this is the House which represents the feeling the country, not Another Place?"

Their lordships whooped at that. Lord Denham, not too reluctantly, conceded that sometimes that might be true.

Godfrey Barker: Daily Telegraph, *18 April 1984*

***

It is always a strange moment when a giant of the Commons lumbers "upstairs", exchanging the party battle for the ermine robes and a life of relative ease. Here Clement Attlee, leader of the post-war reforming Labour Government, takes his seat, as described in *The Manchester Guardian*, as it then was, by Harry Boardman.

"UPSTAIRS": THE HOUSE OF LORDS

ATTLEE'S ASCENT

It was the day of Clement Attlee's ascension. A House of Lords almost bursting at the seams at the floor level and in the public, side, and press galleries looked on as he was received into the bosom of his peers in his hired ermine, which, by the way, was worth every penny of the three guineas he had paid for the loan of it.

The Lord Great Chamberlain would have been justified in putting up a "House Full" notice as is done for more vulgar shows. Mr Gaitskell, for example, was just not shut out from the side gallery, which was just as well, for a leader of the Labour Party should begin early getting acclimatised to his ultimate bourne. Other Labour leaders exercised their right to watch the pantomime from the steps of the throne. Lady Attlee and her family looked down on it from the good view afforded by the side gallery facing the Labour benches.

If ever the House of Lords reminded one of the saying of some old member of it that it is like a ducal mansion with the duke lying dead upstairs, it was yesterday. The silence was unearthly as, first, Black Rod, followed by the Garter King of Arms, followed by the Earl Marshall, followed by the Lord Great Chamberlain, moved with phantom tread up the floor of the Chamber towards the Woolsack where sat the Lord Chancellor with a black tricorne on his head. A Rubens would have been required to do justice to the brilliant colouring of the habiliments of these four. A large bundle of ermine that turned out to be Lord Baldwin, the new earl's first sponsor, followed in the wake of the four demi-gods.

Next, surmounting another bundle of ermine, was the familiar bald cranium of the new earl, and we began to feel we were not complete prisoners of a dream. We have looked down on the late commoner's bald head so long as almost to have a sense of property in it. Lord Huntingdon, the second sponsor, brought up the rear of the erminesque file. Now the pantomime could begin.

The four demi-gods got out of the way of the new earl as he advanced to the Woolsack, bent one knee, and gave the Lord Chancellor the Queen's warrant which was the fount and origin of all this business. He then retreated to the table and the warrant was read by the Clerk. This advanced Clement Attlee by the "abundant and special" royal grace to the state and degree, first, of Viscount Prestwood and then of Earl Attlee. There was something about his being girded with a sword, endowed with a cap of honour, and graced with a coronet of gold.

These symbols of his new dignity did not materialise. They do not belong to this ceremony but they can be hired for such occasions as require them. There may be an odd sword or two at Transport House which they have no use for.

There followed the reading of the writ or summons addressed in the name of Elizabeth II to our "right trusted and well-beloved chevalier". This commands the said well-beloved chevalier to join in deliberating on "certain arduous and urgent affairs" and what not. The former Mr Attlee was now really one with our nobility and he signed the roll in witness of it.

But the play was not finished. He took a seat between his two sponsors. The four demi-gods appeared before him. Three times the Garter Knight dropped his staff and three times the new earl and his sponsors rose, doffed their cocked hats and bowed in the direction of the Lord Chancellor.

All that remained now was for Earl Attlee to go up to the Lord Chancellor, shake him by the hand and depart, which he did to a politely-modulated cheer. Later he returned, having suffered a sea change into nothing stranger than the Attlee of Limehouse and Walthamstow and Cherry Cottage. His peers gave him another cheer. He sat for a while listening to a debate on officers' pay.

Harry Boardman: Manchester Guardian, *26 January 1956*

***

Much earlier, Disraeli made the same journey along the corridor and Henry Lucy described his triumphant arrival, on 20 February, 1877.

LORD BEACONSFIELD

It was the House of Lords that was tonight the hub of the Parliamentary universe, and thither flocked the faithful Commons, as if the occasion were the opening of Parliament, and there were opportunity to the fore of a little horseplay in the lobby. It is years since the two Houses were brought so fully into personal contact. Prince Christian, from his place in the centre of the gallery, by the bevy of fair ladies of whom the flower was the Princess of Wales, looked down on a scene of rare and moving interest. Right before him, full in view, was the late Mr Disraeli, sitting precisely as he used to do in the House of Commons, with legs crossed over knees, arms folded, head hung down, and watchful eyes covertly glancing up and down the Opposition benches.

But what a change in his companions! Instead of Ward Hunt lolling all over the bench, sedately sat the slim and stately Carnarvon. For Stafford Northcote Lord Derby; for Gathorne Heady the Duke of Richmond; and for the ladylike Lord John Manners, ambling across to his seat as if he were going through a quadrille, strode the black-bearded Salisbury, restless and resistless as the sea off Start Point on a stormy morning.

But though the scene has changed the man remains, and there is marvellously little difference between Mr Disraeli in the House of

Commons and Lord Beaconsfield in the House of Peers. In some respects the difference is to his advantage. In the Commons the space between the Treasury Bench and the table is so cramped that a speaker has no room for oratorical gestures, save at the risk of upsetting his own glass of water or treading on the toes of his colleagues. In the Lords there is abundant space, too much, perhaps, for an excitable orator like Argyll, whose nationality sometimes asserts itself by the indication of a disposition to tramp up and down as if he were playing the bagpipes. Beaconsfield enjoys this enlargement, and uses it judiciously, skilfully moving from side to side to address himself in turn directly to the various sections of his audience.

One doubt that hung on the skirts of belief in the Premier's success in the Lords was for ever dispelled by his speech tonight. He can be himself heard in this gilded chamber apparently with as much ease, and certainly with as little effort on the part of listeners, as was his wont in the House of Commons. The House of Lords is, by reason of its defective acoustical properties, the grave of much eloquence. It is not only Lyttleton whom no one can hear beyond a radius of three yards. Derby, who when in the House of Commons was heard without an effort on the part of the listener, may be followed in the House of Lords only by painful straining of the attention. Tonight portions of many of his sentences were lost before they reached the gallery. Granville, who has displayed much personal concern at the inconvenience, and is fully alive to the particular advantage of being heard in the galleries, was inaudible in his opening sentences, and might be followed only when by manifest effort he fixed his voice, and steadily maintained it, at a certain pitch. Salisbury has a powerful voice, but conveys to the listener the conviction that he is shouting. Beaconsfield spoke apparently as if he were in the House of Commons, and it seemed as if the notorious acoustical failure of the House of Lords were a fable. . . .

The House of Lords is not much given to cheering, and studiously eschews the vulgarity of laughter. "In my mind," wrote a formerly distinguished member of the House in a letter to his son, "there is nothing so ill-bred as audible laughter. A man of parts and fashion is only seen to smile, but never heard to laugh."

Men of parts and fashion, of course, abound in the House of Lords, and it follows that, though the august assembly may occasionally be seen to smile, it is rarely heard to laugh. No peer who has not from early life been tainted with the manner of the House of Commons ever lays himself out to draw a cheer, much less to raise a laugh. . . .

Throughout his speech tonight cheers and laughter followed his sentences with a frequency and a heartiness that might not have been excelled in the House of Commons. The deprecating air with which noble lords are accustomed to endure the presence of any man who so far forgets himself as to make a speech gave way to an attitude of earnest attention. It was not a good speech, and in the House of Commons would have been scouted as insufferably heavy. The Premier waded through a recital of events familiar to every one — at least, in their actual occurrence, and the mental excitement of comparing Disraeli's version of facts with accepted records has long worn itself out. But such as it was the speech was eagerly applauded by noble lords, who laughed even at such commonplace witticisms as that by which Granville's disclaimer of an argument attributed to him was somewhat rudely scorned. It is the latest, but surely not the least triumph of a victorious career that Disraeli should thus have subdued the House of Lords.

Henry W. Lucy: A Diary of Two Parliaments

***

It is a place of occasional oratory, as well as ceremony and colour. Of all its maiden speeches few made more impact than that of the young Lord Byron who chose, in 1812, to speak to the Peers on a Bill designed to suppress by threat of death the Nottinghamshire frame-workers, who smashed the machines which were to destroy their livelihoods.

AN EDICT WRITTEN IN BLOOD

Lord Byron rose, and (for the first time) addressed their lordships as follows:

"My Lords; the subject now submitted to your lordships for the first time, though new to the House, is by no means new to the country. I believe it had occupied the serious thoughts of all descriptions of persons, long before its introduction to the notice of that legislature, whose interference alone could be of real service. As a person in some degree connected with the suffering county, though a stranger not only to this House in general, but to almost every individual whose attention I presume to solicit, I must claim some portion of your lordships' indulgence, whilst I offer a few observations on a question in which I confess myself deeply interested. . . .

Setting aside the palpable injustice and the certain inefficiency of the Bill, are there not capital punishments sufficient in your statutes? Is there not blood enough upon your penal code, that more must be poured forth to ascend to Heaven and testify against you? How will you carry the Bill into effect? Can you commit a whole county to their own prisons? Will you erect a gibbet in every field and hang up men like scarecrows? or will you proceed (as you must to bring this measure into effect) by decimation? Place the county under martial law? Depopulate and lay waste all around you? And restore Sherwood forest as an acceptable gift to the crown, in its former condition of a royal chase and an asylum for outlaws? Are these the remedies for a starving and desperate populace? Will the famished wretch who has braved your bayonets, be appalled by your gibbets? When death is a relief, and the only relief it appears that you will afford him, will he be dragooned into tranquillity? Will that which could not be effected by your grenadiers, be accomplished by your executioners? If you proceed by the forms of law where is your evidence? Those who have refused to impeach their accomplices, when transportation only was the punishment, will hardly be tempted to witness against them when death is the penalty. With all due deference to the noble lords opposite, I think a little investigation, some previous enquiry, would induce even them to change their purpose. That most favourite state measure, so marvellously efficacious in many and recent instances, temporizing, would not be without its advantages in this. When a proposal is made to emancipate or relieve, you hesitate, you deliberate for years, you temporise and tamper with the minds of men; but a death-bill must be passed offhand, without a thought of the consequences. Sure I am from what I have heard, and from what I have seen, that to pass the Bill under all the existing circumstances, without enquiry, without deliberation, would only be to add injustice to irritation, and barbarity to neglect. The framers of such a Bill must be content to inherit the honours of the Athenian lawgiver whose edicts were said to be written not in ink but in blood. But suppose it past; suppose one of these men, as I have seen them — meagre with famine, sullen with despair, careless of a life which your lordships are perhaps about to value at something less than the price of a stocking-frame — suppose this man surrounded by the children for whom he is unable to procure bread at the hazard of his existence, about to be torn for ever from a family which he lately supported in peaceful industry, and which it is not his fault that he can no longer so support, suppose this man, and there are ten thousand such from whom you may select your victims, dragged into court, to be tried for this new offence, by this new law; still, there are two things wanting to convict and condemn him; and these are, in my opinion, — Twelve Butchers for a Jury, and a Jeffries for a Judge!"

Lord Byron: Speech, *27 February 1812*

5

Some Wars and Skirmishes

When the 'arf-made recruity goes out to the East
'E acts like a babe and 'e drinks like a beast
An' 'e wonders because 'e is frequent deceased
Ere 'e's fit for to serve as a soldier.
—Rudyard Kipling: *The Young British Soldier*

"Just rejoice! Rejoice!"
—Margaret Thatcher, 1982

PARLIAMENTARY history could be portrayed as a succession of national crises, mainly wars. There is nothing like a foreign war to raise the temperature in the Commons and to convince politicians that this is the moment they have waited for, more or less all their lives. That is not to say it is a bogus emotion — if Governments and MPs do not feel a special responsibility at such moments, they properly belong elsewhere. But warlike noises can be ugly as well as stirring. The clashes of days far gone — like the battles between Pitt and Fox over the war with France — still have the sense in them of immense drama, and in the twentieth century the memory of events is sharp. The Great War is near enough to still have its aura of almost unimaginable horror; World War II is within the memory of many, and a post-war generation has been reared on tales of Churchillian leadership and bold escapades in the field. There have been more minor episodes — the Suez farce and the bizarre events in the South Atlantic in 1982 — which gave rise to their own flashes of passion in Parliament, and fevered debate in the country at large. These four bursts of conflict have provided some Parliamentary moments of high drama.

***

On 5 August 1914, H. H. Asquith rose to tell the Commons what it already knew, that Britain was at war with Germany. Like the statements which were to precede other conflicts in the coming years, it had a dreadful simplicity and bluntness about it.

WAR

"Our Ambassador at Berlin received his passports at seven o'clock last evening, and since eleven o'clock last night a state of war has existed between Germany and ourselves.

We have received from our Minister at Brussels the following telegram:

> 'I have just received from Minister of Foreign Affairs—'

that is the Belgian Minister for Foreign Affairs—

> 'a note of which the following is a literal translation:
>
> Belgian Government regret to have to inform His Majesty's Government that this morning armed forces of Germany penetrated into Belgian territory in violation of enegements assumed by treaty.
>
> Belgian Government are further resolved to resist by all means in their power.
>
> Belgium appeals to Great Britain and France and Russia to co-operate, as guarantors, in defence of her territory.
>
> There would be concerted and common action with the object of resisting the forcible measures employed by Germany against Belgium, and at the same time of guarding the maintenance for future of the independence and integrity of Belgium.
>
> Belgium is happy to be able to declare that she will assume defence of her fortified places.'

We have also received today from the French Ambassador here, the following telegram received by the French Government from the French Minister at Brussels:

> 'The Chef du Cabinet of the Belgian Ministry of War has asked the French Military Attaché to prepare at once for the co-operation and contact of French troops with the Belgian Army, pending the results of the appeal to the guaranteeing Powers now being made. Orders have therefore been given to Belgian provincial governors not to regard movements of French troops as a violation of the frontier.'

This is all the information I am at the moment able to give to the House, but I take the opportunity of giving notice that tomorrow, in Committee of Supply, I shall move a Vote of Credit of £100,000,000."

H. H. Asquith: Speech, *5 August 1914*

The next day Asquith defended the Government's position with regard to the war, explaining the frustration of attempts to keep the peace.

THE SWORD UNSHEATHED

"I am entitled to say, and I do so on behalf of this country — I speak not for a party, I speak for the country as a whole — that we made every effort any Government could possibly make for peace. But this war has been forced upon us. What is it we are fighting for? Everyone knows, and no one knows better than the Government, the terrible, incalculable suffering, economic, social, personal and political, which war, and especially a war between the Great Powers of the world, must entail. There is no man amongst us sitting upon this bench in these trying days — more trying perhaps than any body of statesmen for a hundred years have had to pass through — there is not a man amongst us who has not, during the whole of that time, had clearly before his vision the almost unequalled suffering which war, even in a just cause, must bring about, not only to the peoples who are for the moment living in this country and in the other countries of the world, but to posterity and to the whole prospects of European civilisation. Every step we took we took with that vision before our eyes, and with a sense of responsibility which it is impossible to describe. Unhappily, if in spite of all our efforts to keep the peace, and with that full and overpowering consciousness of the result, if the issue be decided in favour of war, we have, nevertheless, thought it to be the duty as well as the interest of this country to go to war, the House may be well assured it was because we believe, and I am certain the country will believe, that we are unsheathing our sword in a just cause.

If I am asked what we are fighting for I reply in two sentences. In the first place, to fulfil a solemn international obligation, an obligation which, if it had been entered into between private persons in the ordinary concerns of life, would have been regarded as an obligation not only of law but of honour, which no self-respecting man could possibly have repudiated. I say, secondly, we are fighting to vindicate the principle which, in these days when force, material force, sometimes seems to be the dominant influence and factor in the development of mankind, we are fighting to vindicate the principle that small nationalities are not to be crushed, in defiance of international good faith, by the arbitrary will of a strong and overmastering Power.

I do not believe any nation ever entered into a great controversy — and this is one of the greatest history will ever know — with a clearer conscience and a stronger conviction that it is fighting, not for aggression, not for the maintenance even of its own selfish interest, but that it is fighting in defence of principles the maintenance of which is vital to the civilisation of the world. With a full conviction, not only of the wisdom and justice, but of the obligations which lay upon us to challenge this great issue, we are entering into the struggle."

H. H. Asquith: Speech, *6 August 1914*

***

But Asquith's conduct of the war turned to disaster and after months of bitter argument in the Government and outside he gave way in December 1916, with David Lloyd George taking over. In the new Prime Minister's first major speech to the Commons after his appointment, he referred to his relationship with Asquith — often one of bitter rivalry — and looked ahead.

HIGH PURPOSE

"May I say, and I say it in all sincerity, that it is one of the deepest regrets of my life that I should part from the Right Honourable Gentleman (Mr Asquith). Some of his friends know how I strove to avert it. For years I served under the Rt. Hon. Gentleman and I am proud to say so. I never had a kinder or more indulgent chief. If there were any faults of temper, they were entirely mine, and I have no doubt I must have been difficult at times. No man had greater admiration for his brilliant intellectual attainments, and no man was happier to serve under him. For eight years we differed as men of such different temperaments must necessarily differ, but we never had a personal quarrel, in spite of serious differences in policy, and it was with deep, genuine grief that I felt it necessary to tender my resignation to my Rt. Hon. Friend.

But there are moments when personal and party considerations must sink into absolute insignificance and so in this war I have given scant heed to the call of party, although I have been as strong a party man as any in the whole House. If I have not been during this war it is because I realised once the moment of Prussian cannon posed death at a peaceful and inoffensive little country, that a challenge had been sent to civilisation to decide an issue higher than party, deeper than any, wider than all parties — an issue upon the settlement of which will depend the fate of men in this world for generations, when existing parties will have fallen like dead leaves on the highway. Those issues are the issues that I want to keep in front of the nation, so that we shall not falter or faint in our resolve.

There is a time in every prolonged and fierce war, in the passion and rage of the conflict, when men forget the high purpose with which they entered it. This is a struggle for international right, international honour, international goodwill — the channel along which peace, honour and goodwill must flow amongst men. The embankment laboriously built up by generations of men against barbarism has been broken, and had not the might of Britain passed into the breach, Europe would have been inundated with a breed of savagery and unbridled lust for power. The plain sense of fair play among nations, the growth of an international experience, the protection of the weak against the strong by the stronger, the consciousness that justice has a more powerful backing in this world than greed, the knowledge that any outrage upon fair dealing between nations, great or small, will meet with prompt and meritable reaction — these constitute the causeway along which humanity was progressing slowly to higher things. The triumph of Prussia would sweep it all away and leave mankind to struggle helpless in the morass. That is why, since this war began, I have known but one political aim. For that I have fought with a single eye. That is the rescue of mankind from the most overwhelming catastrophe that has ever yet menaced its well-being."

David Lloyd George: Speech, *19 December 1916*

***

As Britain drifted towards the Second World War the government of Neville Chamberlain tried desperately, and with a naiveté which has since become a benchmark of incompetence, to stave off the inevitable. Many scathing accounts of that government's conduct were published, but none more bitter than *Guilty Men*, the first volume in the *Victory Series* produced by Victor Gollancz. It was written by Michael Foot, Peter Howard and Frank Owen in four days in 1940 under the collective pseudonym "Cato" and within days it had sold thousands. Here "Cato" looks back to 1938, to the days when the gleam still shone bright in the appeasers' eyes.

A DANCE OF DELIGHT

On a hot summer afternoon several hundred years ago a Balkan peasant arose from the stone he was squatting upon and began to dance.

Quickly the villagers ran to the spot. They gaped at the remarkable spectacle of a man twirling and gyrating all by himself in the sunlight. They giggled.

But presently the man's dance became more frantic. His eyes began to stare. Foam drooled from his lips and nostrils.

The peasants watching him began to tap their feet in sympathy. Soon they began to dance too.

They streamed across the countryside in a frenzy, dancing all the way. Wherever they went, others joined the dance.

The dance mania spread all over Europe, from country to country.

Women gashed themselves with knives as they capered. Men dashed their heads against walls. When the madness spread across the sea to England, over five hundred deaths were reported as a result of the dancing. The hysteria did not depart from Europe for many months. . . .

At about half-past four on a warm autumn afternoon, September 28, 1938, an exhibition of hysteria, the result of which was also destined to spread over the whole face of Europe, took place in the British House of Commons.

Honourable and right honourable gentlemen yelled and screamed like football fans. Three Tory members put their arms around each other's necks and hopped up and down in the lobby exclaiming, "Thank God for the Prime Minister, thank God for the Prime Minister."

Sixteen men and two women as they walked out of the Chamber, were sobbing and crying with emotion.

The cause of this outburst was physical. For many days MPs had felt that war with Germany over the issue of the Sudeten Deutsch minority in Czechoslovakia was inevitable.

Gas masks had been distributed to all the citizens (except small children. The Government had made no provision for them). Trenches were being dug in the turf of the London parks.

Parliament had met with almost every member of it oppressed by fear. They believed that the Prime Minister was going to announce that we were entering into war with Germany.

Mr Chamberlain, in a sentence, removed that fear. While he was giving his account of events a message from the Foreign Office was passed along the Front Bench and handed to him.

Having glanced at it, Mr Chamberlain's cheeks changed colour. A healthy brown tinge appeared on his ashen countenance. He informed the House of Commons that he was going to Munich next day to meet Hitler. Then the dance of delight began.

Cato: Guilty Men

***

War broke out at 11 a.m. on 3 September 1939, with Chamberlain already a discredited figure, clinging to office in some desperation and destined to fall in less than nine months. Harold Nicolson — diplomat, politician, social observer and diarist — watched the collapse of the "guilty men" in the Commons. In his diary he recorded the appearance of Chamberlain and Arthur Greenwood, Labour's deputy leader, on the day before war was declared.

COLLAPSE

The House is packed and tense and we wait there exactly like a court awaiting the verdict of the jury. At 7.42 the Prime Minister enters with Greenwood. He gets up to speak. He begins with the chronological method: "On Wednesday night Sir Nevile Henderson, our Ambassador in Berlin, handed to Herr von Ribbentrop . . ." — that sort of thing. His voice betrays some emotion as if he were sickening for a cold. He is a strange man. We expected one of his dramatic surprises. But none came. It was evident when he sat down that no decision had been arrived at. The House gasped for one moment in astonishment. Was there to be another Munich after all? Then Greenwood got up. The disappointment at the P.M.'s statement, the sense that appeasement had come back, vented itself in the reception of Greenwood. His own people cheered, as was natural; but what was so amazing was that their cheer was taken up in a second and greater wave from our benches. Bob Boothby cried out, "*You* speak for Britain." It was an astonishing demonstration. Greenwood almost staggered with surprise. When it subsided he had to speak and did so better than I had expected. He began to say what an embarrassing task had been imposed on him. He had wanted to support and was obliged to criticise. Why this delay? We had promised to help Poland "at once". She was being bombed and attacked. We had vacillated for 34 hours. What did this mean? He was resoundingly cheered. The tension became acute, since here were the P.M.'s most ardent supporters cheering his opponent with all their lungs. The front bench looked as if they had been struck in the face.

The House adjourns. The lobby is so dark that a match struck flames like a beacon. There is a great confusion and indignation. We feel that the German ships and submarines will, owing to this inexplicable delay, elude our grasp. The P.M. must know by now that the whole House is against him. He might (had he been a more imaginative man) have got out of his difficulty. It was not his fault but that of George Bonnet (French Foreign Minister). But he is too secretive by nature to be able to create confidence. In those few minutes he flung away his reputation. I feel deeply sorry for him.

Harold Nicolson: Diary, *2 September 1939*

***

By May 1940 Churchill had taken over, and it is his wartime speeches that still capture the atmosphere of the House in those days. He would compose them in his rooms at the top of the Admiralty, pacing the floor and dictating to a secretary late into the night. By the next morning his words would be fixed in his mind and he would prepare for the rigours of the Chamber, which he loved. On 4 June 1940, he spoke of the threat of invasion.

"WE SHALL NOT FLAG OR FAIL"

"Turning once again, and this time more generally, to the question of invasion, I would observe that there has never been a period in all these long centuries of which we boast when an absolute guarantee against invasion, still less against serious raids, could have been given to our people. In the days of Napoleon, of which I was speaking just now, the same wind which would have carried his transports across the Channel might have driven away the blockading fleet. There was always the chance, and it is that chance which has excited and befooled the imaginations of many Continental tyrants. Many are the tales that are told. We are assured that novel methods will be adopted, and when we see the originality of malice, the ingenuity of aggression, which our enemy displays, we may certainly prepare ourselves for every kind of novel strategem and every kind of brutal and treacherous manoeuvre. I think that no idea is so outlandish that it should not be considered and viewed with a searching, but at the same time, I hope, with a steady eye. We must never forget the solid assurances of sea power and those which belong to air power if it can be locally exercised.

I have, myself, full confidence that if all do their duty, if nothing is neglected, and if the best arrangements are made, as they are being made, we shall prove ourselves once again able to defend our island home, to ride out the storm of war, and to outlive the menace of tyranny, if necessary for years, if necessary alone. At any rate, that is what we are going to try to do. That is the resolve of His Majesty's Government — every man of them. That is the will of Parliament and the nation. The British Empire and the French Republic, linked together in their cause and in their need, will defend to the death their native soil, aiding each other like good comrades to the utmost of their strength. Even though large tracts of Europe and many old and famous States have fallen or may fall into the grip of the Gestapo and all the odious apparatus of Nazi rule, we shall not flag or fail, we shall go on to the end, we shall fight in France, we shall fight on the seas and oceans, we shall fight with growing confidence and growing strength in the air, we shall defend our island, whatever the cost may be, we shall fight on the beaches, we shall fight in the fields and in the streets, we shall fight in the hills; we shall never surrender, and even if, which I do not for a moment believe, this island or a large part of it were subjugated and starving, then our Empire beyond the seas, armed and guarded by the British Fleet, would carry on the struggle, until, in God's good time, the new world, with all its power and might, steps forth to the rescue and the liberation of the old."

Winston Churchill: Speech, *4 June 1940*

***

That "rescue and liberation" came in May 1945. Harold Nicolson here describes the atmosphere of Victory in Europe Day.

CHURCHILL'S TRIUMPH

V.E. day. Lunch at the Beefsteak. Up till then everything had been normal, but I then find the streets crowded and people wearing all manner of foolish paper caps and cheering slightly. When I leave the club at 2.15, I find the roads packed. Trafalgar Square is a seething mass of people with figures draped all over the lions. Whitehall is overflowing, but a few buses try to push their way through. After the Cenotaph it is just a jam. I squeeze in behind a car and manage to reach the House about five to three. I pause to recover myself in Palace Yard and regret to observe that I have torn a hole in my new suit. The crowds are packed against the railing and the mounted police have difficulty in clearing a path for the Government cars. Then came the great strokes of Big Ben and thereafter an immense hush. From the loudspeakers in Parliament Square Winston's voice booms out to all those thousands. It echoes on the Palace behind me so that I hear it doubly. He tells of the signature of surrender and its impending ratification in Berlin. He is short and effective. The crowd cheer when he finishes and when *God Save the King* has been broadcast. But it is not frantic cheering.

I then enter the House. The place is packed and I sit on the step below the cross bench. I see a stir at the door and Winston comes in — a little shy — a little flushed — but smiling boyishly. The House jumps to its feet, and there is one long roar of applause. He bows and smiles in acknowledgement. I glance up at the Gallery where Clemmy (Churchill) should be. There is Mrs Neville Chamberlain there instead. And thereupon Winston begins. He repeats the short statement he had just made on the wireless ending up with "Advance Britannia" and then he lays his manuscript aside and with more gesture and emphasis than is customary to him, he thanks the House for its support throughout these years. He then proposes that we adjourn to the Church of St Margaret's Westminster. The Speaker then leaves his seat and the mace is fetched before him. He is in Court Robes with gold facings to his gown and his Chaplain and the Sergeant-at-Arms are also in full dress.

We file out by the St Stephen's entrance and the police have kept a lane through the crowd. The crowd are friendly, recognising some of the Members. I am with Nancy Astor who is, I feel, a trifle hurt that she does not get more cheering. We then have a service — and very memorable it is. The supreme moment is when the chaplain reads out the names of those Members of Parliament who have lost their lives. It is a sad thing to hear. My eyes fill with tears. I hope that Nancy does not notice. "Men are so emotional," she says.

We all go to the smoking-room. Winston comes with us. Passing through Central Hall he is given an ovation by the crowd. They clap their hands. A tiny little boy, greatly daring, dashes up to him and asks for his autograph. Winston solemnly takes out his glasses and signs. He then pats the delighted little boy on the head and grins his grin.

Harold Nicolson: Diary, *8 May 1945*

***

Two great wars dominated the lives of politicians for a couple of generations, straining political loyalties and forging new careers in the heat of the Parliamentary battle. But there were other military affairs that left their mark, and the Suez crisis still stands out as a turning point: it was the test that Anthony Eden failed, and on which his Premiership foundered, and an event which reverberated through the Conservative Party for a decade and more. The storm broke on 30 October 1956 when Eden revealed to the Commons what lay ahead. It was, said Hugh Gaitskell, a statement of "the utmost gravity".

INTERVENTION

"As the House will know, for some time past the tension on the frontiers of Israel has been increasing. The growing military strength of Egypt has given rise to renewed apprehension, which the statements and actions of the Egyptian Government have further aggravated. The establishment of a Joint Military Command between Egypt, Jordan and Syria, the renewed raids by guerillas, culminating in the incursion of Egyptian commandos on Sunday night, had all produced a very dangerous situation. . . .

I must tell the House that very grave issues are at stake, and that unless hostilities can quickly be stopped free passage through the Canal will be jeopardised. Moreover, any fighting on the banks of the Canal would endanger the ships actually on passage. The number of crews and passengers involved totals many hundreds, and the value of the ships which are likely to be on passage is about £50 million, excluding the value of the cargoes.

Her Majesty's Government and the French Government have accordingly agreed that everything possible should be done to bring hostilities to an end as soon as possible. Their representatives in New

York have, therefore, been instructed to join the United States representative in seeking an immediate meeting of the Security Council. This began at 4 p.m.

In the meantime, as a result of the consultations held in London today, the United Kingdom and French Governments have now addressed urgent communications to the Governments of Egypt and Israel. In these we have called upon both sides to stop all warlike action by land, sea and air forthwith and to withdraw their military forces to a distance of 10 miles from the Canal. Further, in order to separate the belligerents and to guarantee freedom of transit through the Canal by the ships of all nations, we have asked the Egyptian Government to agree that Anglo-French forces should move temporarily — I repeat, temporarily — into key positions at Port Said, Ismailia and Suez.

The Governments of Egypt and Israel have been asked to answer this communication within 12 hours. It has been made clear to them that, if at the expiration of that time one or both have not undertaken to comply with these requirements, British and French forces will intervene in whatever strength may be necessary to secure compliance."

Anthony Eden: Speech, *30 October 1956*

***

The Commons debate on Suez rolled on for days, seemingly without pause to those caught up in the crisis. Nothing like it had been seen since the early days of World War II, and the passions were more fervent on the Tory side because of the deep misgivings on the Government benches about Eden's adventure and its likely outcome. For Labour, Aneurin Bevan, the voice of the Left, caught the mood and exploited it. Among his attacks was what has been called his finest Commons speech.

"FOR GOD'S SAKE, GET OUT"

"In more years than I care to remember, even during the days of the war, I do not recollect feeling running so high as it has done today, nor that there has ever been such general uneasiness in the House as exists today or as much private anxiety on both sides. In these debates we necessarily voice our party allegiances and back up our spokesmen in the characteristic fashion of Members of the House of Commons; neverthless, it would be a mistake for anyone to deduce from the events of today that there is any sense of satisfaction with the existing position. There is certainly no sense of satisfaction on this side of the House. We would much prefer that we did not have this case against the Government. We would much prefer that this situation had never arisen.

We have traversed so much of this argument in the last few days that it is familiar to all of us. There is not very much new that anyone can say at this stage of the debate, but I would suggest to hon. and right. hon. Gentlemen that perhaps it is just as well for us to glance for a moment at the background of this debate. I find it hard to believe that Ministers of the experience of members of the Government could have done what they have done or could have defended it so badly unless they were in almost a distraught state of mind. I believe, and we on this side of the House should remember it too, that the members of the Government are in very great difficulties and have been in them for a long time.

I say at once that their difficulties are the difficulties also of other Governments. I do not believe that Her Majesty's Government are alone in their embarrassment. It would a very great mistake for us, even on this side of the House, to indict the existing Government as though they bore the exclusive responsibility for the existing state of affairs.

The fact of the matter is that mankind is faced with an entirely novel situation. There has never been anything like it in the history of nations. Two major events have completely cancelled — if I may be allowed to use the term — all the finesse and the sophistication of conventional diplomacy. There is nothing in the White House, in London, in the Quai d'Orsay or in the Kremlin that furnishes statesmen with lessons from history to enable them to judge what to do in the existing circumstances.

The advent of the hydrogen bomb has stalemated power among the great Powers. The use of the threat of war, which formerly helped to solve many international difficulties — and when the threat could not do it war tried to do it — is no longer available to statesmen. The great Powers are stalemated by their own power. This fact has created a vacuum in diplomatic thinking. In the last four or five years the tragedy of the world has been that the statesmen of the world have not adjusted themselves to that reality. I know it is an obvious thing to say, but we do not leave a thing behind merely because it is obvious. There is an old German saying that to understand is not necessarily to leave behind. . . .

Those are two very important events that lie at the background of what we are discussing this evening. The tragedy has been that in the meantime, although those facts have been there, they have not inspired statesmen to intelligent action. Indeed, there are commentators in the United States, like Mr Lippmann, who, speaking of President Eisenhower the other day, said that the difficulty about the President was that he did not act for peace but merely reacted against trouble.

I am not one, therefore, who is going to say that the British Government are themselves reacting with complete guilt towards this situation, because I think it is one which is shared by everybody, and every public man ought to have a sense of humility in face of these intractable problems. I therefore think that it would be a profound blunder if any party in this State tried to mislead the people of the country into imagining that there is any simple or quick solution to these problems before us.

But having said that, I am bound to say that I have not seen from the Prime Minister in the course of the last four or five months, or even longer, any evidence of that sagacity and skill that he should have acquired in so many years in the Foreign Office. Indeed, I have been astonished at the amateurishness of his performance. There is something the matter with him. I have often listened to bad cases in this House but rarely have I listened to them so badly put as I have heard them in the last few days. The Prime Minister has made several speeches in which he has repeated himself over and over again, but each speech becomes more tawdry and barren than the last.

He made a speech today. It was perfectly obvious from what he said that he had not thought out at all the implications of the actions of the Government. He had no answer to some of the inquiries which were put concerning the legal position of the combatants. We are told that we are not at a state of war with Egypt. We are told that we are in fact in a state of armed conflict.

I have been looking up some of the precedents about this. I thought that I recognised some of the language which the Prime Minister used in justifying himself. He said the other day: 'In the meantime, as a result of consultations held in London today, the United Kingdom and French Governments have now addressed urgent communications to the Governments of Egypt and Israel. In these we have called upon both sides to stop all warlike action by land, sea and air forthwith and to withdraw their military forces to a distance of 10 miles. . . .' (Official Report, 30th October 1956, Vol. 558, c. 1279.) Then he went on to justify it by saying that he did this 'in order to defend British lives and British property'. That was an ultimatum delivered to the Egyptian Government. I have here another ultimatum delivered to Belgium on 2nd August, 1914:

'The German Government cannot but fear . . . that Belgium will be unable, without assistance, to repel so considerable a French invasion with sufficient prospect of success to afford an adequate guarantee against danger to Germany . . . the measures of Germany's opponents force Germany, for her own protection, to enter Belgian territory.'

Will the Prime Minster tell me what single difference there is between that language and the language used by him?

There is another example. The argument advanced by the Prime Minister to this House was that we have in fact taken this action in Egypt in order to safeguard British ships going through the Canal and to safeguard British interests and, of course, stop the war — but, yes, that is what Germany said. Every country that attempts to justify itself uses language of this sort.

Indeed, I could quote almost all the ultimatums given by Hitler to countries that he invaded where he used exactly the same kind of language as the Prime Minister used the other day. . . .

What are we to say at the United Nations, or whenever we go abroad and meet the spokesmen of other people? We say that Great Britain has always stood for civilised principles, and for humanity and justice. How do we answer now, when we drop bombs on helpless people? [Hon. Members: 'Oh.'] Yes, when we drop bombs. How do we answer now at whatever judgment seat any hon. Member likes to mention? A nation more powerful than us may drop even worse bombs on British cities. How answer that? With bombs? Bombs with bombs? That is the bankruptcy of statesmanship. The world has travelled that way in my own lifetime twice. We dare not travel that way again, because this time there would be no return.

We say to the Government, not in any spirit of partisanship — I say so, anyhow, and no one can accuse me of lack of partisanship — not in the spirit of partisanship but with a deep sense of sorrow, that I attack the Government tonight for this policy. I believe that they are not supported by the vast majority of the people of Great Britain. They are certainly not supported by the vast majority of the people right throughout the world.

I do beg and pray of them to retrace their steps even now. It would be evidence of increased status — [Hon. Members: 'Oh.'] — yes, if the Goverment were now able to do that. Having found that their best friends do not sustain them in this action, that their allies are themselves dismayed by it, that the world is shocked, it would be an action of statesmanship for the Government now to say, 'We halt at this point. We are not going any further.' Unless the Government are able to say that, in the name of mankind let them, for God's sake, get out."

Aneurin Bevan: Speech, *1 November 1956*

***

Two days later Gaitskell pressed home the attack on the Government for refusing to go along with the United Nations in trying to get a withdrawal of troops. He pinned the blame firmly on Eden, whose grip on power was already beginning to weaken.

AN OPPORTUNITY LOST

"Do not hon. Members appreciate that at this time above all, when the news of Russian aggression in Hungary is coming through, it is an immense tragedy that the moral strength of this country and of the United Nations, because of our action, is so gravely damaged? We have had a great opportunity — and even now it would have been open to the Government — despite all that has happened, to accept the Resolution of the General Assembly, to say that in the light of this and because we believe in international order and because we believe in the Charter of the United Nations, despite everything that has been said and done in the last few days, we are prepared to accept it.

The Government could, if they had done that, to some extent at least have restored our reputation and moral authority. They could, if they had done that, at once have made it a thousand times easier to deal with the Hungarian situation. [Hon. Members: 'How?'] I beg hon. Members — I repeat that I know how high passions rise — to listen to my words on this. We represent many millions of British people. We represent on this issue the point of view of millions of men and women, not all Labour Party supporters, many of them of no political persuasion, and, I venture to say, many of them persons who have hitherto voted Conservative.

If only the Government had been prepared to accept the Resolution, much of the damage could have been repaired. Unfortunately, they have refused. They have not only refused but are continuing the war against Egypt, continuing the bombing and the destruction and the casualties. All that has been put forward today is a niggling, haggling kind of proposal, which is — *(Interruption)*. Up to this moment, I for my part had hoped for a change in Government policy. I had hoped originally that the Government would have accepted our first proposal to defer action. They refused. I hoped then that the pressure of world opinion upon them would have made them change their mind, and I hoped finally that the passing of this Resolution by such a vast majority in the United Nations Assembly would have brought them to their senses.

Alas, that is not so, and we can draw only one conclusion. That is that if this country is to be rescued from the predicament into which the Government have brought it, there is only one way out, and that is change in the leadership of the Government. Only that now can save our reputation and reopen the possibility of maintaining the United Nations as a force for peace. We must have a new Government and a new Prime Minister. The immediate responsibility for this matter rests upon the only people who can affect the situation — hon. members opposite. I beg them to consider in their hearts to where we are being led at the moment. I beg them to consider the appalling international consequence of this grave error, and I ask them, having done so, to do their duty."

Hugh Gaitskell: Speech, *3 November 1956*

***

Finally, inevitably, there came withdrawal, more than a month after a cease-fire had been agreed. Eden was convalescing in Jamaica as the

Commons gathered to hear the announcement. Harry Boardman described the scene in the *Manchester Guardian.*

THE END?

Neither intrinsically nor in externals can one recall anything comparable to yesterday's happenings in the House of Commons. It was an hour that will be memorable historically and for the deep passions it stirred. The Foreign Secretary had come to the House to announce a decision which, beyond any concealment, could not but be humiliating for the Government. It was admittedly as trying an ordeal as a Foreign Secretary has had to face, and Mr Selwyn Lloyd proved once again that he has nerve and courage.

So much so that he could spend twenty minutes seeking to persuade the House, along the old lines of Tory apologetic, that the Government's policy has been abundantly vindicated; that it has succeeded in stopping a local war and even preventing a larger war; that it has unmasked Soviet penetration in the Middle East and driven the United Nations to create an international force.

During these twenty minutes the Opposition reminded one of nothing so much as an audience at a vaudeville entertainment. Its laughter was almost continuous and shook the Chamber. It brought Mr Selwyn Lloyd to a dead stop more than once. To make what the Opposition regarded as a justificatory speech, rather than a statement of intentions, and one that it considered an extravagant absurdity, may have been a mistake. But this riotous hilarity, it must be said, did no credit to the House of Commons at such a grave moment.

Mr Bevan knew a better way. He derives from the pre-war House of Commons. After all, it is the word that does the damage in the House of Commons, not blaring laughter. Mr Bevan welcomed the withdrawal of the forces even though it was being done, as he said, reluctantly. He was also glad the Government was no longer attempting to dictate to the United Nations by making the retreat, as he called it, conditional on the future control of the Canal.

As an answer to the Foreign Secretary's apologia, nothing was, or could have been, said that was more destructive than to describe it, as Mr Bevan did, as sounding the bugle to advance in order to cover the retreat. Nor could anything have been more effective than the commiseration he professed for Mr Lloyd. He pulled himself up abruptly in the course of some reflections on how we are now back where we were before the armed intervention. He had said enough. "I feel," he remarked, with affected tenderness, "I should be a bully if I proceeded any farther."

The two principals having had their say, the mêlée, which the excitement and high feeling had already promised, began. Members were charging into conflict from all parts of the House. Perhaps charging hardly describes Mr Waterhouse's manner. He rose on the scene with a fine dignity. His voice reminds you of old port. The Opposition regards him as an amusing relic but it also respects him as an honourable man.

He was the first of the Suez men to speak, and the great question over the Government and the House is how the Suez men are going to take the withdrawal. The fate of the Government could be in their hands.

Harry Boardman: Manchester Guardian, *4 December 1956*

***

On Friday, 2 April 1982, Argentina invaded the Falkland Islands, precipitating war, and the conversion of Mrs Margaret Thatcher from a position of notable weakness in the opinion of the polls into a heroine-figure with an appeal which infuriated her opponents as much as it delighted her supporters and came as a surprise to those who had thought that war fever was a condition of the past. For ten weeks, while the fleet steamed to the southern seas and then recaptured the islands, Britain was in the grip of an extraordinary bout of patriotic fervour which, though it alarmed many, came as a new lease of political life for "the Iron Lady". But before the victory it had been different, with the Government shaking at the shock of invasion. The first statement to the Commons came on the Friday morning, from Humphrey Atkins, the Lord Privy Seal and deputy Foreign Secretary.

THE FIRST NEWS

"Over the past twenty-four hours the situation has become increasingly grave. There is now a real expectation that an Argentine attack against the Falkland Islands will take place very soon. It was for this reason that we sought an emergency meeting of the Security Council yesterday and associated ourselves immediately with a request from the President of the Security Council that both Britain and Argentina should exercise restraint and refrain from the use or threat of force, and continue the search for a diplomatic solution. There was no Argentine response to this; nor has the Argentine President responded to the many appeals that have been made to him to draw back from the use of force.

We are taking appropriate military and diplomatic measures to sustain our rights under international law and in accordance with the provisions of the United Nations charter. The House will not expect me to give details at this stage of the military steps we have taken to respond to the worsening situation. In the meantime, we continue to hope that the Argentine Government even at this late stage will reconsider their rejection of the diplomatic channel as a means for settling the differences between our two countries."

Humphrey Atkins: Speech, *2 April 1982*

***

Twenty-four hours later the Commons had an emergency debate, the first Saturday sitting since Suez. Mrs Thatcher, who was to face the resignation of three Ministers and was to send an armada to the South Atlantic before the weekend was over, rose to defend her Government.

INVASION

"The House meets this Saturday to respond to a situation of great gravity. We are here because, for the first time for many years, British sovereign territory has been invaded by a foreign power. After several days of rising tension in our relations with Argentina, that country's armed forces attacked the Falkland Islands yesterday and established military control of the islands.

Yesterday was a day of rumour and counter-rumour. Throughout the day we had no communications from the Government of the Falklands. Indeed, the last message that we received was at 21.55 hours on Thursday night, 1 April. Yesterday morning at 8.33 a.m. we sent a telegram which was acknowledged. At 8.45 a.m. all communications ceased. I shall refer to that again in a moment. By late afternoon yesterday it became clear that an Argentine invasion had taken place and that the lawful British Government of the islands had been usurped.

I am sure that the whole House will join me in condemning totally this unprovoked aggression by the Government of Argentina against British territory. [Hon. Members: 'Hear, hear.'] It has not a shred of justification and not a scrap of legality.

It was not until 8.30 this morning, our time, when I was able to speak to the governor, who had arrived in Uruguay, that I learnt precisely what had happened. He told me that the Argentines had landed at approximately 6 a.m. Falklands time, 10 a.m. our time. One party attacked the capital from the landward side and another from the seaward side. The governor then sent a signal to us which we did not receive.

Communications had ceased at 8.45 a.m. our time. It is common for atmospheric conditions to make communications with Port Stanley difficult. Indeed, we had been out of contact for a period the previous night.

The Governor reported that the Marines, in the defence of Government House, were superb. He said that they acted in the best traditions of the Royal Marines. They inflicted casualties, but those defending Government House suffered none. He had kept the local people informed of what was happening through a small local transmitter which he had in Government House. He is relieved that the islanders heeded his advice to stay indoors. Fortunately, as far as he is aware, there were no civilian casualties. When he left the Falklands, he said that the people were in tears. They do not want to be Argentine. He said that the islanders are still tremendously loyal. I must say that I have every confidence in the governor and the action that he took.

I must tell the House that the Falkland Islands and their dependencies remain British territory. No aggression and no invasion can alter that simple fact. It is the Government's objective to see that the islands are freed from occupation and are returned to British administration at the earliest possible moment."

Margaret Thatcher: Speech, *3 April 1982*

***

The debate that followed was fevered and intense: exciting to some and troubling to others. Here is *The Scotsman*'s account, published the following Monday.

THE FALKLANDS DEBATE

At the end of the tumultuous debate on the Falkland Islands on Saturday, as the Commons erupted in a babble of chatter, abuse and congratulations, Mr John Nott, Her Majesty's Secretary of State for Defence, found around him a still and awful calm.

Mrs Thatcher sat by him as he shuffled his papers at the Dispatch Box, but offered not a word. Mr Willie Whitelaw, who had wrapped his head in his hands more than once during Mr Nott's speech, was sitting alongside, but he could have been 1,000 miles away for all the notice he took. On a day when the Commons had been at their best, Mr Nott had been at his worst and his humiliation, caught in that little scene as the noise subsided, was the measure of the emotion expended in those three hours.

From the start, for those of us facing the prospect of our first war, the day had a strange atmosphere: perhaps we almost expected to see them piling sandbags up in Parliament Square, or starting the community singing in the Tube. All the harbingers were there. Crowds spilled down Whitehall and clustered round the gate at the Commons where ministerial cars were inspected by the curious and the ghoulish as they spun inside. Yesterday's billboards still said: "Invasion Under Way".

Like Budgets, wars are guaranteed to fill the chamber. By the time Mrs Thatcher and her white-faced Cabinet filed along the Front Bench the place was boiling with rage. Too often the Commons forces a mood on itself by creating a phony storm, but on Saturday there was no need for artificial stimulants. It was effortless.

Mrs Thatcher rose, and spoke badly. With no hope of convincing MPs that the Government performance had been anything but lamentable, she seemed to lose all that self-assurance which usually carries her through. Her defiant promise of an Argentine-bashing expedition got its cheer, but the mood was one of black despair with most MPs believing, behind the bellicosity, that the battle for the Falklands was already over.

Many MPs, in all parties, have campaigned long and hard for the islanders, constantly pushing the Government for guarantees that the Falklands were safe. These guarantees have always been given and as a result what we saw at the weekend was one of those rare moments when the authority of Ministers crumbles, like some ancient statue turning to dust in the wink of an eye.

One minute they are in charge, the next they are stumbling and stuttering, looking anxiously across crowded benches for a friend. When they get to that stage it is usually too late to find one. Mrs Thatcher bravely tried to hold the line as the debate began but within a few minutes it became clear that her efforts were doomed.

For a start Mr Michael Foot — who had climbed off a plane from Germany only about an hour earlier — found the elusive combination of passion and rational argument which has deserted him in the Commons since he became Leader of the Opposition. He was devastating in his assault on Ministers for "betraying" the Falklanders, and in his denunciation of the "foul and brutal" aggression of the Argentinians. His raving was purposeful again.

That speech set the tone: shock at the invasion; a sense of shame at the plight of the islanders; disbelief at the apparent blunders by the Government.

What concerned some of his backbenchers was Mr Foot's apparent support for military retaliation, but what moved the Commons as a whole was the swashbuckling attack on ministerial incompetence the like of which has not been seen since Labour lost the election.

With the mood established, all Mrs Thatcher, Mr Nott and the others could do was to brace themselves for an onslaught. It came. From the Labour, Liberal, SDP and SNP benches came speeches of real ferocity, and from the Tory side there were barbs sharper than any Mrs Thatcher has so far known.

Like all such debates where the tide of emotion is running strong, there were a few moments when the scene seemed to freeze for a second or two, and an almost visible chill settled on the Government Front Bench.

Mr Edward du Cann, the grandest of Tory grandees, was the first to strike. He is renowned as a master of the political *double entendre*: praise from Mr du Cann should always make you look behind you. On this occasion he succeeded in making a speech which he can defend as loyal, but which offered biting criticism. "I don't remember the Duke of Wellington whining before Torres Vedras," he said. Such reference to the Iron Duke must have pierced the Iron Lady.

Mr Enoch Powell, as usual, spoke quietly and with deadly effect. Over the next week he would see just what metal the Iron Lady was made of. Mrs Thatcher in a little-noticed and perhaps alarming gesture, looked across, nodded vigorously and said: "Right", several times. Mr Powell, though, will suspend his judgment.

Dr David Owen, a former Foreign Secretary, found more eloquence than he had in office and delivered a devastating indictment of what he described as lack of preparations by the Government for an Argentinian invasion — in sharp contrast, he pointed out, to the action taken in 1977 by the Labour Government. For Mrs Thatcher to hear her own back-benchers muttering their approval for David Owen as he praised Labour defence strategy must have been a painful experience, a nightmare played out in slow motion before her eyes.

But worse was to follow. Mr Patrick Cormack, a Tory back-bencher, recalled how constituents had complained to him on the evening of the invasion that they had thought it possible to sleep safe and sound with a Conservative Government in office. "What a blunder!" he roared. And he ended with the phrase which has Whips reaching for their revolvers: "Many of us will have to question our position on these benches."

As if it were not enough to have these hand grenades dropping around her like a deadly hailstorm, the Prime Minister had to contend with the revolt of the ancient Tory Right, outraged by the infamy of a dago invasion. Mr Julian Amery, one of the dwindling band of Empire Loyalists who still trundle to their places when the world is up for discussion, growled across at the Cabinet. It was sad, he said, to see such "unpreparedness and feeble counsel" in a Conservative administration.

Then in one of those splendidly extravagant images with which such grand old stagers gild their speeches, he called on Mrs Thatcher to "make the Argentinian dictator disgorge what he has taken". To such veterans of world diplomacy, the great Powers — and some of the lesser ones — still feast on the spoils of conquest.

As the debate rolled on the calls for retaliation became stronger. It bred its own emotions. Mr Donald Stewart, for the SNP, and Mr Russell Johnston, for the Liberals, both spoke powerfully in defence of the islanders against the incompetence of the Government and argued for military efforts to free them. Such was the passion unleashed in the Commons during such speeches that even those — like Dr Owen — who are highly sceptical of a naval rescue operation, believed the Government had left themselves with little choice.

There were two speeches solidly against such a course. Mr Ray Whitney, a Right-wing Conservative from Buckinghamshire, recalled his own diplomatic tour of duty in Buenos Aires and argued for talks rather than naval engagements. He was more or less shouted down by Tory colleagues who made clear their view that here in their very midst was a representative of what they most despised at the moment — a Foreign Office toady.

But there was another speech from Mr George Foulkes, MP for South Ayrshire, which stood out from the throng. With real passion he warned of the consequences of war: the loss of British lives as well as Argentinian would be colossal. MPs might not like hearing it, he went on, but war would not be pleasant. His words were remarkably well received and the time may yet come when such speeches are commonplace.

"Thousands of Argentinians will be killed and we may not wish to weep any tears over that. But inevitably thousands of British troops must be killed and we must face the consequences," he said.

So after nearly three hours of passionate debate, Mr Nott rose in his place. If he had little authority left when he stood up, by the time he sat down only about 15 minutes later he was a wreck, a shrunken skeleton of the Minister who has so often dominated from the Dispatch Box, earning Prime Ministerial favours for his quick-witted and sometimes arrogant dismissal of the Government's critics.

In front of him, Opposition MPs jeered and shouted: "Resign"; behind him Tories banged their benches in frustration and shook their heads in bewilderment, alongside his Cabinet colleagues paled and moved delicately away from him. In a particularly gauche moment, he tried to introduce a partisan note about nuclear policy and was promptly shouted down.

Like so many politicians faced with that last terrifying stand at the Dispatch Box, Mr Nott's wit and surefootedness deserted him at the end. He fumbled and footered, raising hoots of laughter with his boast that new Navy vessels were even now undergoing sea trials, that the task force would be led by HMS *Invincible* (which the Government have decided to sell), that, yes, Britain had the capacity to protect the Falklands. It was a dismal scene and as the Tories filed away there was hardly one to be found who would offer a halfpenny for Mr Nott's survival in office, even if the *coup de grace* is briefly delayed.

So it was over. Old hands recalled the Suez debate on November 3, 1956, and we gradually realised that what we had heard was probably a declaration of war. That thought takes time to get a hold, but the immediate impressions were vivid enough.

Dr Owen telling Mr Nott that if he did not know the value of negotiating from a position of strength he had no right to be Defence

Secretary; Mr Ted Rowlands shouting out the news that the Foreign Office had been reading official Argentinian telegrams for years; a Labour MP demanding that Lord Carrington should be brought to the Bar of the House to be questioned; a Conservative declaring that Mr Michael Foot had "spoken for Britain".

How politics changes. From a Government whose well-developed resilience had belied the dismal facts of economic life, Ministers were transformed in a flash to a huddle of nervous and fearful figures. It can, for once, be said with justice: the Government has been shaken to its foundations.

And as for the Commons? For long hours it fails to deliver what its members want, and falls short of fulfilment in testing the Government, or expressing a united sentiment, or simply being genuine. Yet for once, despite the excesses of jingoism which marked passages of Saturday's debate, it was an occasion when we all lived a heady and frantic year or two in the course of three short hours.

In the weeks ahead there may be reversals as swift as that which has humbled the Government this weekend, there may be resignations and sackings, there may be war. Even the passion and melodramatic flourishes of Saturday's debate may have been no more than an overture to what is yet to come.

James Naughtie: The Scotsman, *5 April 1982*

***

More than two months later, after abortive diplomacy and much bloodshed, the Argentine forces surrendered. Mrs Thatcher savoured her victory, and rose to tell the Commons that it was over — and to signal her determination to pursue a "fortress Falklands" strategy. Britain's latest war was over.

VICTORY

"Early this morning in Port Stanley, 74 days after the Falkland Islands were invaded, General Moore accepted from General Menendez the surrender of all the Argentine forces in East and West Falkland together with their arms and equipment. In a message to the Commander-in-Chief Fleet, General Moore reported:

'The Falkland Islands are once more under the Government desired by their inhabitants. God Save the Queen.'

General Menendez has surrendered some 11,000 men in Port Stanley and some 2,000 in West Falkland. In addition, we had already captured and were holding elsewhere on the islands 1,800 prisoners, making in all some 15,000 prisoners of war now in our hands.

The advance of our forces in the last few days is the culmination of a determined military effort to compel the Argentine Government to withdraw their forces from the Falkland Islands. . . .

We must now bring life in the islands back to normal as quickly as possible, despite the difficult conditions and the onset of the Antarctic winter. Mines must be removed, the water supply in Stanley is not working and there will be other urgent tasks of repair and reconstruction.

Mr Rex Hunt and members of the Islands Council at present in this country will return as soon as possible. Mr Hunt will concentrate on civilian matters. General Moore will be responsible for military matters. They will act in effect as civil and military commissioners and will, of course, work in the closest co-operation.

After all that has been suffered it is too early to look much beyond the beginning of the return to normal life. In due course the islanders will be able to consider and express their views about the future. When the time is right we can discuss with them ways of giving their elected representatives an expanded role in the government of the islands.

We shall uphold our commitment to the security of the islands; if necessary we shall do this alone."

Margaret Thatcher: Speech, *15 June 1982*

6

Constitutional and Imperial Ramblings

If it be said that there is an evil in change as change, I answer that there is also an evil in discontent as discontent.

—Thomas Babington Macaulay

Learn to think Imperially.

—Joseph Chamberlain

CONSTITUTIONALISTS have a way of either becoming great figures of the Commons, or its great bores. Sometimes, an observer might conclude, both at once. The lure of constitutional wrangle and reform to the barrack-room lawyers, not to mention the real ones, is irresistible. There are some Parliamentarians for whom all-night battles on the fine print of an obscure Bill is the essence of the politician's business; others for whom constitutional reform is the great theme rolling along beneath the day-to-day business of the place and the object of their noblest purposes. The great debates are occasions for confusion and double-dealing, but they also produce political heroism and memorable performances. Where else to start but the Great Reform Bill, and the first genuine step in widening the franchise? Of all the speeches made in its support, one still holds a special place — Lord Macaulay's.

***

REFORM

"The question of Parliamentary Reform is still behind. But signs, of which it is impossible to misconceive the import, do most clearly indicate that unless that question also be speedily settled, property and order, and all the institutions of this great monarchy, will be exposed to fearful peril. Is it possible that gentlemen long versed in high political affairs cannot read these signs? Is it possible that they can really believe that the Representative system of England, such as it now is, will last to the year 1860? If not, for what would they have us wait? Would they have us wait merely that we may show to all the world how little we have profited by our own recent experience? Would they have us wait that we may once again hit the exact point where we can neither refuse with authority nor concede with grace? Would they have us wait that the numbers of the discontented party may become larger, its demands higher, its feelings more acrimonious, its organisation more complete? Would they have us wait till the whole tragi-comedy of 1827 has been acted over again? Till they have been brought into office by a cry of 'No Reform', to be reformers, as they were once before brought into office by a cry of 'No Popery', to be emancipators? Have they obliterated from their minds — gladly, perhaps, would some among them obliterate from their minds — the transactions of that year? And have they forgotten all the transactions of the succeeding year? Have they forgotten how the spirit of liberty in Ireland, debarred from its natural outlet, found a vent by forbidden passages? Have they forgotten how we were forced to indulge the Catholics in all the licence of rebels, merely because we chose to withhold from them the liberties of subjects? Do they wait for associations more formidable than that of the Corn Exchange, for contributions larger than the Rent, for agitators more violent than those who, three years ago, divided with the King and the Parliament the sovereignty of Ireland? Do they wait for that last and most dreadful paroxysm of popular rage, for that last and most cruel test of military fidelity? Let them wait, if their past experience shall induce them to think that any high honour or any exquisite pleasure is to be obtained by a policy like this. Let them wait, if this strange and fearful infatuation be indeed upon them, that they should not see with their eyes, or hear with their ears, or understand with their heart. But let us know our interest and our duty better. Turn where we may, within, around, the voice of great events is proclaiming to us, Reform, that you may preserve. Now, therefore, while everything at home and abroad forebodes ruin to those who persist in a hopeless struggle against the spirit of the age; now, while the crash of the proudest throne of the Continent is still resounding in our ears; now, while the roof of a British palace affords an ignominious shelter to the exiled heir of forty kings; now, while we see on every side ancient institutions subverted and great societies dissolved; now, while the heart of England is still sound; now, while old feelings and old associations retain a power and a charm which may too soon pass away; now, in this your accepted time; now, in this your day of salvation, take counsel, not of prejudice, not of party spirit, not of the ignominious pride of a fatal consistency, but of history, of reason, of the ages which are past, of the signs of this most portentous time, Pronounce in a manner worthy of the expectation with which this great debate has been anticipated, and of the long remembrance which it will leave behind. Renew the youth of the State. Save property, divided against itself. Save the multitude, endangered by its own ungovernable passions. Save the aristocracy, endangered by its own unpopular power. Save the greatest, and fairest, and most highly civilised community that ever existed from calamities which may in a few days sweep away all the rich heritage of so many ages of wisdom and glory. The danger is terrible. The time is short. If this bill should be rejected, I pray to God that none of those who concur in rejecting it may ever remember their votes with unavailing remorse amidst the wreck of laws, the confusion of ranks, the spoilation of property, and the dissolution of social order."

Lord Macaulay: Speech, *1 March 1831*

***

Parliamentary reform itself dominated many sessions as the century rolled on, but by 1886 another battle was under way, over Ireland. W. E. Gladstone tried, and failed, to get the Commons to accept his Home Rule Bill, warning that if the issue of reform was not grasped, only disaster could follow. The scene, as a crucial debate neared its end, was described by John Morley, Gladstone's biographer, Chief Secretary for Ireland and a convinced Home Ruler. The Government lost the vote and resigned the next day.

HOME RULE

Then came the unflagging veteran with the last of his five speeches. He was almost as white as the flower in his coat, but the splendid compass, the flexibility, the moving charm and power of his voice, were never more wonderful. The construction of the speech was a masterpiece, the temper of it unbroken, its freedom from taunt and bitterness and small personality incomparable. Even if Mr Gladstone had been in the prime of his days, instead of a man of seventy-six years all struck; even if he had been at his ease for the last four months, instead of labouring with indomitable toil at the two bills, bearing all the multifarious burdens of the head of a government, and all the weight of the business of the leader of the House, undergoing all the hourly strain and contention of a political situation of unprecedented difficulty — much of the contention being of that peculiarly trying and painful sort which means the parting of colleagues and friends — his closing speech would still have been a surprising effort of free, argumentative, and fervid appeal. With the fervid appeal was mingled more than one piece of piquant mockery. Mr Chamberlain had said that a dissolution had no terrors for him. "I do not wonder at it. I do not see how a dissolution can have any terrors for him. He has trimmed his vessel, and he has touched his rudder in such a masterly way, that in whichever direction the winds of heaven may blow they must fill his sails. Supposing that at an election public opinion should be very strong in favour of the bill, my right hon. friend would then be perfectly prepared to meet that public opinion, and tell it, 'I declared strongly that I adopted the principle of the bill.' On the other hand, if public opinion were very adverse to the bill, he again is in complete armour, because he says, 'Yes, I voted against the bill.' Supposing, again, public opinion is in favour of a very large plan for Ireland, my right hon. friend is perfectly provided for that case also. The government plan was not large enough for him, and he proposed in his speech on the introduction of the bill that we should have a measure on the basis of federation, which goes beyond this bill. Lastly — and now I have nearly boxed the compass — supposing that public opinion should take quite a different turn, and instead of wanting very large measures for Ireland, should demand very small measures for Ireland, still the resources of my right hon. friend are not exhausted, because he is then able to point out that the last of his plans was for four provincial circuits controlled from London. All these alternatives and provisions were visibly "creations of the vivid imagination, born of the hour and perishing with the hour, totally unavailable for the solution of a great and difficult problem".

Now, said the orator, was one of the golden moments of our history, one of those opportunities which may come and may go, but which rarely return, or if they return, return at long intervals, and under circumstances which no man can forecast. There was such a golden moment in 1795, on the mission of Lord Fitzwilliam. At that moment the parliament of Grattan was on the point of solving the Irish problem. The cup was at Ireland's lips, and she was ready to drink it, when the hand of England rudely and ruthlessly dashed it to the ground in obedience to the wild and dangerous intimations of an Irish faction. There had been no great day of hope for Ireland since, no day when you might completely and definitely hope to end the controversy till now — more than ninety years. The long periodic time had at last run out, and the star had again mounted into the heavens.

This strain of living passion was sustained with all its fire and speed to the very close. "Ireland stands at your bar expectant, hopeful, almost suppliant. Her words are the words of truth and soberness. She asks a blessed oblivion of the past, and in that oblivion our interest is deeper even than hers. You have been asked tonight to abide by the traditions of which we are the heirs. What traditions? By the Irish traditions? Go into the length and breadth of the world, ransack the literature of all countries, find if you can a single voice, a single book, in which the conduct of England towards Ireland is anywhere treated except with profound and bitter condemnation. Are these the traditions by which we are exhorted to stand? No, they are a sad exception to the glory of our country. They are a broad and black blot upon the pages of its history, and what we want to do is to stand by the traditions of which we are the heirs in all matters except our relations with Ireland, and to make our relation with Ireland to conform to the other traditions of our country. So we treat our traditions, so we hail the demand of Ireland for what I call a blessed oblivion of the past. She asks also a boon for the future; and that boon for the future, unless we are much mistaken, will be a boon to us in respect of honour, no less than a boon to her in respect of happiness, prosperity and peace. Such, sir, is her prayer. Think, I beseech you; think well, think wisely, think, not for the moment, but for the years that are to come, before you reject this bill."

John Morley: Life of Gladstone

***

Reform of the Lords has been a recurring theme, as it still is. Before Asquith's Government succeeded in 1911 in passing its Parliament Bill to restrict the powers of the Upper House, having won a general election on the question and with the threat in reserve that George V would agree to create enough Peers to force through reform, there were rough times for the Prime Minister from the diehard opponents of reform. On 25 June 1911 a scene took place in the Commons that encapsulated the fierce split of opinion over Asquith's proposals. A. J. Balfour, the leader of the Conservative opposition, acquiesced in the assault by Asquith's enemies, some of whom were to help depose the Tory leader a year later because of his advice to them to surrender.

A PRIME MINISTER AT BAY

Asquith was to outline the Government's intentions on the motion to consider the Lords' amendments. He was cheered by crowds in the streets as he drove with his wife in an open motor car from Downing Street, and he was cheered by his own back-benchers as he walked up the floor of the House of Commons. But as soon as he rose to speak he was greeted by a roar of interruption. "Divide, divide," was the dominant shout, but interspersed with it were cries of "Traitor", "Let Redmond speak", "American dollars" and "Who killed the king?". For half an hour the Prime Minister stood at the box, unable to make any full sentence heard to the House, and unable to fill more than a staccato half-column of Hansard. F. E. Smith and Lord Hugh Cecil were manifestly the leaders (Will Crooks, the Labour Member for Woolwich, proclaimed that "many a man has been certified insane for less than the noble Lord has done this afternoon"), but there were many others who took a full part. In a moment of comparative calm, Sir Edward Carson attempted to move the adjournment of the debate. Balfour sat unruffled in his place throughout these proceedings. He took no part in the scene, but he did not make any attempt to restrain his followers.

At last Asquith gave up. With a remark about "decline to degrade himself further", he sat down. Balfour followed and was heard in silence throughout his speech. He had begun with a very mild implied rebuke to those who had perpetrated the scene, but made no further reference to it. Then Sir Edward Grey rose. He had been subjected to a perhaps understandably hysterical note passed down from the Ladies' Gallery by Mrs Asquith, but it is not clear whether or not this was the decisive cause of his intervention. "They will listen to you," the note had run, "so for God's sake defend him from the cats and the cads!" This Grey made some attempt to do, and his performance satisfied Mrs Asquith at least.

> "Arthur Balfour followed," she wrote in her diary, "and when Grey rose to speak the silence was formidable. Always the most distinguished figure in the House, he stood for a moment white and silent, and looked at the enemy: 'If arguments are not to be listened to from the Prime Minister there is not one of us who will attempt to take his place,' he said, and sat down in an echo of cheers . . . I met Edward Grey for a moment afterwards alone, and, when I pressed my lips to his hand, his eyes filled with tears."

In Hansard, however, the firm and clear-cut statement which Mrs Asquith recorded was lost in a column of repetitive, diffuse and inconclusive sentences. The speaker appeared to know neither what to say nor when to sit down. Perhaps in the actual performance Grey's widely acclaimed gifts of character shone through and gave dignity to his intervention.

When Grey had finished F. E. Smith rose and attempted to carry on the debate. Not unreasonably, the Government back-benchers who had listened in silence to Balfour decided that this was too much. Uproar again developed, and after five minutes the Speaker suspended the sitting on the ground that a state of "grave disorder" had arisen. Standing Order 21, under which he did this, had not previously been invoked since 1893, and a precedent for the refusal of a hearing to a Prime Minister could not be found without a much longer research.

The incident aroused great resentment, and not only amongst normal supporters of the Government. Even Lord Halsbury, we are informed by his biographer, took exception to the scene, "for it was as alien from his principles as it was temporarily damaging to his cause". *The Times, Daily Telegraph*, and some leading Unionist papers in the provinces delivered stern rebukes to the ringleaders, and a number of Opposition Members of Parliament, led by Sir Alfred Cripps and Colonel Lockwood, sent a letter of apology to the Prime Minister. But the bitterness could not easily be undone, especially as those who had provoked the incident were in no way repentant. "The ugliest feature," Mr Churchill had accurately reported to the King, was the absence of any real passion or spontaneous feeling. It was a squalid, frigid, organised attempt to insult the Prime Minister

Roy Jenkins: Mr Balfour's Poodle

***

Lords reform came back to the Commons in 1969, when Harold Wilson's Labour Government tried to push through a Bill to reshape the Upper House, and failed. A notable feature of the debates was the strange alliance between two extrovert constitutionalists, Michael Foot and Enoch Powell, who found common cause across the party divide, though their purposes were quite different — Foot an abolitionist and Powell a preservationist. It was their backbench campaign which, more than any other single factor, destroyed the Bill. Foot defended his opposition to his own Government on the issue of "the other place" as the voice of consistency, and attacked the front-bench spokesmen of the Conservative opposition.

FOOT REBELS

"We are holding consistently to the view of the Labour Party, although I will not elaborate this, in the sense that we have a mandate for what we propose, which is to strip the other place of its powers. Indeed, that is the compromise which the Government will eventually have to reach, and when they return to that they will be exactly in line with Labour Party policy. But there is not a scrap of mandate for the kind of body for which they ask, and least of all is there any support in the Labour Party policy for the idea of the payment of peers with all the consequences which have been described.

The debate that we have had on payment brings us once more to the question of how we are to resolve these problems in the House, how we are to deal with a political situation where the Government seek to force through the House a measure which is bitterly opposed on both sides, a measure for which, although the Government can get majorities, as the Home Secretary says, any fair observer of what is happening in the House would agree that there has been hardly any support from the back benches, except perhaps from my hon. Friend the Member for Luton, and to which there has been growing opposition.

As I have said and as the right hon. Member for Wolverhampton, South-West (Mr Powell) and others have said, the proposal that is now going through the House is a different one from that which was originally proposed to the other place, bad as most of us think that was. It is my judgment, and I may be quite wrong, that when this Bill reaches the other place, if it ever does, there will be a very different reaction to it, particularly on this Clause. If that occurs then the Government will really be in the soup. If there is a revolt of the peers against what is now proposed then the Government will suffer the gravest humiliation. That is why some of us are pleading with them still to look at the matter again.

That brings me to the attitude of the Opposition Front Bench. The experience we are having with the Opposition Front Bench is unique in my recollection of Parliament, in this sense. Here is a major issue, nobody disputes that this is a constitutional measure of first-class importance; nobody can dispute that if this measure goes through and is passed it will alter the whole nature of the British Constitution, maybe for generations to come. That is the intention and the purpose of it. It is not a short-term measure, a minor amendment Act, it is a major change in the constitution.

I do not believe that in the whole history of Parliament there can have been a single example of a measure of such constitutional importance, with Clauses such as we are now discussing which alter the nature of the constitution, upon which we are given no advice of the official view of the Conservative Party. It is no business of mine to protect them, but it is a matter of extreme discourtesy towards their own back-benchers, their own right hon. Friends who make very powerful speeches in this matter. It is an extraordinary state of affairs when the Opposition Front Bench does not even attempt to answer the arguments on these questions which their right hon. Friends think are of such importance.

We have had the extraordinary spectacle of the right hon. Member for Enfield, West (Mr Iain MacLeod) who spoke on the White Paper; he came in for a few minutes and went out without a word. Other Front Benchers have come in and gone out without a word. The right hon. Member for Barnet (Mr Maudling), who we hoped would contribute to the debate, has not uttered a word. I have never seen anything like them. Look at them, these unlikely novices for a new Trappist order, these bashful tip-toeing ghosts, these pale effigies of what were once sentient, palpable, human specimens, these unlarynxed wraiths, these ectoplasmic apparitions, these sphinix-like sentinels at our debates, why are they here?"

Michael Foot: Speech, *25 February 1969*

***

Earlier, at the start of the long committee stage on the Bill, Powell had made a typical speech, demolishing the whole scheme of the Bill. He prepared the ground for long nights of debate on the detailed provisions with a characteristically surprising argument that many of the attacks on the House of Lords were based on false premise.

A POWELLITE ARGUMENT

"In the course of his introductory speech to this part of our proceedings, the hon. Member for Ashton-under-Lyne (Mr Sheldon), whose remarks I shall not at present attempt to emulate in respect of length, among much other highly mythical history founded his argument upon an entirely false assumption. That false assumption was the the so-called hereditary principle on which the House of Lords is at present constituted is the principle of heredity.

The hon. Member spent much of his time demolishing a structure which, in fact, did not exist — his assumed House of Lords founded on the principle of heredity. If the House of Lords were founded on the principle of heredity, a peerage would not descend to the eldest son. It would descend to all sons, since there can be no ground for selecting in respect of ability or other characteristic one rather than another of the offspring of a sire.

Secondly, the descent of peerages would universally be, as it is called, in tail general, that is, through the female as well as through the male, since there is equally no reason for supposing that whatever virtues may be transmissible hereditarily are not just as transmissible through the female as through the male.

But, of course, all this has nothing to do with the constitution, or the principles of the constitution, of the House of Lords. The House of Lords is a prescriptive House. It consists partly of members who are nominees in that they are peers of first creation; but it consists also and preponderantly of members by hereditary succession who are there by prescription, because prescriptive right to succeed in a certain way to a seat and to a writ of summons to the Upper Chamber has come down in the course of our history.

The fact that elder son succeeds arises from the convention — an old convention, but still a convention, and an arbitrary convention — of primogeniture. The fact again that some peers and peeresses sit in the other place by descent through the female arises from a long and tangled story in the 14th and 15th centuries, when the Parliamentary barony was superseding the feudal barony and the old feudal baronies which still survived had to be interpreted in terms of those Parliamentary baronies by creation with which men were then predominantly familiar. These are matters of convention which, in the course of time, have come to be the prescriptive right on which the institution is founded.

The argument which the whole Bill raises is whether we shall be the gainers by replacing an Upper Chamber partly consisting of nominees and partly consisting of peers by succession but constituted on the principle of prescription, by a Chamber constituted by nomination in obedience to a formula which is not even written into the Bill. Here, in the very first debate on the very first Amendment, the Committee comes right up against the difficulty that the heart of the Bill, any sense there may be in it — and I think that there is not a great deal — is in the Preamble and what lies behind the Preamble. It is only if one accepts the scheme alluded to in the Preamble that the Bill becomes intelligible, and that it becomes possible to argue about it at all."

Enoch Powell: Speech, *12 February 1969*

***

A decade later another celebrated constitutional imbroglio engulfed a Labour Government, this time over the issue of devolution — in particular, the scheme for an elected Assembly in Edinburgh produced by James Callaghan's minority Government to hold on to the support of Scottish Nationalist MPs and Liberals and, therefore, power itself. After months of debate, Labour rebellions and a long battle against his Government's plan by Tam Dalyell, the MP for West Lothian, the Scotland Act was passed, on the promise of a referendum in which 40 per cent of those entitled to vote would have to say "yes" for the Assembly to be set up. The referendum failed by a hairsbreadth to meet that 40 per cent requirement and when the Conservatives arrived in office after Labour lost the general election in May 1979 they moved quickly to repeal the Act. On a long, hot night in June George Younger, the Secretary of State for Scotland, urged the Commons to put devolution aside.

THE LAST RITES

Scots enjoy a good wake. There is nothing quite like a bit of gloom to get the old Calvinistic juices running and nothing like a burial for bringing a sparkle to the eye and a rosy blush to the cheek. So it was last night when the Scotland Act was laid to rest.

Not a black tie was in sight, and there seemed to be plenty of joviality on the Labour side (although they were meant to be gloomy) and plenty of gloom on the Tory benches (although they were meant to be jolly). This adds weight to the theory that a Scot smiles only when things are going against him.

All these feelings swirled round the Commons as the old devolution hacks settled down with the new boys to work over the familiar ground and draw a last veil over the Act. Mr Tam Dalyell brooded on his bench; Mr John Smith appeared for the final act, Mr George Younger prepared to say the last rites and a selection of Empire Loyalists shuffled in to mark the survival of "the unity of the Kingdom".

That kenspeckle figure Mr Teddy Taylor was nowhere to be seen, of course. Instead of his fire we had Mr Younger's gentle glow as he painstakingly raked over the 40 per cent argument and said that there would be talks to decide what there was going to be to talk about in the all-party talks. Invitations, he said confidently, had already gone out.

Mr David Steel was a little piqued. If these invitations had been winging their way hither and thither none had landed on the Liberal bench, he pointed out. There will have to be talks to see why he has not been invited to the talks.

Through it all the Labour benches were quite jovial, never more so than when they were shouting "Shame" and "Oh, oh".

Mr Younger ploughed on and decided to pay a compliment to Mr Dalyell, who he said had given his constituency the fame (or should it be the notoriety) of Schleswig-Holstein as the nub of a great constitutional question, doubtless destined to be wheeled out to torment generations of schoolchildren.

Mr Younger spent much time on 40 per cent calculations, a dangerous pastime. A vision was conjured up of thousands of people sitting at their firesides confident that in so doing they were voting "No". Consequently, we must assume, most people were voting against Europe in that recent jamboree.

But after a very difficult speech he finally pronounced the death sentence and resumed his seat. Mr Dennis Canavan then shouted rather unnecessarily, "Sit down." That is the sort of thing you say on such occasions.

Mr Bruce Millan strove to keep the thing going by accusing Mr Younger of utter humbug, which is what Tories traditionally shout at Socialists. But nothing from Mr Millan could compete with the entertainment of the following contribution from Mr Julian Amery, MP for Brighton Pavilion and the Empire.

He told us at great length how we had just escaped disaster in the Scotland Act. It sounded as if it was an outrage only narrowly beaten in the disaster stakes by the Indian Mutiny. At this stage, unaccountably, Labour MPs began to giggle and leave the chamber.

Mr Amery went on to award his own medals for persistence in opposing devolution, and poor Mr Dalyell was singled out for praise.

Then there was praise for the national mix in the United Kingdom, illustrated by Mr Amery by reference to the London telephone directory. For one ghastly moment we wondered if this was some new sophisticated filibuster.

But no, he sat down to pave the way for the last hours of the Scotland Act. A queue of MPs waited to pronounce their various eulogies, and a long night began. The honourable member for Schleswig-Holstein brooded on his bench.

James Naughtie: The Scotsman, *21 June 1979*

The most important constitutional change of recent years was Britain's accession to the European Community, successfully negotiated by Edward Heath's Government despite opposition from a large group of Conservatives, who fought their leader every step of the way. It was the great cause of his life as a political leader, well expressed in his closing speech in a genuinely historic debate on Britain's entry into Europe in October 1971. He won the vote by 356 to 244.

INTO EUROPE

"I do not think that any Prime Minister has stood at this Box in time of peace and asked the House to take a positive decision of such importance as I am asking it to take tonight. I am well aware of the responsibility which rests on my shoulders for so doing. After ten years of negotiation, after many years of discussion in this House and after ten years of debate, the moment of decision for Parliament has come. The other House has already taken its vote and expressed its view — [Hon. Members: 'Backwoodsmen!']: 451 frontwoodsmen have voted in favour of the motion and, for the rest, 58.

I cannot over-emphasise tonight the importance of the vote which is being taken, the importance of the issue, the scale and quality of the decision and the impact that it will have equally inside and outside Britain. On one thing I agree very much with the right hon. Member for Cardiff, South-East (Mr Callaghan). He finished by saying that he wished to set this against a world canvas. It has been said that this is a historic decision; it is being taken in what many would describe as a historic week.

Earlier, the world was watching New York. They were waiting to see whether China was going to become a member of the Security Council and of the General Assembly. Tonight, the world is similarly watching Westminster, waiting to see whether we are going to decide that Western Europe should now move along the path to real unity — or whether the British Parliament, now given the choice, not for the first time but probably for the last time for many years to come, will reject the chance of creating a united Europe.

There can be absolutely no doubt of the world interest in this matter — of those physically watching and those waiting for the outcome. Nor can there be any doubt of the reasons why. It is natural that we in this House, in this long debate, have been largely concerned with the impact on our own country, but our decision tonight will vitally affect the balance of forces in the modern world for many years to come.

It will affect the sort of world in which we British people and many generations to come will live their lives. Even since we last debated this in the House in July, the situation has been transformed by China showing that, certainly within this century, it will be the third super Power. We could not tell, when this decision was taken in the United Nations, what the consequences of it would be, either for China or for the rest of us in the western world. But we thought that decision right: it is one that British Governments have worked for since 1961. . . .

I have sometimes felt that among those who have been in this debate seeking to balance up the advantages and disadvantages there was a desire for a degree of certainty which is never obtainable in human affairs. Hon. Members will not ask for it in their lives, in their own businesses. As a nation we have never hitherto asked for it in a trading agreement or in international affairs, either economic or political. Anyone who studies the length of our trading agreements outside will accept that that is the case.

It may be that it is showing a lack of confidence in ourselves, but I suggest that, whatever the explanation, we are worrying about the wrong question. Surely the right question to ask ourselves is this: has the Community the necessary and appropriate means for dealing with the problems of its members, whether they arise out of these present negotiations in which we have taken part or whether they arise from any other cause in the life of the Community? . . .

Surely we must consider the consequences of staying out. We cannot delude ourselves that an early chance would be given us to take the decision again. We should be denying ourselves and succeeding generations the opportunities which are available to us in so many spheres; opportunities which we ourselves in this country have to seize. We should be leaving so many aspects of matters affecting our daily lives to be settled outside our own influence. That surely cannot be acceptable to us. We should be denying to Europe, also — let us look outside these shores for a moment — its full potential, its opportunities of developing economically and politically, maintaining its security, and securing for all its people a higher standard of prosperity.

All the consequences of that for many millions of people in Europe must be recognised tonight in the decision the House is taking. In addition, many projects for the future of Europe may have been long delayed. There has been great uncertainty, and tonight all that can be removed—[Hon. Members: 'No.']

The right hon. Gentleman the Member for Cardiff, South-East was very kind in the personal remarks he made about myself. Throughout my political career, if I may add one personal remark, it is well known that I have had the vision of a Britain in a united Europe: a Britain which would be united economically to Europe and which would be able to influence decisions affecting our own future, and which would enjoy a better standard of life and a fuller life. I have worked for a Europe which will play an increasing part in meeting the needs of those parts of the world which still lie in the shadow of want. I always understood that the right hon. Gentleman wanted that. I want Britain as a member of Europe which is united politically, and which will enjoy lasting peace and the greater security which would ensue.

Nor do I believe that the vision of Europe — and the right hon. Gentleman raised this specific point — is an unworthy vision, or an ignoble vision or an unworthy cause for which to have worked — *(Interruption)*. I have always made it absolutely plain to the British people that consent to this course would be given by Parliament —[Hon. Members: 'Resign.'] Parliament is the Parliament of all the people.

When we came to the end of the negotiations in 1963, after the veto had been imposed, the negotiator on behalf of India said:

'When you left India some people wept. And when you leave Europe tonight some will weep. And there is no other people in the world of whom these things could be said.'

That was a tribute from the Indian to the British. But tonight when this House endorses this motion many millions of people right across the world will rejoice that we have taken our rightful place in a truly United Europe."

Edward Heath: Speech, *28 October 1971*

***

Later, much later, there came the question of the European Assembly and as the pact between Callaghan's Government and David Steel's Liberals began to dissolve the question of Proportional Representation in the coming Assembly elections assumed a sudden new significance. For the Liberals, who had been obsessed like the rest of the nation with the resignation of their leader, Jeremy Thorpe (and were to be haunted by his subsequent arrest, trial and acquittal on a charge of conspiracy to murder), it was an important moment: the test of the pact was to be an effort to obtain from Callaghan a commitment to PR. Naturally, it was to fail. James Fenton watched the goings-on as the pact started to fall apart.

DAVID STEEL'S PREDICAMENT

Foolish men have compared the debate on direct elections to the European Assembly with the contest over the Reform Bill of 1832. Wise men cannot see the case for such an august comparison. Your reporter is, however, obliged to say that the scenes in the Commons on Tuesday night during the last stages of the debate were exciting enough to behold, even if the issue itself is hardly the most burning question of the day. Were you in favour of the regional list or did you want first-past-the-post? Myself, I rather fancied a sort of first-past-the-regional-list — get the matter over with as soon as possible. And so, as the House filled up (for most of the debate there had been only 30 or 40 Members on either side), and it became clear that there would be no late-night sitting, not even an extension to 11 p.m., my spirits rose.

It is marvellous to look down from the gallery during a major vote, and see absolutely *tout le monde* pass well within spitting distance. Just a little effort and splat! I could have landed one on Nigel Lawson, old Blaby-face. On the Government front bench sat Jim Callaghan, enjoying a little discussion with Dennis Skinner. I gather that Skinner, always the optimist, made a final attempt to persuade Callaghan to vote for first-past-the-post (the system the PM, were it not for the pact, would undoubtedly have preferred to put forward). In the Strangers' Gallery sat Mrs Paul Channon, explaining PR to her daughter: "You see, er, everyone has two or three votes, and, er, you all vote, and then, um, all the votes are sort of put together. Oh look, look! There's Mrs Thatcher." "Bleeugh." "And look, look! There's daddy. He's one of the tellers." "Is he pleased?" "Um, I'm not sure."

Earlier in the evening, the following conversation was heard in the corridors. First PR enthusiast: "Bryan Magee is going to come back from the opera at ten." Second PR enthusiast: "I wonder what time the vote will be. You know how bored Bryan gets. He may not stay till eleven."

The great set-piece of the debate was Ted Heath's speech. It pleased nobody. Loyalist Tories were annoyed: "Trains and trouble, that's what Ted means nowadays." One of them quoted Talleyrand on Napoleon: "I am amazed that such a great man could be so badly brought up." As for the PR-loving Tories, they left the Chamber swearing that Heath had single-handedly lost them 30 votes by his manner during the debate. Certainly the old boy was not on form. "Suffering from train-lag," muttered a colleague of mine. But I cannot help wondering whether we are not beginning to see the decline of an elder statesman. I detect all the symptoms of the *lues wilsoniana*, Wilson's Disease — an excessive devotion to making large sums of money by the publication of worthless books. The Tories are of course all in favour of making large sums of money — but they would prefer the method to be slightly less vulgar.

In addition to their annoyance at the book-signing spree, the Tories have begun to notice that Heath is actually a pompous old wind-bag. Last autumn in Blackpool they thronged to his CPC lecture (so much so that a larger hall had to be used). They came away from the lecture bored stiff. Two years ago when Heath spoke in the House he was heard with great respect. He had approximately the same effect as Banquo's ghost (although he did *not*, as in the recent television version of Verdi's *Macbeth*, appear in the middle of a bowl of jelly). On Tuesday night the House filled up to hear him — and he was mocked. His argument in favour of PR was so vaguely phrased and aimlessly delivered that it was a relief when Robert Adley intervened to ask Heath how he was to reply to a party worker who had said: I took your advice on local government reform — how can you expect me to believe you on *this*?

Throughout the debate the mood of the House had been fractious and quibbling. There seemed to be many more interventions than usual, and there was no shortage of subversive comment. This was not the sort of climate in which one would expect Merlyn Rees to thrive. Nor did he. In his early speech he gave the impression of a man who was struggling desperately to conceal either the fact that he did not know what he was talking about or his lack of conviction in the case he was making.

But just how embarrassed should the Government be? Certainly the whole drafting of the Bill and the manoeuvrings on the voting had been from the start an exercise in political expediency rather than principle. Callaghan, Foot and Rees were simply mounting a be-nice-to-David campaign, and if the campaign did not come off in quite the way intended — well, they had tried. Almost at once, the Liberal Party showed signs of recurrent Pardomania. Pardoe: "If the Labour Party is incapable of continuing the pact like this, it is incapable of governing the country and should be turned out immediately." This is surely a non-sequitur, borne of the mad Pardovian notion that the country is becoming ungovernable merely because Pardoe isn't getting what he wants. Cyril Smith: "I am delighted from the point of view of the future of the pact. I think it has laid the foundations of erosion for the pact." This is a pretty dotty metaphor.

The House broke up, for the most part, in a genial mood. It had been good fun all round. But as the first editions of the next day's papers came on the street, there must have been some very worried Liberals indeed. For once again, the Thorpe affair had hit the headlines, this time in the *Daily Mirror*, who promised a new set of revelations on the alleged cover-up. The Thorpe affair is in a curious state at the moment — you have to read all the papers in order to keep track of it. Nobody seems to pick up anybody else's story. All the advances are piecemeal. But to any Liberal proposing to plunge the country into a general election, the risk should be obvious.

For the scandal is by no means over. As the *Mirror* put it: "The drama has been played out in public over the past 22 months. The final act is yet to come." And until the final act is over, the most absorbing questions about the Liberals are questions about the Thorpe affair. In vain does Steel tour the country outlining his political philosophy. In vain does Michael Steed explain the virtues of PR to the long-suffering *Guardian* readership. In vain will any special assembly debate the merits and demerits of the pact. What we want to know is: who hired Newton, and why?

Steel's position this week, then, was doubly awkward. On the one hand, the mysterious return of the bloodstain in the carpet. On the other, the unreasonable insistence of party elements on the full pound of flesh.

Steel himself might well consider that the vote on PR was a sufficient improvement on previous votes to count as a small achievement. But he was boxed in by loonies and forced to agree to Wednesday morning's statement, calling for a meeting with the Prime Minister.

In doing so he had everything to lose, and very little to gain. Whatever was on his shopping-list this time, by way of profit-sharing schemes and so forth, his bargaining position was non-existent. How can one strike a bargain on the basis of other people's pique? How indeed can one negotiate on the basis of a threat of political suicide? It might suit Callaghan, it might turn out possible for him to throw a lifeline to Steel. But if this was inconvenient, Steel would leave the meeting empty-handed, to face his hysterical troops.

This, I'm afraid, is where we must leave Steel, on Wednesday afternoon, waiting for Downing Street to return his call, wondering how long his policies can last, when the next general election will be and what, if anything, he can rescue from the fiasco. We are sorry for Steel. We like him. We recommend that he has a good rest over Christmas, and that on his return he should do the decent thing, join the Labour Party and forget he ever knew his silly friends.

James Fenton: New Statesman, *16 December 1977*

***

The recent arguments over constitutional change have been bound up with one of the Commons' main post-war concerns, the retreat from Empire, its troubles and its benefits. It has provided a stage for the old-timers to have one last outing, in defence of Britain's world role, and a few moments of crisis. When Ian Smith issued his illegal declaration of independence in Rhodesia in November 1965, Harold Wilson made the mistake of believing the rebellion would be over — in a notorious phrase — "in weeks rather than months". It is worth recording his remarks, during the debate on the Queen's Speech, just after UDI, as he appealed for national unity in the struggle against the Smith regime.

UDI

"I warned the House yesterday that the problems arising from this could quickly get out of hand on an international scale. If that were to happen no assertion of our imperial responsibilities could stop it. It is not good enough to say that this is a matter for Britain only. One will not stop this by procedural amendments, whether in this House or in the United Nations. Debates about the use of words, whether 'punitive' or anything else, will not stop military aircraft crossing national frontiers. Hon. Members may dismiss, and are perfectly entitled to dismiss, from their minds the resolutions of the O.A.U., or the announcements made this morning about the use of parachutists, as impracticable or nonsense. They may dismiss these, but one thing that they cannot dismiss is the danger of major Powers getting a foothold on the Continent of Africa.

After the Commonwealth Conference last summer I referred in the House to 'the struggle for the soul of Africa' going on between countries such as ours and China, whose attempts at penetration in Africa have become a byword. But there are other nations beside China. There are other nations, who, perhaps, might feel competitively stimulated by the success they think China is having.

There may be other nations seeking a foothold, perhaps a military foothold, on the Continent of Africa, who would be glad of the opportunity of establishing that foothold with the substantial backing, with the aura of legitimacy from a resolution of the United Nations. I must ask hon. Gentlemen putting this argument, who are prepared to say that we might perhaps go a bit slow on our own economic measures, whether they have considered where this might lead us? If we are not able to show world opinion and those who have it in their power, whatever we do, to go in for military action, that we ourselves mean business and are carrying out effective measures, unless we are prepared to face that, then hon. Gentlemen may be inviting a prospect which is not one that I find comforting — the prospects of a Red Army in blue berets.

The issues that we are facing today cannot be dismissed by a play on words. We have to get down to real issues. They cannot be assessed in terms of the nicely calculated less or more. They cannot be assessed and decided by pure considerations of private profit. Still less, I think, can they or should they be settled in terms of purely party considerations.

I am not prepared to go to my colleagues in the Commonwealth and say that what we said before this illegal declaration we did not mean, that it was all bluff. I am not prepared to go to them and say, and nor is my right hon. Friend in the United Nations prepared to say, that the national unity to which we appealed was a facade. I believe that it is not a facade. I believe that it is a real national unity, and what the right hon. Gentlemen the Leader of the Opposition said yesterday and today, I think has made that clear. But this means that our measures must be effective.

Nearly 30 years ago, Winston Churchill, in a debate in the House on Abyssinia, used these words:

> 'We cannot undo the past, but we are bound to pass it in review in order to draw from it such lessons as may be applicable to the future, and surely the conclusion from this story is that we should not intervene in these matters unless we are in earnest and prepared to carry out intervention to all necessary lengths.'
> [Official Report, 6th April 1936; Vol. 310, c. 2482.]

I cannot think of a better text on which to build our national unity than those words of Sir Winston Churchill.

Harold Wilson: Speech, *12 November 1965*

***

Of the imperial headaches which have afflicted post-war governments one of the most gentle — though it once promised to be fearsome — was the repatriation of the Canadian constitution in 1982. Godfrey Barker watched the denouement for the *Daily Telegraph*.

THE SUN SETS ON CANADA

The sun set by 334 votes to 44 upon another part of the British Empire last night. We gave Canada away.

It was the second reading in the Commons on whether to hand back what Mr Denis Healey told the more backward MPs was "the second largest land area in the world" with 24 million people on it.

Only a thin red line of 44 MPs rebelled against the overwhelming will to surrender on both Front Benches — barely enough to man three canoes up the Red River.

So you should get out your globe and paint out, after 218 years, the red bit between the North-West Passage and Baffin Island. Paint it maple.

The House was crowded with lawyers and Red Indians to consider this request to have his country back from a Mr Pierre Trudeau, a nightclubber known to certain Members.

The Red Indians, rather needlessly, had their pow-wow head-dress removed by the Sergeant-at-Arms before entering the Chamber. Despite this slight, they were on the British side against Trudeau (funny thing, history).

Rumours abounded before the debate began that there was going to be a final Empire Loyalist assault on the Red River with points of order.

It would have required about 400 of these to have talked out the entire time from 3.30 to 10 p.m., well within the capacity of MPs. But the revolt crumbled after only four.

Even Cut Knife himself, the great logic-chopper Mr Robin Maxwell-Hyslop, seemed not to have his heart in it.

To ensure that any resistance to the Canada Bill would fall asleep over the camp fire, the Government put on Mr Humphrey Atkins, the Lord Privy Seal.

One was reminded after a while that Choral Evensong was on at this hour on the Third Programme, which was, of course, much more exciting. But for your, and the Empire's, sake one stayed to hear him.

Mr Atkins said that Canada was a wonderful country and that it was "incongruous", "an anachronism", etc. for it to have to ask the Commons to pass constitutions for it.

This, of course, is nonsense. British MPs have an unrivalled habit of meddling in the internal affairs of other countries.

Your average MP has passed 30 British North America Acts from 30 Vict. C.3 to 24-24 Eliz. II C.53, one learned from some enlivening small print while Mr Atkins was droning on.

Anyway, the Lord Privy Seal was determined to house the white flag at Moose Jaw.

"No Act of the Parliament of the U.K. passed after the Constitution Act 1982 comes into force shall extend to Canada as part of its law," he read out from the big print.

So who would fight for England? After Labour had abjectly surrendered and Sir Derek Walker-Smith had reminded us why Const. Hist. was the dullest subject in Oxford Mods, the Commons man of steel turned out to be Sir Bernard Braine.

Sir Bernard (C., S.E. Essex) and Lord Denning are, it seems, going to mount a re-invasion. Sir B. boomed out an appeal court judgment that "the Dominion of Canada is still not completely independent. It is still bound hand and foot by the British North America Acts."

He wanted nothing of the soothing appeals from both Front Benches to get out of the North-West Passage. Sir B. was worried about the Indians and their rights.

He kept dashing out of the Chamber into the central lobby, reportedly to consult two gents called Chief Jack Weasel-Moccasin and Chief Short-Both-Sides (or it may be Shout).

From a learned tome I see that in March 1867, the Canadians were appalled by the "scant attention" given by MPs to passing their previous constitution. They remarked bitterly on the eagerness, in contrast, with which MPs turned to a dog tax Bill immediately afterwords.

On the strength of last night's vote, they may deduce that we gave Canada back with as little resistance as we acquired it.

Godfrey Barker: Daily Telegraph, *18 February 1982*

***

So Canada went, meekly. Recreating the atmosphere of the debate over the colonies and the Empire means going back much further — and, perhaps, to the loss of America. The case for the colonies was put often enough with great feeling but, as a reminder of the greatest breach with the Crown, the obvious speeches to recall are those of Edmund Burke. Here, as a proper end to a selection of passages dealing with constitutional affairs, he argues for conciliation with the rebels.

A LOVE OF LIBERTY?

"My hold of the colonies is in the close affection which grows from common names, from kindred blood, from similar privileges, and equal protection. These are ties which, though light as air, are as strong as links of iron. Let the colonies always keep the idea of their civil rights associated with your government; they will cling and grapple to you, and no force under heaven will be of power to tear them from their allegiance. But let it be once understood that your government may be one thing and their privileges another, that these two things may exist without any mutual relation; the cement is gone, the cohesion is loosened, and everything hastens to decay and dissolution. As long as you have the wisdom to keep the sovereign authority of this country as the sanctuary of liberty, the sacred temple consecrated to our common faith, wherever the chosen race and sons of England worship freedom, they will turn their faces towards you.

The more they multiply, the more friends you will have; the more ardently they love liberty, the more perfect will be their obedience. Slavery they can have anywhere. It is a weed that grows in every soil. They may have it from Spain, they may have it from Prussia. But until you become lost to all feeling of your true interest and your natural dignity, freedom they can have from none but you. This is the commodity of price of which you have the monopoly. This is the true act of navigation which binds to you the commerce of the colonies, and through them secures to you the wealth of the world. Deny them this participation of freedom and you break the sole bond which originally made and must still preserve the unity of the empire. Do not entertain so weak an imagination as that your registers and your bonds, your affidavits and your sufferances, your cockets, and your clearances are what form the greatest securities of your commerce. Do not dream that your letters of office, and your instructions, and your suspending clauses are the things that hold together the great contexture of the mysterious whole. These things do not make your government. Dead instruments, passive tools as they are, it is the spirit of the English communion that gives all their life and efficacy to them. It is the spirit of the English constitution which, infused through the mighty mass, pervades, feeds, unites, invigorates, vivifies every part of the empire, even down to the minutest member.

Is it not the same virtue which does everything for us here in England? Do you imagine then that it is the Land Tax Act which raises your revenue, that it is the annual vote in the committee of supply which give you your army? or that it is the Mutiny Bill which inspires it with bravery and discipline? No! surely no! It is the love of the people, it is their attachment to their government from the sense of the deep stake they have in such a glorious institution, which gives you your army and your navy, and infuses into both that liberal obedience, without which your army would be a base rabble, and your navy nothing but rotten timber.

All this, I know well enough, will sound wild and chimerical to the profane herd of those vulgar and mechanical politicians, who have no place among us; a sort of people who think that nothing exists but what is gross and material; and who, therefore, far from being qualified to be directors of the great movement of empire, are not fit to turn a wheel in the machine. But to men truly initiated and rightly taught, these ruling and master principles which, in the opinion of such men as I have mentioned, have no substantial existence, are in truth everything and all in all. Magnanimity in politics is not seldom the truest wisdom; and a great empire and little minds go ill together. If we are conscious of our situation, and glow with zeal to fill our place as becomes our station and ourselves, we ought to auspicate all our public proceedings on America with the old warning of the Church, *'Sursum corda'*. We ought to elevate our minds to the greatness of that trust to which the order of Providence has called us. By adverting to the dignity of this high calling, our ancestors have turned a savage wilderness into a glorious empire, and have made the most extensive, and the only honourable conquests, not by destroying, but by promoting the wealth, the number, the happiness of the human race."

Edmund Burke: Speech, *22 March 1775*

7

Four Spies and a Scandal

To betray, you must first belong.

—Kim Philby

BELONGING, in Philby's sense, was feeling — and certainly enjoying — the embrace of an Establishment ready to trust its own, almost unquestioningly. Presumably it made the act of betrayal more satisfying: certainly it gave the revelations surrounding the spies who turned to their trade in the 1930s a fascination which has gripped the public imagination for thirty years. The idea of a secret world turned inside out, with trust among its inhabitants and with the outside world made impossible, has proved potent — spawning recollections and biographies and ever-more elaborate theories to explain "the real story". No one, probably, yet knows the story in full. But never mind that other spies — the MI6 man George Blake and the computer spy Geoffrey Prime — may have wreaked more harm, it is the names of Guy Burgess, Donald Maclean, Harold Philby and Anthony Blunt that have become the pantheon of demons in the public mind. Their ideological conversions at Cambridge, which led them to work for the Soviet Union, and their simultaneous acceptance into the established circles of power have provided curious outsiders with an irresistible saga of intrigue, unfolding year by year. Yet when it began, when someone warned Burgess and Burgess warned Maclean and they fled across Europe, only the smallest hint of the story was given to the public. It was to be nearly 30 years before an even reasonably full version of the tale was available.

It has kept its appeal as a story because it has afforded the nation at large a tantalising glimpse of an hitherto unknown world. It was also a very Establishment scandal, as the best ones are. So there is a natural association between the story of the Cambridge spies and the Profumo affair. The same sense of shock was accompanied by the same lurid fascination for every salacious detail of the tale. An element of the traditional faith in those "natural" rulers in British society was destroyed (and did as much as anything else to give the Macmillan Government its lasting image of a decaying élite, ready for the knackers yard). There was plenty sensation, and plenty hypocrisy. The four spies and the promiscuous Minister have, between them, hovered in the public mind for a generation.

In as much as there was a beginning in the Commons it was in 1955, long after the revelation that Guy Burgess and Donald Maclean, the two missing Foreign Office diplomats whose disappearance had caused a flurry of speculation in 1951, were in Moscow. Colonel Marcus Lipton, the Labour MP for Brixton, asked a question the answer to which was to become notorious.

***

A THIRD MAN?

Lieut.-Colonel Lipton asked the Prime Minister whether he will move to appoint a Select Committee to investigate the circumstances of the disappearance of Burgess and Maclean in particular, and the efficiency of Civil Service security arrangements in general.

The Prime Minister: No, Sir.

Lieut.-Colonel Lipton: Has the Prime Minister made up his mind to cover up at all costs the dubious third man activities of Mr Harold Philby, who was First Secretary at the Washington Embassy a little while ago; and is he determined to stifle all discussion on the very great matters which were evaded in the wretched White Paper, which is an insult to the intelligence of the country?

The Prime Minister: My answer was "No" to the hon. and gallant Member's Question, which was not about all that but asked for the appointment of a Select Committee. My answer remains "No". So far as the wider issues are concerned, the Government take the view that it is desirable to have a debate, and an early debate, on this subject, in which I as Prime Minister will be glad to take part.

Hansard: *25 October 1955*

***

So, Philby was no "third man" and a debate on Burgess and Maclean was promised. It took place thirteen days later, and Harold Macmillan, Eden's Foreign Secretary, rose to speak, and to reveal — though in a guarded way — the Government's concern over Soviet penetration. It was, aside from the hostage to fortune in the form of the public exoneration of Philby, the most revealing account of the Foreign Office's backstairs world ever given to the Commons. But still it was only a corner of the veil that he lifted.

TWO SPIES

"It can rarely have happened in our long Parliamentary history that the political head of a department should have to unfold to the House of Commons so painful a story as that which it is our duty to consider today. To understand — though not, of course, to excuse — this story, it is necessary to cast our minds back to the 1930s and to recall the kind of background against which the two principal characters grew up.

At that time all kinds of violent opinions were being expressed. The circumstances of the Spanish Civil War, with Fascists and Communists backing the rival forces, divided British and, indeed, European opinion acutely. This had a particularly disturbing effect upon young people, many of whom, we remember, thought it their duty actually to take part in these fierce revolutionary struggles.

When Hitler had made his pact with Stalin and the Second World War began, some of those who had espoused extremist views found that their ideological beliefs exerted a pull which was to prove stronger than their patriotism. This clash of loyalties was buried in 1941 by our alliance with Russia. But, when the war ended and there came an estrangement between this country and Communist Russia, it revived.

Thus it was that men could be found in Britain who could put the interests of another country before those of their own, and could commit the horrible crime of treachery. This occurred not only among criminals and degenerates, but in men holding high technical and scientific posts, among men of philosophic and literary attainments, and, finally, in these two cases, the subject of this debate, in the Foreign Service.

There are many on both sides of the House who, as Ministers or as private Members, have seen the work of the Foreign Service at home and abroad. I know they will agree with me when I say how fortunate we are in this country to have a Foreign Service of the highest quality, giving the most loyal and devoted service to the Crown and to the nation. I think that all of us today are feeling how severe is the blow that has been struck against its reputation. Our Foreign Service regards this case as a personal wound, as when something of the kind strikes at a family, or a ship, or a regiment. We must recognise, too, that this case has caused a profound shock to Parliament and to the general public, both at home and abroad. . . .

Ministers, and Ministers alone, must bear the responsibility for what goes wrong. After all, they are not slow to take credit for anything that goes right. This does not mean that they have to accept responsibility for wrongful acts on the part of their officials of which they have no prior knowledge. But in discussing this case it is quite wrong to assert that the Foreign Office, if by that is meant 'officials' made decisions of their own.

Ministers are responsible and, in fact, took all the important decisions. Moreover, they took those decisions in full knowledge of all the relevant facts so far as they were known at the time.

The House will realise that both the Opposition and the present Government share the responsibility. The main acts in the drama took place while the Opposition were in power. The investigation into the leak, the narrowing of the suspicion down to Maclean, and the escape of the two traitors — that Government took a number of steps before, during and after their flight.

When the present Government succeeded in October, 1951, much had already been done to investigate the whole circumstances of the case and to improve our security measures. From that point, the responsibility rests with them. . . .

Although, as I say, the circumstances are explanatory in the terms of a 'tip off', they are not necessarily the effect of that. That is what I am trying to say. However, the possibility of a 'tip off' had to be seriously considered and searching and protracted investigations into this possibility have been undertaken, and are proceeding even at the present time.

In this connection, the name of one man has been mentioned in the House of Commons, but not outside. I feel that all hon. Members would expect me to refer to him by name and to explain the position. He is Mr H. A. R. Philby, who was a temporary First Secretary at the British Embassy in Washington from October, 1949, to June, 1951, and had been privy to much of the investigation into the leakage. Mr Philby had been a friend of Burgess from the time when they were fellow undergraduates at Trinity College, Cambridge. Burgess had been accommodated with Philby and his family at the latter's home in Washington from August, 1950, to April 1951, and, of course, it will be realised that at no time before he fled was Burgess under suspicion.

It is now known that Mr Philby had Communist associates during and after his university days. In view of the circumstances, he was asked, in July, 1951, to resign from the Foreign Service. Since that date his case has been the subject of close investigation. No evidence has been found to show that he was responsible for warning Burgess or Maclean. While in Government service he carried out his duties ably and conscientiously. I have no reason to conclude that Mr Philby has at any time betrayed the interests of this country, or to identify him with the so-called 'third man', if, indeed, there was one."

Harold Macmillan: Speech, *7 November 1955*

***

Later that evening the Prime Minister wound up the debate. Eden made an offer to the Opposition. Privy Councillors from all parties should meet to discuss security procedures in the public services. It was the act of a Premier aware of the shock the recent revelations had sent through Parliament, and a break — though perhaps an insignificant one — with the tradition of absolute silence on security matters.

FEARS AND ANXIETIES

"Behind all that the House has been discussing this afternoon, behind the anxieties, the fears — to some extent the confusion — there is a larger question, and it is this. How far are we to go in pursuit of greater security at the cost of the essential liberties of the British people? That is why I have suggested Privy Councillors — who are not judges. This is not, I think, a matter for judges, but for Parliament. The only reason that I said Privy Councillors is that they are Members of Parliament. It is essentially Parliament's decision.

For instance, it has been suggested that Burgess and Maclean should not have been allowed to escape. All right. Under the law as it stands today they could not have been prevented from escaping, unless a charge could have been preferred. No charge could be preferred. Now, would the House like that law altered? Would the House agree that the law should allow any British subject to be detained on suspicion? [Hon. Members: 'No.'] But we have to face these questions. When there is no evidence on which a man can be charged, would the House be willing that people should be held indefinitely by the police while evidence is collected against them? In this case, as we now know, detention would have been justified; but some hon. Gentlemen think, too easily, that because that was so it would always be justified. It is not so in the least. Who could tell then, at the time when the right hon. Gentleman rightly took his decision to take the action he did, whether Maclean was innocent or guilty? No one knew. British justice over the centuries has been based on the principle that a man is to be presumed innocent until he can be proved guilty. Are we going to abandon that principle? Perhaps, worst of all, are we to make an exception for political offences?

In this debate I have said something in defence of the Security Service because I think that it has been criticised, but the last thing that I would wish to see in this country is the Security Service having the power to do some of the things which some of our friends of the Press do not seem to realise would flow from what they advocate.

It may be true — it probably is true — that if the Security Service had those powers, Burgess and Maclean would not be where they are today. I think that is true. I think that if the right hon. Gentleman had had the power — and Burgess and Maclean is not the only case; we have had problems of this kind, he and I; certainly I have had them many times arise — if he had had those powers, they would not be where they are today. But what would have been the consequences, if he had had these powers, to British freedom and the rights which this House so far has always been determined to defend? I want to make one thing quite clear before I sit down. I would never be willing to be Prime Minister of a Government which asked those powers of this House."

Anthony Eden: Speech, *7 November 1955*

***

Eight years passed before Philby's guilt, suspected by many senior intelligence officials for more than a decade and accepted as a fact by the Americans since 1951, was made public. Edward Heath, the Lord Privy Seal, rose to make a statement in the Commons. It was brief, perhaps misleading in one or two respects, and of course gave no hint of the importance of Philby's former post in the Secret Intelligence Service, but it broke the silence. And in two words, Marcus Lipton's question was answered at last.

KIM'S GAME

"With your permission, Mr Speaker, and that of the House, I wish to make a statement on the case of Mr Harold Philby.

I informed the House on 20th March that shortly after the disappearance of Mr H. A. R. Philby from the Lebanon Mrs Philby received messages purporting to come from him from Cairo. At the request of his wife and of a British newspaper which he was representing, Her Majesty's Government made inquiries concerning his whereabouts from the Governments in both Cairo and Beirut, without success.

I can now tell the House that more recently Mrs Philby has received messages purporting to come from Mr Philby from behind the Iron Curtain. On the other hand, the Soviet newspaper *Izvestiya* reported on 3rd June that Mr Philby was with the Imam of the Yemen. There is no confirmation of this story.

Although there is as yet no certainty concerning Mr Philby's whereabouts, there has been a development which may throw light on the question. On 7th November, 1955, my right hon. Friend the Prime Minister, at that time Foreign Secretary, told the House that it had become known that Mr Philby had had Communist associations and that he was asked to resign from the Foreign Service in July 1951, which he did. My right hon. Friend also said that his case had been the subject of close investigation and that no evidence had been found up to that time to show that he was responsible for warning Burgess and Maclean or that he had betrayed the interests of this country.

My right hon. Friend added that inquiries were continuing. In fact, the security service have never closed their file on this case and now have further information. They are now aware, partly as a result of an admission by Mr Philby himself, that he worked for the Soviet authorities before 1946 and that in 1951 he in fact warned Maclean through Burgess that the security services were about to take action against him.

This information, coupled with the latest messages received by Mrs Philby, suggests that when he left Beirut he may have gone to one of the countries of the Soviet *bloc*.

Since Mr Philby resigned from the Foreign Service in July, 1951, he has not had access of any kind to any official information. For the last seven years he has been living outside British legal jurisdiction. . . .

As to the evidence, I have said that the security services have never closed their files on this matter and, therefore, over this long period of twelve years, they have continued with persistence to endeavour to find the truth about this matter. From time to time, they have been able to obtain items of information and finally, as I have said, there was, in part, the admission of Mr Philby himself.

Mr Patrick Gordon Walker: To the security services?

Mr Heath: I did not say that.

Mr Gordon Walker: To whom?

Mr Heath: I am not prepared, nor would it be right, to give information about the way this information was finally brought together. That, however, is the conclusion we have reached.

As to Mr Philby's activities in the Foreign Service, he was a temporary First Secretary up to July, 1951, in the Foreign Service and in that capacity, as has already been stated, he had knowledge of certain information which he was then able, we now know, to pass to Burgess and Maclean.

Mr Gordon Walker: Can the right hon. Gentleman answer my other question, whether, in 1955, if the matter had been more diligently pursued, the other evidence that is now apparently available could have been discovered?

Mr Heath: No, Sir; I do not think it could have been discovered. The inquiries made at that time were extensive and intensive and I do not believe that at that particular moment it was possible to come to any other conclusion than my right hon. Friend the Prime Minister, as Foreign Secretary, announced to the House in the debate.

Mr Lipton: Does the Lord Privy Seal's statement mean that Mr Philby was, in fact, the "third man" that we were talking about at the time of the disappearance of Burgess and Maclean?

Mr Heath: Yes, Sir."

Edward Heath: Statement, *1 July 1963*

***

But there was to be no more. Macmillan appealed for the veil to be drawn back over the unsavoury scandal in British intelligence and in exchanges with Harold Wilson, the Leader of the Opposition, and Jo Grimond, the Liberal leader, he found Wilson a willing partner.

A PRIME MINISTER'S SECRET

"We lead from one question to another and one question leads to another. It is dangerous and bad for our general national interest to discuss these matters. It has been a very long tradition of the House to trust the relations between the two parties to discussions between the Leader of the Opposition of the day and the Prime Minister of the day. I ask the House now to revert to the order tradition — [Hon. Members: 'No.'] — which I think is in our real interest. Otherwise, we would risk destroying services which are of the utmost value to us.

Mr H. Wilson: Is the right hon. Gentleman aware that I can confirm what he has just said? In the two meetings which we have had, he has given my right hon. Friend and me a very full and frank account of this case, which raises a number of issues which, frankly, cannot be discussed across the floor of the House. While we still have some grave anxieties about the way in which it has been handled, which I think it best we should pursue in further confidential discussions with the right hon. Gentleman, we feel that in the public interest this is a matter which should now be left where it is and not made the subject of further public discussion or public inquiry.

The Prime Minister: I am grateful to the right hon. Gentleman. As he knows, I am always willing to discuss with him, as I was with his predecessor, all these matters which always, through our history, have been questions outside party and which the Leader of the Opposition of the day and the Prime Minister of the day have a right and duty to discuss with each other.

Mr Grimond: While appreciating what the Prime Minister has said, may I ask him whether he is aware that the Government and the House also have a duty to the public? A statement was made in the House, no doubt quite rightly, and the public are naturally interested in certain aspects, there has been considerable speculation about how it came that this man was recommended to a newspaper, which apparently was not informed or warned or in any way asked about the inquiries which subsequently went on. It would be useful for the public at large if the Prime Minister could assure us that there was no lack of liaison between whatever branch is inquiring into Mr Philby's activities and the Foreign Office, which apparently was not in a position to warn the *Observer* what was going on.

The Prime Minister: This question is just an example of the danger of being led into answering exactly the kind of points which the right hon. Gentleman has made. If he had any experience — which, alas, I have and which others have — of the operations which we are forced to undertake in the present condition of the world, he would not have put this question."

Harold Macmillan: Statement, *16 July 1963*

***

Candidates for the role of the "fourth man" came and went over the years, and there was speculation about the fifth, the sixth, and, no doubt in the secret places, the seventh and his successors. But it was not until 1979 that another piece of jigsaw dropped into place in the public gaze when Mrs Thatcher's Government, alarmed by Andrew Boyle's book *The Climate of Treason*, decided to unmask Professor Sir Anthony Blunt, the Surveyor of the Queen's pictures, as another of the Cambridge spies. It was an incongruous public entrance for the latest of the "moles" — as they now were in the *patois* of the espionage romances — for the news was given in a mere written Commons answer, released while Sir Geoffrey Howe, the Chancellor of the Exchequer, was making his autumn economic statement.

THE FOURTH MAN

Saatchi & Saatchi could not have planned it better. Unmask the Fourth Man and everyone will forget about monetary policy. A mole is always likely to be more interesting than Sir Geoffrey Howe.

The possibilities are endless. Prepare for the entrance of the Fifth Man at the height of the coming winter's unpleasantness, and for the Sixth to arrive as *deus ex machina* when Mrs Thatcher rises finally to announce her incomes policy/wage freeze/U-turn and the rest of it.

Even as the snout of the mole was emerging into the open, Sir Geoffrey was plodding away in the mysteries of "sterling M3" (otherwise known as the money supply) and blaming the increase in the public sector borrowing requirement on the men who crank the phone-bill computer.

He was greeted by some rather too well-rehearsed cries of "Resign" and a feeble onslaught from Mr Denis Healey, who has in his time talked passionately about controlling the money supply. Mr Healey looked menacing, but his claws need sharpening. Between them the two old sparring partners landed nothing more than some gentle pats.

The chamber was packed, but the centre of attraction was not there. Nothing, except maybe inflation, escalates faster than a good old-fashioned Westminster scandal, particularly if it involves a spy, and an upper-class, artistic, titled one at that.

Sir Geoffrey's statement, after all, was like the rerun of an old movie, albeit through a mirror. Mr Healey was wearing his Budget suit, a well-worn one, and there were the usual insults about who had got the inflation rate higher sooner, and when and with which monetary instruments. The imagination begins to wander.

And of course it wends its way into the secret world. Who is that little man in the public gallery with the pin-striped suit, the concave specs and the hatchet face? Was that the whirring of a tape recorder, or just some heavy breathing from a Tory elder statesman?

The advantage of secrets is that they are secret. Nothing is ruled out. Is Sir Geoffrey talking in code? The number of MPs who were shaking their heads suggested that it was a secure one.

And talking of spies, what of Mr Joel Barnett, the former Treasury Chief Secretary? Mr Barnett has given the Thatcher Government a priceless asset in the form of a newspaper article written after the election calling for a reduction in our old friend the money supply, and Ministers now batter Mr Healey regularly with the words of his old mate. Mr Barnett's cover is now truly blown.

Yet even more interesting than the plethora of agents great and small lining the green leather benches is the memory of the faces of old. How many of the older members were recalling Colonel Marcus Lipton's question to Mr Anthony Eden questioning the loyalty of a Mr H. A. R. Philby? There was, of course, nothing in it.

And who are the "sleepers" in the Government and Opposition these days (apart from Mr Angus Maude, the Paymaster-General, who dozes off regularly on the Front Bench)? Maybe, after all, there are none at all.

Perhaps our MPs and Ministers are just what they seem. A setting at once more seedy and more intriguing is necessary for the great game. Footsteps need to echo on darkened pavements and bowls of flowers need to bristle with bugs. Westminster is much too mundane, and a quite different kind of circus.

Yet it protects its mysteries well. The Fourth Man seemed cloaked in permanent anonymity, but now we know everything. We know much more about Sir Anthony Blunt than some of us know about the money supply.

James Naughtie: The Scotsman, *16 November 1979*

***

A week later the Commons debated the Blunt affair and Mrs Thatcher sketched in the background of the man now stripped of his knighthood.

MR ANTHONY BLUNT

"In the early part of last week, Professor Blunt was publicly identified as having been a suspect Soviet agent. This disclosure understandably gave rise to grave concern.

Last Thursday, in response to a priority written question from the hon. Member for Hartlepool (Mr Leadbitter), I thought it right to confirm that Professor Blunt had indeed been a Soviet agent and to give the House the salient facts. Today we have an opportunity to debate the whole matter. It may be convenient, therefore, if I start by setting out the facts in greater detail.

Professor Blunt had admitted that he was recruited for Russian intelligence when he was at Cambridge before the war. In 1940 he joined the Security Service.

To us today it seems extraordinary that a man who had made no secret of his Marxist beliefs could have been accepted for secret work in any part of the public service, let alone the Security Service. Perhaps standards were relaxed because it was a time of considerable expansion and recruitment to deal with the wartime tasks of the service, which were directed against Hitler's Germany.

Professor Blunt has said that during his period in the Security Service from 1940 to 1945 he regularly passed to Russian intelligence anything that came his way which would be of interest to them. We do not know exactly what information he passed; we do know, however, to what information he had access by virtue of his duties. There is no doubt that British interests were seriously damaged by his activities. But it is unlikely that British military operations or British lives were put at risk. Further, the story that he jeopardised the lives of secret agents in the Netherlands is without foundation; he was never in the Special Operations Executive.

After he left the Security Service in 1945 and resumed his career as an art historian, Professor Blunt ceased to have access to classified information. He has said that from 1945 to 1951 he passed no information to the Russians.

In May 1951 an investigation which had continued for some years caught up with Donald Maclean. It was Philby who warned Burgess to tell Maclean that he was about to be interrogated. And it was Burgess who used Blunt as a contact with the arrangements for Maclean's flight to Russia — a journey in which he was joined by Burgess.

Blunt admits that on one occasion between 1951 and 1956 he assisted Philby in contacting Russian intelligence. He has said that he has had no contact with Russian intelligence since then.

The defection of Burgess and Maclean led to intense and prolonged investigations of the extent to which the security and other public services had been infiltrated by Russian intelligence.

At an early stage in these investigations Professor Blunt came under inquiry."

Margaret Thatcher: Statement, *21 November 1979*

***

He had been interviewed by MI5 eleven times in eight years, said the Prime Minister, but it was left to Sir Michael Havers, the Attorney General, to complete the story.

A CONFESSION

"Before attempting to deal as fully as I can with the main points made in the debate, I should first, as my right hon. Friend the Prime Minister foreshadowed, like to deal with the question of immunity, a matter at the heart of this affair.

The granting of immunity is a promise that a man will not be prosecuted, and it is given when the public interest in obtaining the man's co-operation is judged to be sufficient to forego the opportunity or possible opportunity of prosecuting him. It may — and this is more usually the case nowadays — be a more limited affair — that is, limited to saying that a man's confession would not be used against him, but leaving open the question of his prosecution based on admissible evidence from sources other than his confession.

In that kind of case any confession given becomes unstable as a matter of law because no statement is admissible unless it is voluntary; and it is not voluntary if there has been a promise or inducement. In the case of Mr Blunt that was a situation in which there was no admissible evidence against him and little, if any, prospect of ever obtaining any. His denials had been firm over a number of years. What was given to him, therefore, was not merely a promise that his confession would not be used against him, but in return for his co-operation and his giving of information useful to the Security Service he was given a promise that he would never be prosecuted for his previous spying activities.

One of the issues that has been raised is whether the immunity should have been granted. I shall summarise what happened when Professor Blunt was interviewed by the Security Service on 23 April 1964 at his home. He was told of the new information to which my Rt. Hon. Friend the Prime Minister has referred. He maintained his denial. He was offered immunity from prosecution. He sat in silence for a while. He got up, looked out of the window, poured himself a drink and after a few minutes confessed. Later he co-operated, and he continued to co-operate. That is how the immunity was given and how Blunt responded.

Sir Michael Havers: Speech, *21 November 1979*

In *The Guardian*, Michael White, a sketchwriter with a touch of class, gave this account of the debate.

AN ENJOYABLE DISGRACE

Like all the best advertised Big Parliamentary Occasions, this one rapidly went true to form as a Little Parliamentary Occasion.

It was 5.36 before the magic words "Establishment protecting its own" and "squalid conspiracy" frothed from the lips of Willie Hamilton in a rabble-rousing speech worthy of the publicity.

Nothing yesterday — not even Mr Benn in full flow — could break the grip of the Established front benches, reinforced by Heath (forthright) and Callaghan (calculated candour).

Like a good spy story it improved and culminated at 10 o'clock in the Attorney General's exclusive on Blunt's confession.... "He got up, looked out the window, poured himself a drink and a few minutes later confessed."

Mundane reality — Rhodesia's raids on Zambia and Sir Keith's on the NEB — had already pushed the big moment back 45 minutes. Mrs Thatcher, dressed in what seems to be the smart green uniform of a government chauffeur, made a measured and sober contribution, her "Mrs Deedes Comes To Town" inclination to disown the whole incompetent shower evidently well under control.

Le Carre buffs waited expectantly. Would she name Bill Haydon as the Fifth Man? She flashed out a few new details but conspicuously fudged a few more.

Every incoming Prime Minister and Home Secretary since 1967 had been told all about it. We trivia mongers were puzzled. Why had so many of them forgotten when they managed to remember some extraordinarily boring things?

There was some doubt about whether the Home Secretary of the day had told his Prime Minister in 1964. The Home Secretary had definitely been told, said Mrs Thatcher. He had simply forgotten when asked last week, which was "quite understandable".

To anyone over thirty it was indeed understandable for the gent in question was the luckless Henry Brooke who at the time was probably capable of forgetting before getting round to telling Sir Alec.

"He's now been told what to say," chipped Dennis Skinner. Mrs Thatcher snapped back angrily — and loyally — that Lord Brooke was "an honourable and devoted servant" but it did not stop cries of "Just before the election".

This aspect of events in 1964 would not go away despite Mr Rees's lofty dismissal — "These are honourable men." Why the 1964-67 gap, asked Philip Whitehead and others. Why weren't Labour's 1964 Home Secretary and Attorney General told?

But this kind of talk would not do yesterday. Mr Rees, who followed Mrs Thatcher, is a deeply respectable and respectful chap who seems to favour the status quo (he is a good Labour man). And not for the first time yesterday reporting of his speech was protected — not by the Official Secrets Act but by the rich unintelligibility of his oratory.

The debate dragged on. Then came the People's Willie to give vent to vulgar passion. All afternoon, all week actually, there has been repressed aggro about who should get the black mark for Mr Blunt.

Was he an upper-class traitor and therefore the Tories' fault or a Marxist traitor and down to Labour?

There had been nasty scenes during Mrs Thatcher's party political tailpiece about not being "so obsessed with yesterday's danger that we fail to detect today's . . .".

"Skinner," cried Preston's over-excitable Robert Atkins who is a Tory pink and evidently anxious to prove his loyalty to Control.

Whereupon some Labour MPs erupted, notably Eric Heffer who genuinely fears a witch-hunt or an Eric Hunt. But it fell to Mr Hamilton to strike the counter-blow. If Mrs Thatcher was looking for a fifth man, she wouldn't find him in the Labour movement or the comprehensive schools.

Try public schools, homosexuals, Tory voters and social groups one and two. "Perm any three out of four and she will be on the right track," cried the old brute. It was disgraceful, but enjoyable.

Michael White: The Guardian, *22 November 1979*

***

The revelation of Blunt's secret confession and the clandestine unmasking of the Fourth Man in an elegant Mayfair flat in 1964 brought a whiff of old times to the Commons, throwing its mind back to the last days of the Macmillan Government when the atmosphere seemed heavy with tales of espionage — Philby and Vassal, the Admiralty spy — and the odour of scandal, clinging especially to one name, John Profumo, the Secretary of State for War. The affair, which was to become a sort of emblem of the end of an old kind of public morality and the new code of the 1960s, began late one night in 1963 when Mr George Wigg, a Labour backbencher with a nose for scandal, rose to put to the Government rumours which had been swirling around Fleet Street for weeks.

A MINISTER'S HONOUR

"There is not an hon. Member in the House, nor a journalist in the Press Gallery, who in the last few days has not heard rumour upon rumour involving a member of the Government Front Bench. The Press has gone as near as it could — it has shown itself willing to wound but afraid to strike. This all comes about because of the Vassall Tribunal. In actual fact, these great Press Lords, these men who control great instruments of public opinion and of power, do not have the guts to discharge the duty that they are now claiming for themselves.

That being the case, I rightly use the Privilege of the House of Commons — that is what it is given to me for — to ask the Home Secretary, who is the senior member of the Government on the Treasury Bench now, to go to the Dispatch Box — he knows that the rumour to which I refer related to Miss Christine Keeler and Miss Davies and a shooting by a West Indian — and, on behalf of the Government, categorically deny the truth of these rumours. On the other hand, if there is anything in them, I urge him to ask the Prime Minister to do what was not done in the Vassall case — set up a Select committee so that these things can be dissipated, and the honour of the Minister concerned freed from the imputations and innuendoes that are being spread at the present time.

George Wigg: Speech, *21 March 1963*

***

The next day Profumo made the personal statement which was to bring on his downfall, denying any impropriety in his relationship with Christine Keeler. But the story, with its tales of riotous living, the involvement of Captain Ivanov of the Soviet Embassy and the sad career of the osteopath Stephen Ward (whom we now know to have had an arrangement with MI5), rolled on. Profumo resigned, Macmillan was shaken, the Commons prepared for a debate and Harold Wilson prepared for the attack.

THE PROFUMO DEBATE

"This is a debate without precedent in the annals of this House. It arises from disclosures which have shocked the moral conscience of the nation. There is the clear evidence of a sordid underworld network, the extent of which cannot yet be measured and which we cannot debate today because of proceedings elsewhere.

I believe that the feelings that have been aroused throughout the nation are similarly echoed in this House and that there are many hon. and right hon. Gentlemen opposite who are as sick at heart by what has been disclosed as those on this side of the House. There is the personal and family tragedy of a man lately our colleague here. However much we condemn him — and we must condemn him — that is not the issue today.

What concerns us directly is that the former Secretary of State for War, faced with rumours and innuendoes that could not be ignored, chose deliberately to lie to this House, and in circumstances in which this House allows freedom of personal statement without question or debate on the premise that what is said is said in good faith.

What does concern us, too, is the question whether any other Minister in any sense connived at this action through foreknowledge or, being in a position to ascertain the truth, failed to take steps that were necessary to fulfil the duty that he owed to the House.

What concerns us, also, is whether a man in a position of high trust, privy to the most secret information available to a Government, through a continuing association with this squalid network, imperilled our national security or created conditions in which a continuing risk to our security was allowed to remain.

We are not here as a court of morals, though the nation as a whole cannot escape the responsibility so to act. But questions affecting national security, questions affecting the duty of Ministers to this House, must be pressed and probed today, and this debate, in one form or another, must continue until the truth is known so far as it can ever be known. . . .

For reasons which I have given, I have not dealt with the moral challenge with which the nation is faced. The uncovering of this sleazy sector of society in London and elsewhere is a matter to be pursued elsewhere. But the papers day by day add to the odious record. Saturday's papers told of an opportunist nightclub proprietor who had offered Miss Christine Keeler — or should I refer to her as Miss Christine Keeler Ltd. — a nightclub job at a salary of £5,000 a week, and I say to the Prime Minister that there is something utterly nauseating about a system of society which pays a harlot 25 times as much as its Prime Minister, 250 times as much as it pays its Members of Parliament, and 500 times as much as it pays some of its ministers of religion.

But they are wrong at home and abroad who see this as a canker at the heart of our society. I believe that the heart of this nation is sound. What we are seeing is a diseased excrescence, a corrupted and poisoned appendix of a small and unrepresentative section of society that makes no contribution to what Britain is, still less to what Britain can be. There are, of course, lessons to be drawn for us all in terms of social policy, but perhaps most of all in terms of the social philosophy and values and objectives of our society — the replacement of materialism and the worship of the golden calf by values which exalt the spirit of service and the spirit of national dedication.

I once heard the Archbishop of York say that we were in danger of creating a system of society where the verb 'to have' means so much more than the verb 'to be', and now we are seeing the pay-off for that system of society. But our friends abroad are wrong if they draw the hasty conclusion that this country is entering the era of corruption which has heralded the decline of the great civilisations of the past. The sickness of an unrepresentative sector of our society should not detract from the robust ability of our people as a whole to face the challenge of the future. And in preparing to face that challenge, let us frankly recognise that the inspiration and leadership must come first here in this House."

Harold Wilson: Speech, *17 June 1963*

***

The Prime Minister responded, and asked for the confidence of the House. He explained in detail, at great length, the background to the case but the most affecting passage of his speech was its opening — his expression of horror at the breach of honour committed in his own Cabinet.

DILIGENCE AND PRUDENCE?

"As the right hon. Member for Huyton (Mr H. Wilson) observed, this debate takes place on conditions which are wholly unprecedented. A great shock has been given to Parliament, and, indeed, to the whole country. On me, as head of the Administration, what has happened has inflicted a deep, bitter, and lasting wound. I do not remember in the whole of my life, or even in the political history of the past, a case of a Minister of the Crown who has told a deliberate lie to his wife, to his legal advisers and to his Ministerial colleagues, not once but over and over again, who has then repeated this lie to the House of Commons as a personal statement which, as the right hon. Gentleman reminded us, implies that it is privileged, and has subsequently taken legal action and recovered damages on the basis of a falsehood. This is almost unbelievable, but it is true.

Before I went away for my short holiday on 30th May, I felt pretty sure that this incident, as I knew it then, raised no serious security issues, and I shall explain why. Nevertheless, I had arranged for the Lord Chancellor to make an inquiry in circumstances about which the right hon. Gentleman has said something and about which I shall have more to say later. It was also my conviction that Mr Profumo had not deceived me, his colleagues, or the House, but spoke the truth, and I was fortified in this belief by the successful action that he had taken.

On the fifth day of my holiday I was informed of the truth. Since we cannot now, I fear, put much confidence in anything that he has said, the problem of security is now enhanced, but, in addition, moral issues of the deepest kind are involved. For what greater moral crime can there be than to deceive those naturally inclined to trust one, those who have worked with one, served with one, and are one's colleagues?

The right hon. Gentleman has put a number of questions to me, and I can assure him and the House that they will be answered in the course of my speech, but I trust that hon. Members will allow me to deal with these points as they occur in the narrative which it is only right that I should give to the House. This is more convenient, though long I fear, and it is the proper way to deal with it. This means covering both the action I took before Mr Profumo's statement and the action which I took to deal with any matters after it, but before his confession. However, there are certain aspects of this case to which I would first like to refer, as they affect myself.

In a period of Ministerial office which runs altogether to 17 years, and more especially during the last six years as Prime Minister, I have had to face, like all Ministers, grave and baffling difficulties. Sometimes, the House probably realises, looking back on their character, that they involved great strain and pressure, but these burdens were all bearable because whatever the different point of view between both sides of the House, whatever the degree of political argument and conflict, whatever the international dangers involved, these have been questions of policy. This is different. I find it difficult to tell the House what a blow it has been to me, for it seems to have undermined one of the very foundations upon which political life must be conducted.

However, in recent days I have been trying to search my heart and conscience, and I have approached the matter in this way: there is the question of good faith; there is the question of justice, and there is the question of good judgment; I know that I have acted honourably; I believe that I have acted justly, and I hope that when it has heard my account the House will consider that I have acted with proper diligence and prudence."

Harold Macmillan: Speech, *17 June 1963*

***

But he was gravely damaged. Within six months he would have left office because of ill-health, and an air of decay would cling to his Government. The Profumo debate had a speech from the Tory benches which caught just that feeling that for Macmillan it was all over. It was from Nigel Birch, the MP for Flint West.

THE LOST LEADER

"In many organs of the Press and, to a certain extent, during the latter part of the speech of the Leader of the Opposition, there has been a suggestion that the whole moral health of the nation is at stake and is concerned in this debate. I do not believe that that is true. As far as the moral health of the nation can be affected by any human agency, it is affected by prophets and priests and not by politicians. But this certainly has been one of the best field days that the self-righteous have had since Parnell was cited as co-respondent in O'Shea's divorce case. In all these miseries, the fact that so many people have found some genuine happiness is something to which, in all charity, we have no right to object.

I must say that I view the activities of the editor of *The Times* with some distaste.

He is a man about whom it could have been predicted from his early youth that he was bound to end up sooner or later on the staff of one of the Astor papers.

Nor do I think that this debate is primarily concerned with the security aspect, although that, of course, is important. It was fully dealt with by my right hon. Friend the Prime Minister and, for my part, I am perfectly prepared to accept everything that the Prime Minister said about security. I believe that what he said was right and true and I am not prepared to criticise my right hon. Friend in any way concerning the question of security.

What seems to me to be the real issue is something much simpler and much narrower. The real issue seems to be whether it was right to accept Profumo's personal statement. . . .

He was not a man who was ever likely to tell the absolute truth in a tight corner, and at the time the statement was made he was in a very tight corner indeed. There are people — and it is to the credit of our poor, suffering humanity that it is so — who will tell the whole truth about themselves whatever the consequences may be. Of such are saints and martyrs, but most of us are not like that. Most people in a tight corner either prevaricate — if anyone is interested in prevarication they will find the *locus classicus* in the evidence given before the Bank Rate Tribunal by the Leader of the Opposition — or, as in this case, they lie.

This lie was accepted. I have meditated very deeply on this, and though I have given some rather tough reasons for not accepting that Profumo's statement was credible, I have after deep consideration come to the conclusion that my right hon. Friend did absolutely genuinely believe it. I will give my reasons now for taking that view, and these reasons concern the competence and the good sense with which the affair was handled.

Profumo on his own admission had been guilty of a very considerable indiscretion, for a Minister at any rate. He was not a particularly successful Minister. He had no great place in this House or in the country. I cannot really see that the Prime Minister was under any obligation whatever to retain his services, nor do I think that getting rid of Mr Profumo would, in fact, have made the political situation any worse than it then was. On the other hand, to retain him entailed a colossal risk and a colossal gamble. The difficulties and dangers were obvious enough. The Press were in full cry. They were in possession of letters. They were hardly likely to have bought letters unless they had something of interest in them. Miss Keeler was pretty certain to turn up again, and if she did, editors were sure to make use of her literary talent. The dangers were enormous, and yet this colossal gamble was taken, and in this gamble, as it seems to me, the possible gain was negligible and the possible loss devastating.

The conclusion that I draw from that is that the course adopted by my right hon. Friend the Prime Minister could have been adopted only by someone who genuinely believed the statements of Profumo, and therefore, I absolutely acquit my right hon. Friend of any sort of dishonour. On the other hand, on the question of competence and good sense I cannot think that the verdict can be favourable.

What is to happen now? I cannot myself see at all that we can go on acting as if nothing had happened. We cannot just have business as usual. I myself feel that the time will come very soon when my right hon. Friend ought to make way for a much younger colleague. I feel that that ought to happen. I certainly will not quote at him the savage words of Cromwell, but perhaps some of the words of Browning might be appropriate in his poem on 'The Lost Leader', in which he wrote:

> '. . . let him never come back to us!
> There would be doubt, hesitation and pain.
> Forced praise on our part—the glimmer of twilight,
> Never glad confident morning again!'

'Never glad confident morning again!' — so I hope that the change will not be too long delayed.

Ahead of us we have a Division. We have the statement of my right hon. and noble Friend Lord Hailsham, in a personal assurance on television, that a Whip is not a summons to vote but a summons to attend. I call the Whips to witness that I at any rate have attended."

Nigel Birch: Speech, *17 June 1963*

8

A Government Falls

A majority is always the best repartee.
—Benjamin Disraeli

IN March 1979 the Government lost a vote of confidence in the Commons, by 311 votes to 310, and James Callaghan announced that he would go to the Queen the next day to offer his resignation. He was the first Prime Minister to be removed from office by such a vote for more than fifty years. The minority Labour Government had been kept alive for three years and more by a bewildering series of deals and policy manoeuvres, through the pact with the Liberals (until 1978) and by Cabinet support for the Scotland Bill setting up a devolved Assembly in Edinburgh. After the devolution referendum in March 1979 produced only a narrow "Yes" vote, Callaghan dithered. The Scottish Nationalists pressed him for a statement of intent on the implementation of the Act. He delayed, and they withdrew their support and tabled a motion of no confidence, followed within an hour or two by Mrs Thatcher's Conservatives, who saw their chance at last. The Government, which had looked tired and bedraggled for months, needed one more effort to give it the extra weeks Callaghan wanted, to allow him a general election date of his own choosing. On the afternoon of 28 March the motion on the order paper was "That this House has no confidence in Her Majesty's Government". A Government might fall before the day was out, but another deal might yet be struck with a maverick Independent or a minority party. Even as Mrs Thatcher rose to open the debate, Ministers were trying to find a last means of escape, and a heady uncertainty reigned.

***

Robert Rhodes James, the historian who is Conservative MP for Cambridge, published his own recollections of that day nearly a year later.

A GOVERNMENT FALLS

A STORMY CALM

In politics, luck is virtually everything. And it was, at least in retrospect, in March 1979 that Labour ran out of it. On 2 March, the burly and strong-willed Labour stalwart, Tom Swain, was killed when his Mini was in collision with a lorry. On Monday 26 March — two days before the day of decision — Tim Kitson lost the rear axle and a wheel off his car as he was motoring somewhat rapidly down the M1. Miraculously, after a spectacular crash, he was completely unhurt. Sir Alfred Broughton, Labour MP for Batley and Morley, was now so seriously ill that it was doubtful whether he could come to Westminster at all. With the Government's hairline majority, these facts began to assume great importance.

But this was not all. For months, Gerry Fitt, the intrepid and immensely popular SDLP Member for Belfast West, had been conducting an increasingly bitter feud with the Northern Ireland Secretary, Roy Mason, which had now reached the point when Gerry was totally disillusioned with the Government. We were not certain what Gerry would do, but all the signs were that he would abstain, and some even hazarded that he might actually vote against the Government.

In order to counter this appalling and unexpected defection, Ministers and Government Whips were reduced to looking eagerly towards the almost mythical Independent MP for Fermanagh and South Tyrone, Frank Maguire.

Like most MPs, I had never even seen Mr Maguire. He was said to run a pub in his constituency and to have marked distaste for the Westminster scene. But he had shown that he had been open to argument from the Government Whips on special occasions in the past. Would he come to their rescue? In the agitated counting of heads, Mr Maguire suddenly assumed an awesome significance.

On the evening of 27 March I had a hint that my assiduity in the defence debate had not gone unnoticed and would not be unrewarded in the confidence debate. I spent the morning of the 28th working on my speech, trying to boil my thoughts down to the five-minute standard which had been my regular norm since my long maiden speech of 23 minutes, which had prompted Ted Heath to remark, "Congratulations on *both* your maiden speeches!" I also dealt with constituency correspondence with my secretary, Polly Andrews, in my tiny office in Dean's Yard.

As I walked slowly to the Palace of Westminster I was surprised to realise that I was curiously unexcited. Here was a momentous day, in which I, an historian, was playing a part, but it seemed as if there was nothing ahead except a debate on the Cheshire County Council Bill. There were no eager crowds, although one did notice the television and radio caravans and impedimenta being languidly established outside the Palace.

The Palace itself was strangely quiet. But as soon as I walked into the Members' Lobby there was an urgent message to ring Polly. She had heard that a special announcement had been made at Lloyd's to the effect that Callaghan, anticipating defeat, was to make a pre-emptive strike by calling a general election in his opening speech.

I put down the telephone, looked round, and immediately saw Tony Berry, one of our Whips, and himself a Lloyd's underwriter. He took the news seriously enough to ask me to see the Chief Whip, Humphrey Atkins, at once. Humphrey told me to tell Adam Butler, one of Margaret Thatcher's two Parliamentary Secretaries, and I went — almost ran — to her office at the end of the long corridor behind the Speaker's Chair.

The atmosphere in the outer office was, as always, one of controlled chaos. Caroline Stephens and Alison Ward, Mrs Thatcher's two secretaries, were coping heroically with the telephone and were also trying to type. Airey Neave was waiting to see Margaret, calm and quiet as ever in the general bedlam. Adam was somewhere off-stage, but was summoned while I chatted to Airey, always a strange, remote, but kindly man, particularly to young people. I told him that I hoped to be called in the debate, and he gave me some very wise advice on the highly precarious Ulster situation. While he did not venture to advise me on what I might say, he was very clear on what I must *not* say. As it happened, I had no intention of unwittingly upsetting his elaborately created strategy, which was a minor masterpiece (to which future historians and his biographer should devote close attention), but I was glad to have his confidence and kind suggestions.

Adam Butler appeared, and I told him my story. Margaret Thatcher herself came in almost immediately I finished, and I repeated my account. She was highly sceptical, but Adam was dispatched to check. While I waited, Airey repeated to her his latest information on the Ulster position. Maguire was definitely coming, but whether he would stick to his magnificent purpose "to personally abstain" was uncertain. There were dark doubts about Harold McCusker, the Ulster Unionist from Armagh.

That brief episode sticks firmly in my memory. The telephones ringing behind us, and the voices of the two secretaries. The sun streaming through the window. Margaret, very understandably, extremely tense. Airey, calm and quiet-spoken, solicitous, but with an aura of detached matter-of-factness which I found immensely impressive. He reminded me of a family doctor informing an old friend that, although her condition had some complications, everything could be sorted out and there was little to worry about if certain courses of action were duly taken. It was a brief vignette of one of the most interesting and important personal relationships in modern British politics. I was reminded of one of Churchill's favourite comments: "Here firm, though all be drifting."

I left them together, and went to the library to work on my speech.

During the course of the early afternoon I saw Douglas Hurd in the Members' Lobby. Douglas, *inter alia*, writes the best and the funniest political thrillers, and I asked him whether he could ever have dreamt up a situation remotely comparable to this. We agreed that if he had, no one would have believed it.

For the Palace was now definitely alive. High comedy — which is never far removed from politics — intervened in the form of a lightning strike by the catering staff. There would, accordingly, be no food or drink for MPs, journalists, officials and visitors for the rest of the day. The journalists took refuge in a conveniently located hostelry; those of us who had to sit through the great debate had to accept literally hours of hunger and thirst. Ministers with private caches in their offices became highly popular, but not for us Tories.

After an hour of somewhat forced ribaldry at Question Time, the debate itself got off to a mixed start. Margaret Thatcher's nervousness was as evident as her determination, and her speech — like so many others of hers in Opposition — was excellent in content but lacking in impact in delivery. And now, because the debate was being broadcast live, she had a much vaster audience than only the House of Commons. Because of this, the Labour Party had been warned not to give her a rough ride, but she was frequently and noisily interrupted from the Government benches. Not for the first time I was struck by the fundamental male chauvinism of the Labour Party and the trade union movement, and the vulgar coarseness of so many of its leading figures. I was watching some of them very closely, as I was sitting immediately behind her, and it was difficult to know whether they were prompted by genuine distaste for her views, personal dislike, or simple prejudice against women in politics. Whatever the cause, it was an unlovely spectacle.

Robert Rhodes James: The Listener, *8 May 1980*

***

Mrs Thatcher ended her speech with the themes that were to dominate her election campaign.

A CHALLENGE

"Go anywhere in the country, and one finds that the demand is for two things — less tax and more law and order. The phrase 'law and order' does not refer only to vandalism and violence — although that is uppermost in many people's minds. It means that our citizens expect and are not getting an ordered or orderly society. They expect the rubbish to be cleared, the schools to be open and the hospitals to be functioning.

They are not. They expect each man and woman to rise to his obligations in an orderly and decent way. They expect bargains to be kept between trade unions and employers. Finally, they expect Ministers to support them in those views.

In the recent closure of schools, the authorities did not support the law-abiding citizen or his children. It was the citizens who had to go to the courts when their children were denied access to the schools. It was the law that upheld the parents when they could not persuade the council or Ministers to help them. The Secretary of State for Education took the view — astonishing as it may seem — that the council had not failed to discharge its duty. The right hon. Lady (Mrs Williams) has been prepared to pass new laws to close good schools. It is a pity that she has not been as eager to use existing laws to keep present schools open.

At least there was a law to invoke. There are many cases when the interests or livelihood of a person can be changed or taken away and there is no remedy at law. That is the legacy of this Government. After five years, it is not surprising that our people want the benefit of a Government who regard the maintenance of the rule of law as the foremost of their tasks.

There we have the record, and some of the reasons for failure. Each crisis, industrial or financial, has been met by short-term measures, but there has been no serious attempt to deal with the underlying problems. On the contrary, they are worse.

The Government have doubled prices, doubled dole queues, doubled debt, diminished our defences and undermined public respect and confidence in the law. There has been a failure not only of policies but of the whole philosophy on which they are based — the philosophy which elevates the State, dwarfs the individual and enlarges the bureaucracy. Across the Western world the tide is turning against that, and soon the same thing will happen here.

I return to the occasion for this motion, which arose out of a constitutional matter affecting the whole House. Hon. Members from both sides made an eminently reasonable request to the Prime Minister that he should determine the matters outstanding from the referendums by the end of this month. He deliberately chose not to make a matching response but to try to manipulate the situation for his own ends. He can have no grounds for anger if others judge it for the manoeuvre that it was. Nor, in view of the Government's conduct of parliamentary matters during the past three years, can he complain if his present action is dubbed characteristic.

It is not usual for minority Governments to carry on for a considerable time, as this Government have. What condemns the Prime Minister now is the justified feeling that the substance of matters before the House takes second place to the survival of the Government. That feeling is widespread, and it robs the Government and the Prime Minister of authority, credibility and dignity. The only way to renew the authority of parliamentary government is to seek a fresh mandate from the people and to seek it quickly. We challenge the Government to do so before this day is through."

Margaret Thatcher: Speech, *28 March 1979*

***

As the Prime Minister rose to reply, the preparations were going on in the Whips' offices for what they knew would be a close vote. The next day Simon Hoggart wrote in *The Guardian* of the scene outside the Chamber.

THE LAST HOURS

The letter from the Government Chief Whip was perfectly clear: all Labour MPs were to be in the building by 7 p.m. — a full three hours before the big vote. And they were to telephone the Whips' office to say that they had arrived, so that they could be crossed off the scores of lists being endlessly perused in the office at the corner of the lobby.

A Tory MP said indignantly: "We have been instructed to 'clock in' with our Whips. I'm quite certain I don't know what the phrase means."

Suddenly the Whips' nail-biting job was made vastly more difficult when the whole Commons catering staff — who man the bars, cafeterias, tearooms and restaurants — staged a lightning strike over their pensions.

MPs discovered a desperate need for refreshment, chiefly liquid, and one Government Minister who confessed he had an electric kettle and some teabags in his room was quickly surrounded by new-found friends.

The scene in the dive bar in the pub over the road was, according to the harrowing accounts of those who went in, hellish. Vast groups of MPs and journalists stood shoulder-to-shoulder attempting to get served in the muggy heat at the bar. The question was: would they all survive these black hole conditions?

The tension in the Members' Lobby, which had been growing all morning, suddenly snapped at 1 o'clock when a loud bang was heard. As Members spun round they saw it was a bottle of pop accidentally dropped by a visitor, a small boy. The resulting mess was swept up by a swift squadron of cleaners in case someone should slip, break his back, and so change the course of British history by being dead for the crucial vote.

As the afternoon progressed and the Labour Whips began to look more cheerful, it became clear that the Government's fate rested on the still unpredictable behaviour of the Ulster Unionists. MPs rushed up to inquire of any Unionist who showed his face in the lobby, or any journalist who had talked to a Unionist or to anybody who might have an Irish grandmother.

The Unionists were to have had a formal meeting at 3 o'clock to discuss any possible offer from the Government on cutting Northern Ireland's fuel bills. But there was no offer so they held an informal meeting instead. Then they were 6-1 for the Tories, but there were doubts that one or two would stay the course. Would they vote solidly? one was asked. He went away, muttering: "Hard to know, it's hard to know."

Rumours swelled and then ebbed. Mr Frank Maguire, the Independent Republican, was over with his wife. Would he vote Labour? Mr James Kilfedder, the Independent Unionist, was said to be a possible abstainer. "He wants to make a V-sign to both main parties but he can't think of the best way to do it," a friend said.

The Welsh Nationalists were quickly pleased. They saw their Bill for compensation for slate quarrymen yesterday morning, and then two of them met Mr Michael Foot just before lunch to confirm that the scheme applied to widows. They were satisfied with what he said.

The Liberals held their routine meeting at 6 o'clock, and as they do every week they went through next week's business — the business that would happen without an election. This includes matters of pressing moment such as the Weights and Measures Bill, the Legal Aid Bill, control of off-street parking in Scotland and, of course, Mr Healey's 427th Budget.

Simon Hoggart: The Guardian, *29 March 1979*

***

The speech of the debate was Michael Foot's, as expected. The Lord President of the Council and Leader of the Commons, he had cobbled together most of the deals to keep his Government in business and now he knew it was slipping away. But he was, as Frank Johnson put it in the *Daily Telegraph*, "in full Footage", waving his arms and his white mane at the Dispatch Box, speaking without notes and managing to stir the place up with humour as well as a passionate defence of his Government. He enjoyed himself especially in mocking the decision of David Steel and the Liberals — his erstwhile partners — to support Mrs Thatcher, identifying Humphrey Atkins, the Tory Chief Whip, as the matchmaker. And he scorned the eleven SNP MPs under Donald Stewart, their leader, for their support for the Tories. But as well as the fun, Foot engaged in a last-minute effort to persuade Gerry Fitt to support the Government (and failed).

FOOT'S LAST STAND

"First I should like to refer to some of the extremely important speeches that have been made by representatives of the smaller parties in the House. I do not know whether all hon. Members understand that this is a House in which smaller parties have rights. [Hon. Members: 'Hear, hear.'] I do not know why Conservative Members should jeer so readily. It would be discourteous of me not to reply to those speeches.

I refer first to the speech of my hon. Friend the Member for Belfast, West (Mr Fitt). I am glad that there were a considerable number of hon. Members in the Chamber for my hon. Friend's speech. All those who heard it, whatever their views, would have been deeply moved. My hon. Friend proved again what we on this side of the House have always recognised — that he is a man of great courage and great honour. The House is wise to heed what he says.

I did not agree with everything that my hon. Friend said about the Government and our conduct in Northern Ireland. My hon. Friend is one of my oldest friends in the House, and I believe that when he comes to review everything that he said he will recognise that there were some unjust comments on what has been done by my right hon. Friends. Nevertheless, I respect his speech. Of course, I would have preferred that my hon. Friend could have made a peroration in which he said that he would come into the Lobby with us, but even though that peroration was absent it does not detract from the admiration felt by every hon. Member who heard his speech.

The hon. Member for Antrim, South (Mr Molyneaux) also speaks for Northern Ireland. He is well aware that my right hon. Friend the Secretary of State for Northern Ireland made a statement just under a year ago on many of the matters that the hon. Gentleman touched on. We are pursuing those policies faithfully and properly. Anyone who reviews what the Government have done in that area cannot doubt the straightforwardness and honesty with which we have approached the problems. I do not believe that the hon. Members who represent Northern Ireland, on both sides of the House, can question what I am saying.

I believe that the right hon. Member for Western Isles (Mr Stewart) and his party have made an error in the way that they propose to vote. However misguided the right hon. Gentleman may be if he adheres to his apparent resolution to vote in the Lobby with those who are most bitterly opposed to the establishment of a Scottish Assembly, hon. Members who heard his speech must acknowledge the remarkable allegiance that the right hon. Gentleman commands from his followers. It is one of the wonders of the world. There has been nothing quite like it since the armies of ancient Rome used to march into battle. It is only now that we see the right hon. Gentleman in his full imperial guise.

'Hail Emperor, those about to die salute you.'

Which brings me to the Leader of the Liberal Party. He knows that I would not like to miss him out. I am sure that I shall elicit the support and sympathy of the right hon. Lady when I say that she and I have always shared a common interest in the development of this young man. If the right hon. Lady has anything to say about the matter, I shall be happy to give way to her. I should very much like to know, as I am sure would everybody else, what exactly happened last Thursday night. I do not want to misconstrue anything, but did she send for him or did he send for her — or did they just do it by billet-doux? Cupid has already been unmasked. This is the first time I have ever seen a Chief Whip who could blush. He has every right to blush. Anybody who was responsible for arranging this most grisly of assignations has a lot to answer for.

That brings me to the right hon. Lady. I have never in this House or elsewhere, so far as I know, said anything discourteous to her, and I do not intend to do so. I do not believe that is the way in which politics should be conducted. That does not mean that we cannot exchange occasional pleasantries. What the right hon. Lady has done today is to lead her troops into battle snugly concealed behind a Scottish nationalist shield, with the boy David holding her hand.

I must say to the right hon. Lady — and I should like to see her smile — that I am even more concerned about the fate of the right hon. Gentleman than I am about her. She can look after herself. But the Leader of the Liberal Party — and I say this with the utmost affection — has passed from rising hope to elder statesman without any intervening period whatsoever. . . .

Some of us believe that a major purpose in politics is to ensure that our country shall not again have to live through the situation in the period 1970 to 1974. What the right hon. Lady is proposing, which is confirmed by Mr Maudling's experience inside the Shadow Cabinet, is retreading that path. Nothing more disastrous could happen to our country, not only in industrial relations, which is perhaps most strongly branded on the public's mind, but in almost all areas. It was part of the Selsdon Park policy to abandon support for British industry, drive us into the Common Market on the most disadvantageous terms, and return to the naked *laissez-faire* policies of the right hon. Member for Leeds, North-East (Sir K. Joseph). Those are the policies to which the right hon. Lady has led her party. I give her full credit. She does it because she believes in it. She would hardly deny it. Or will she deny it and pretend that on this issue she has some special new policy of her own? . . .

It is not the case that we have failed to grapple with all the problems in the past four years. We have started to deal with them, even with the limited power that we have had in this House. We have also, despite all the storms, despite all the setbacks, despite all the hardships, carried out major programmes of social reform at the same time. It is because we were determined to carry out those social changes, those social reforms, those improvements in the social services, despite all the difficulties, determined to share better the wealth produced by this country, even if that wealth was not as great as we wanted it to be, that we have been able to weather the storm and prepare for other times.

So what will happen? What will once again be the choice at the next election? It will not be so dissimilar from the choice that the country had to make in 1945, or even in 1940 when the Labour Party had to come to the rescue of the country — [Hon. Members: 'Oh.'] It was on a motion of the Labour Party that the House of Commons threw out the Chamberlain Government in 1940. It was thanks to the Labour Party that Churchill had the chance to serve the country in the war years. Two-thirds of the Conservative Party at that time voted for the same reactionary policies as they will vote for tonight. It is sometimes in the most difficult and painful moments of our history that the country has turned to the Labour Party for salvation, and it has never turned in vain. We saved the country in 1940, and we did it again in 1945. We set out to rescue the country — or what was left of it — in 1974. Here again in 1979 we shall do the same —[*Interruption.*]

Mr Speaker: Order. The noise in the Chamber prevents me from hearing what the Lord President is saying.

Mr Foot: They are trying to stop me from getting your vote as well, Mr Speaker. [Hon. Members: 'Shame.'] I do not know why Conservative Members are saying that this is shameful. I think that it is high time that the Tory Party recovered some sense of humour, even if it has lost everything else — [*Interruption.*] Conservative Members really ought to have had plenty of practice at laughing at themselves over these recent years, and they should make better effort on this occasion.

I repeat — and I hope within your hearing, Mr Speaker — that over the coming weeks and months the British people will make the decision. If the debate is any test, if argument counts for anything, and if overwhelming support from the Government benches counts for much, it will of course be a very good election and there will be a thumping Labour majority, too.

We are quite prepared to have an election, but the Conservative Party has always had the idea that it was born to rule, although I should have thought that the country had been cured of that impression long since. It has always thought that everything must be decided according to the desires and whims of Conservative Central Office, that everything else is unpatriotic. Well, we say that this House of Commons should decide when an election takes place, and that the people will decide which Government they will have to follow this one.

We believe that once the record is fully put to the country we shall come back here with the real majority that the Labour Government require to govern for the next five years."

Michael Foot: Speech, *28 March 1979*

Foot sat down to an enormous cheer from the Labour benches. The Prime Minister patted him on the back, the Speaker put the question, and the division bells rang.

THE VOTE

And so, at 10 p.m., we voted. The atmosphere in our Lobby was now one of gloom. The word went round that Margaret had calculated that we would lose by one. Harold McCusker and John Carson had bolted; Frank Maguire was in the Speaker's Lobby behind the Chair, surrounded by urgent and gesticulating Socialists; we had lost the Welsh Nats. One colleague even had doubts about the Scots Nats.

The procession past the Clerks' desks seemed endless. I returned to the House to find every place taken, and the gangways crammed. I eventually finished up in the far corner under the public galleries beside the little box where party officials and Denis Thatcher were sitting. We exchanged nervous and not very confident looks. Denis was very calm, but evidently worried. So were we all.

The Government benches, meanwhile, were beginning to glow. Then, a Labour Whip, Jimmy Hamilton, marched in triumphantly and raised a thumb as he went to the Table. The Labour benches erupted. On our front bench Margaret was with Humphrey Atkins and Francis Pym, and all looked miserable. In fact, Peter Morrison had told them that we had won; they were unconvinced until Tony Berry confirmed it. None of this, of course, was known to us.

Then we could see the tellers from the "No" Lobby, struggling to the Table. They gave their figures to the Clerk. He seemed to take an age to transfer them to the official slip which is handed to the senior teller for the winning side. He took so long, and then turned to have a quick word with the Speaker, that we thought the vote was tied and that the Speaker was being warned that he would have to cast his vote for the Government.

And then the Clerk handed the paper to our Whip, Spencer Le Marchant. And then there was bedlam. Spencer barked out the figures. We had won by one vote, 311 to 310. Maguire had abstained, after all!

In the tumult I turned to Denis Thatcher, and we shouted joyously at each other. Margaret then rose to ask the Government's intentions, and Callaghan announced an immediate general election with a defiant confidence and spirit that one could only admire; a group of Labour backbenchers began to sing "The Red Flag", somewhat reedily; there was a sporadic and swiftly doomed attempt from our side to respond with "Land of Hope and Glory". But our main desire was to leave the Chamber.

In the Lobby there were wild scenes. Bitter enemies, although nominal colleagues, virtually hugged one another. A Conservative peeress was startled to be much kissed. Margaret went to the Whips' Office for champagne and was greeted with a roar of exultation from her exhausted aides, and Airey Neave, still outwardly calm, happily twirled a champagne glass.

Under normal circumstances there would have been much jollification in the Smoking Room, but it was silent and dark, still strike-bound.

As I walked out I came across the wife of a Labour MP sobbing bitterly, her husband trying to console her. In an odd way, this little scene immediately ended my mood of stunned exultation. There was champagne and joy at Tim Sainsbury's house in Great College Street, a splendidly Disraelian occasion. And then we returned to Barton Street, exhausted.

Two days later, close to 3 p.m. on the afternoon of 30 March, while the House was debating the postponed Credit Unions Bill, Airey Neave was killed in the precincts of the Palace by a bomb placed under his car. We were already under the shadow of a Parliamentary Dissolution and an impending general election. That shadow was now darkened immeasurably further, and abruptly stilled our rejoicings. As I drove home from a funeral in Cambridge I heard the first reports on my car radio. Not for the first time, I reflected on the fact that there are more important things than politics and the winning of elections. The sweet taste of triumph had been swiftly and brutally soured.

This ended my week.

Robert Rhodes James: The Listener, *8 May 1980*

***

FAILED MANOEUVRES

According to those who witnessed the incident, Ted Heath smiled, shook his head, and walked away. It was an unbearably poignant footnote to Mrs Thatcher's triumph, late on Wednesday night. She had been hugged and kissed by her husband Denis, then almost manhandled into the Whips' office for a bottle of champagne by her henchmen Willie Whitelaw and Humphrey Atkins. Ted Heath was invited, almost implored to join in, but at the greatest moment so far of her leadership he could not bring himself to come.

It is certainly true that the Tory victory was the result as much of good luck as the wheeling and dealing which went on — much of it unsuccessful. For example, Mr Clement Freud, Liberal MP for the Isle of Ely, insists that Government supporters offered him Part Two of his controversial Official Information Bill if he agreed accidentally on purpose to miss the train from Liverpool, where he has been campaigning, and so miss the vote.

PLAYING THE PALACE

The Government have made it plain that even without an election it intended to let the Bill die. But it was less opposed to Part Two, which would have reformed the Official Secrets Act, than to Part One which gave right of access to official documents. Freud had no intention of bucking the party line; yet he kept the tension up by arriving in the Aye lobby only thirty seconds before the vote.

Meanwhile Sir Alfred Broughton, Labour MP for Batley, was lying in bed at home, tucked away in his bedroom with his wife, seriously ill. There was never any possibility that Sir Alfred could have come to Westminster to vote without a serious danger to his life; yet even an hour before the vote Labour Whips were claiming he had arrived.

Probably fewer than half a dozen people, including the Chief Whip, Michael Cocks, knew he was not coming, but it was essential to their plans for everyone else to think he would be there. For which minority MPs would dare to vote with the Government if they thought Labour was destined in any case to lose? In particular the news was kept from Harold McCusker, the Unionist MP for Armagh, who had decided to defy his colleagues and vote Labour. Now Mr McCusker has the worst of all worlds.

There was no actual "deal" with Mr McCusker, though Ministers had acquainted him with certain facts not known to his colleagues. In particular the Government expects to announce shortly a new factory in his constituency, American-owned, which will provide several hundred jobs. On top of this, Mr McCusker had been told the contents of a Government Green Paper on energy supplies to Ulster.

Simon Hoggart: The Guardian, *30 March 1979*

***

Now the Commons was preparing for a general election but business had to be tidied up before the campaign could begin. In particular, an emasculated Finance Bill had to be passed. So, six days after the Government's defeat, Denis Healey rose for the last time as Chancellor.

HEALEY'S CURTAIN CALL

When Chancellor Healey was finally called yesterday afternoon, almost an hour late, he modestly declared: "I feel like the man who turns up to play the leading role in an opera, and all they want him to do is to help hold the scenery steady."

In the extraordinarily downbeat circumstances of yesterday's non-Budget this was surely an exaggeration. Going to the opera induces a sense of occasion if only on account of the price of the tickets. Mr Healey's performance yesterday, so far as one could tell, was not even going to cost us anything at all.

As for the opera, the nearest we got to Covent Garden was the sight of Mr Bryan Magee, the Wagnerian Labour egghead, in the Chamber. Mr Magee is the kind of MP who is normally only seen hanging around the place for adjournment debates on Wittgenstein.

Yesterday he was present before the Chancellor rose and stayed to listen to his speech for, oh, several minutes.

This was more than some people could manage. The House was no more than moderately full, nor was the public gallery. Mrs Edna Healey was present but Mrs Thatcher evidently thought now was the time to adopt her election low profile and slipped away.

But first the important business of the day. It is difficult to know where to start. Temperatures rose so rapidly over hospital waiting lists that Speaker Thomas diagnosed election fever, a recurring condition yesterday.

Later Labour's George Cunningham revealed that governments of both parties had been "acting illegally (pause) though entirely innocently (pause) for the last 28 years" over the (sighs of relief) appointment of Council of Europe delegations. Oh yes, and there was an error reported in the Price of Beds Order.

In between time Liberal David Alton — presumably down from Edge Hill on an away-day ticket — was introduced, and both the Prime Minister and John Silkin turned in formidable final performances.

Jim's day was marred by a minor tragedy — for Tory David Atkinson. He tried unsuccessfully to floor Jim with a quote from page 505 of the Collected Works of Marx and Engels.

He is a new MP and apparently unaware that in the Toffs Party it does not pay to admit to being able to read. He will be a marked man from now on.

Even more impressive, a few minutes later Jim courted the ecology vote after David Steel had raised the Harrisburg incident. It was clear that Britain's Polaris nuclear power station will be safe as long as he is in charge.

Yesterday's unexpected twist, however, was the sheer length of Mr Silkin's now traditional Roman triumph. These are always pretty pagan occasions with the Agriculture Minister returning from Brussels, his chariot heaped with devalued green pounds and things like revised coefficients for bacon dragged along in chains behind him.

As usual Mr Silkin saw off the Opposition to his own (considerable) satisfaction. But it went on and on for 40 minutes. The only explanation was that the Speaker was giving the chance of a last ego-trip to MPs that are not going to return from the Ballotbox Massacre on May 3.

"Anyone else with a swing of less than 4 per cent?" one expected him to ask as waves of Labour MPs had their say.

At last Mr Healey's fifteenth Budget. For a man who has inflated the number of Budgets presented even more than he has the currency it was a suitably devalued occasion. But then who knows . . . at one point Denis referred to the "next Chancellor".

You, Jim indicated. Denis demurred. He wished to be released. On the other hand, brightening up, "if the Prime Minister wishes me to continue to carry this heavy burden for the benefit of the nation then I will have no hesitation. . . ."

Michael White: The Guardian, *4 April 1979*

9

Order! Order!

> The office of Speaker does not demand rare qualities. It demands common qualities in rare degree.
>
> —Speaker Lowther

THE Speaker's cry from the chair is now carried on the air waves into every home, where it seems to have become a daily reminder, like the pips before the news, of an enduring truth: that MPs are restless, even rowdy, and seldom deserving of the public respect which, it is assumed, was granted to them and to Parliament in palmier days. That golden age is, of course, an illusion. Dickens wrote in 1855: "I really am serious in thinking that representative government is become altogether a failure with us. . . . The House of Commons is become just the dreariest failure and nuisance that ever bothered this much-bothered world." Quite what the small enfranchised public would have made of most Victorian Parliaments had they been able to hear the hubbub we can only guess, but today's critics who express shock at the antics in the Chamber could be expected to pale quickly if they could see Parnell's Irish members being carried feet-first by policemen from the Commons. They might revise their opinions of today's leaders if the could, by a trick of time, watch Mr Asquith lolling on the front bench, apparently unable to rise in his place through the effects of strong drink. The truth is that a tight little community, bound together by the lure of power and ambition, will never behave in a fashion considered normal outside (and if it did would become a mouse of a Parliament). No doubt there are plenty of just criticisms of the ya-boo style of politics traditional in the little Commons Chamber — which was deliberately not enlarged, on Churchill's recommendation, to preserve that intimacy when it was rebuilt after World War II — but they should surely not be allowed to distort the human character of the place by being given too much importance. It is one of the principal arguments for televising Parliamentary proceedings — a reform which now seems likely, at last — that the peculiarities of MPs' behaviour will seem less bizarre if they are seen and not just heard.

These strange practices are, of course, controlled by the Speaker as the guardian of the House's own rules. He interprets them, but does not make them. It was Speaker Lenthall, an otherwise unimpressive character, who gave the immortal description of his role when confronted by Charles I, come in January 1642 to arrest five members on charges of treason. When he took Lenthall's chair and demanded to know where the five were, the Speaker responded: "May it please your Majesty, I have neither eyes to see nor tongue to speak in this place but as the House is pleased to direct of me, whose servant I am; and I humbly beg your Majesty's pardon that I cannot give any other answer than this to what your Majesty is pleased to demand of me." Weak Speakers and strong Speakers have come and gone, but it is the Commons itself that has written its rules. They are the rules by which the struggle between Opposition and Government is waged (and, just as important, the struggle between the back benches on both sides and those who sit on the authority of their parties on the front benches). Naturally in such a place they have Byzantine qualities, and some strange purposes, and they provide opportunities for procedural wrangles which are nearly incomprehensible to the outsider. The maintenance of order is seldom easy: if there is not an angry challenge to the chair on a matter of principle, there is likely to be an argument about what the rules mean. Politicians, and sometimes even Speakers as well, love it. They know that the consensus required to process the business of the House is always fragile, and that nothing in the Commons rules is immutable. So, they squabble.

***

CROMWELL THROWS THEM OUT

Yet the most powerful personage in the country was not William Lenthall, Speaker of the House of Commons, but Oliver Cromwell, Captain-General of the Army. In 1653 the Commons and Cromwell were at variance. The Commons, indeed, were but the "Rump", or those Members who survived "Pride's Purge", which was administered on December 6, 1648, and had become a mere clique of crotcheters and talkers. On April 20, 1653, as they were discussing a Bill for the constitution and election of a new representative Assembly, Lenthall being in the Chair, Cromwell came in, wearing plain black clothes with grey worsted stockings, and sat and listened to the debate. But when the Speaker rose and put the question, "That this Bill do pass", he sprang to his feet and contemptuously putting on his hat strode up and down the floor, berating the House for their neglect of the public good and their desire only to perpetuate themselves in power. From this general attack he proceeded to revile individual Members as whoremasters and drunkards. Sir Peter Wentworth ventured to rise in protest. Such language, he said, was most unbecoming from the servant whom the House had so highly trusted and honoured. "Come, come! I will put an end to your prating," cried Cromwell. "You are no Parliament. I say you are no Parliament. I will put an end to your sitting." At his word, Thomas Harrison called in the guard, and thirty or forty musketeers tramped into the Chamber.

Lenthall's conduct was manly and dignified. He refused to leave the Chair. Cromwell directed Harrison to bring him down. One contemporary description says that Harrison caught the Speaker by the gown and roughly pulled him out of the Chair. But Harrison, in an account which he furnished in 1660, when, after the Restoration, he was sentenced to death for his part in the execution of Charles I, denies that he used any compulsion. "I went to the Speaker," he says, and told him, "Sir, seeing things are brought to this pass, it is not requisite for you to stay there. He answered he would not come down unless he was pulled out. Sir, said I, I will lend you my hand; and he, putting his hand in mine, came down without any pulling, so that I did not pull him."

There remained the Mace. Cromwell's eye fell upon it as it lay at the end of the Table. He was in a most irreverent and sardonic humour. The emblem of the Speaker's authority reminded him of the jester's staff with bells. "What shall we do with this bauble?" he first asked. Then he quickly answered the question himself by turning to the Captain of the musketeers and saying, "Here, take it away!" He also got the Bill of Elections from the Clerk. Finally, he saw that the doors of the Chamber were locked. That evening some wit scribbled on the doors — "This House to be let unfurnished". Cromwell himself said that after he had thus dispersed the House of Commons by force not a dog barked.

Michael MacDonagh: The Speaker of the House

***

MacDonagh, who chronicled affectionately the life of the reporters' gallery as well as the story of the office of Speaker, also described one of the most extraordinary incidents involving an occupant of the chair and one which, it is safe to say, is unlikely to be seen again.

A DUEL

Addington presided over the House of Commons for twelve years, and in a time of partisan Speakers had the confidence of the Whigs as well as of the Tories. When his father died, in March 1790, the House adjourned for two days. Only once was his impartiality questioned. The occasion was a dispute between the First Minister, Pitt, and Tierney, the leader of the Opposition. On May 25, 1798, Pitt brought in a Bill for increasing the Navy by 10,000 men, and as the nation was at war with France he asked the House to pass it through all its stages that evening. Tierney said he knew of no sudden emergency which made the Bill necessary; and in any case time ought to be allowed for examining into the claim of urgency. "No man," said Pitt, "could oppose the Bill in the manner Mr Tierney has done, unless it were from a wish to impede the defence of the country." Tierney, thus almost stigmatized as a traitor, appealed to the Speaker for protection. Addington said that any words which tended to cast a personal imputation upon a Member were unparliamentary, and added that the House would wait to hear the explanation of the Minister. Pitt replied that the House must wait a long time before it heard any such explanation from him. Later on in the discussion he was more definite. "I gave no explanation," said he, "because I wished to abide by the words I had used." Thus he set at naught the authority of the Chair. But the Speaker did not move. Tierney, to emphasise his resentment of the words of Pitt and the inaction of Addington, rose and left the Chamber. In the fashion of the time the matter could only be settled by pistols.

The quarrel arose on a Friday. The next day Pitt sent for the Speaker, and apprised him that arrangements had been made for the duel to take place on Putney Heath at three o'clock on Sunday afternoon. Addington not only did nothing to stop the meeting, but mounting his horse after luncheon on Sunday rode out to Putney to see the uncommon spectacle of the Leader of the House and the Leader of the Opposition shooting at each other with something more serious than partisan arguments. "When I arrived on the hill," said Addington, in an account he gave of the occurrence, late in life, "I knew from seeing a crowd looking down into the valley that the duel was then proceeding. After a time I saw the same chaise which had conveyed Pitt to the spot mounting the ascent, and riding up to it I found him safe, when he said, 'You must dine with me today'." Two shots were fired by the combatants without effect, after which the seconds decided that enough had been done for honour.

Michael MacDonagh: The Speaker of the House

***

The great Speakers are usually remembered for a moment of courage in adversity rather than for such happy acquiescence in physical conflict as that displayed by Addington. Speaker Brand has that distinction. In 1881, Charles Stewart Parnell led his Irish Land Leaguers in a spectacular rearguard action against the Protection of Person and Property (Ireland) Bill which would allow the Government to suspend the ordinary processes of the law in districts of Ireland. On 31 January the House began a sitting which lasted for 41 hours. In February Speaker Brand made his move. Henry Lucy, naturally, was in the gallery to record the scene as the first closure was imposed on a debate.

THE FIRST CLOSURE

All night long the babble continued, with more or less volume of sound, according as passion was momentarily raised or remained dead under the weight of sleep and infinite weariness. Now, at nine o'clock, some flux of life pulsated through the chamber. The relays had begun to come in, fresh from bed, and bath, and breakfast. The men who had borne the heat and weariness of the night shook themselves together, yawned, and made for the door. Having reached the lobby they came back again with quickened step and freshened vigour. Something was going to happen. No one quite knew what; but, with the quick intelligence which at particular crises runs through the House of Commons like an electric shock, everybody was certain that momentous events were at hand.

At a quarter to nine Mr Gladstone entered; the pent-up feelings of the now crowded assembly broke forth in a ringing cheer. Dr Lyon Playfair was in the chair, which he had occupied all night. Suddenly and unexpectedly the stately figure of the Speaker in wig and gown was discovered standing by the chair, which Dr Playfair with joyful alacrity vacated. Mr Biggar was on his legs, his rasping voice filling the chamber with nothingnesses, a process on which he had been engaged for upwards of an hour. Mr Biggar looked up astonished at the thunderous cheer that welcomed the coming of the Speaker. What he saw was the Speaker on his feet bidding him with peremptory gesture be seated.

Mr Biggar thought his hour was surely come. He had already been suspended, had since been frequently warned, and more than once had been on the very verge of further suspension. This quick gathering of members gently filling the House but just now empty, this eager expectation on every face, this solemn entry of the Speaker, and these ringing cheers must portend something out of the common. It might be "the axe in the lobby" which Mr O'Donnell's prophetic vision had beholden some days earlier. Whatever might be in store for him, Mr Biggar's present duty was to obey the Speaker, and he made haste to sit down, thereafter leaning forward, the customary grin that festoons his countenance being displaced by a look of genuine anxiety.

Amid breathless silence the Speaker began to read from a paper that trembled like an aspen-leaf in his hand. For all his grave aspect and stately quietude, the Speaker is a nervous man, and always brings to the performance of his duty a disturbing consciousness of its momentous character. The task he was now engaged upon was enough to shake the nerves of a stronger man. Never since Cromwell entered the House at the head of his men-at-arms had regular Parliamentary procedure been subject to this swift and arbitrary cutting off by the mandate of a single man. But the Speaker got through his task with great dignity, being strengthened by the burst of enthusiastic cheering that filled up each slightest pause in the reading. When he had made an end of speaking he proceeded in customary manner and in ordinary tone to put the question.

Meanwhile the followers of Mr Parnell clustered together below the gangway in speechless amazement. The blow was all the more confusing since it found them as sheep without a shepherd. Mr Parnell had been in his place the greater part of the night, and was now peacefully in his bed, securing the rest necessary for continuing the contest throughout the coming day and the following night. In accordance with Parliamentary usage, the Speaker put the amendment first, a verbose proposition worthy of the genius of Dr Lyons. The reading of it occupied some appreciable time, affording opportunity to the Parnellites so far to recover as to shout a defiant "No!" when the Speaker declared that he "thought" the ayes "had it".

Then followed the interval for the clearing of the House. Whilst the sand swiftly spread through the glass on the table before the Speaker a deafening buzz of conversation filled the chamber. Members gathered together in little groups excitedly discussing this new and dramatic episode. The prevailing aspect on the crowd of eager faces was one of uncontrollable delight. It was as if to a multitude of hopeless and despairing men there had suddenly come from an unexpected quarter news of complete deliverance. One exception to this general aspect was found below the gangway to the left of the Speaker. Here the Home Rulers gathered together round Mr Justin McCarthy, each asking the other what was to be done. For the present there was only one thing to be done, and that was to vote for Dr Lyons's amendment. This they did, forlornly filing out, nineteen all told.

Henry W. Lucy: A Diary of Two Parliaments

***

Even in Parliament, attempts are made to let the punishment fit the crime. The most severe punishment that a Speaker can impose is the "naming" of a member for disregarding his authority, suspending him from the service of the House. The aftermath of Speaker Brand's closure, not surprisingly, was uproar. Parnell was named and thirty-six of his Irish colleagues followed.

PARNELL SUSPENDED

The Speaker ruled Mr Gladstone was in possession of the House, whereupon Mr Parnell, rising amid cheers from the Irish members, moved that Mr Gladstone be not heard. The Speaker again calling upon Mr Gladstone, Mr Parnell shouted out, "I insist upon my motion being put." The Speaker having warned Mr Parnell that his conduct was wilfully obstructive, again called on Mr Gladstone, who had not proceeded beyond his first sentence when Mr Parnell, rising again, excitedly insisted upon his right to be heard.

"I name Mr Parnell as disregarding the authority of the Chair," said the Speaker, and Mr Gladstone moved his suspension.

The House was again cleared for the division, Liberals and Conservatives walking out in the usual manner; but the Irish members remained seated, Mr R. Power, the whip, walking round and round as a shepherd's dog guards a flock of sheep. The majority were a long time clearing out, members lingering in the passages to watch the result of this new proceeding. Having communicated with the Irish members, Lord Richard Grosvenor, approaching the table, reported to the Speaker that certain members declined to leave the House. Mr Sullivan shouted out, "We contest the legality of the proceeding." The Speaker quietly answered that if members did not go into the division lobby their votes could not be counted. After a brief pause the Sergeant-at-Arms was directed to open the door of the "Aye" lobby, and the majority came pouring in. In this division 405 voted for the suspension of Mr Parnell and 7 against. The figures being announced, the Speaker reported to the House that certain members had challenged the division, declined to leave and that their votes had not been recorded. He then called on Mr Parnell to withdraw, an invitation which the gentleman, always "respectfully", declined. The Sergeant-at-Arms was then ordered to remove him. Mr Parnell declining to retire except by superior force, four assistants were called in, at the sight of whom his scruples vanished, and he at once rose and left the House amid cheers from the Irish party.

Henry W. Lucy: A Diary of Two Parliaments

***

Irish brawls were a feature of the Commons and a torment to Speakers. It was Speaker Peel who was in the chair during one of the most memorable during the committee stage of the Home Rule Bill of 1893, like the committee stages of all constitutional Bills, on the floor of the Chamber itself.

THE BRAWL

The most splendid exhibition of Mr Peel's influence and authority took place on a night the record of which would have otherwise disgraced irretrievably the annals of the House of Commons. It was the night of the brawl in Committee on the Home Rule Bill of 1893.

On July 27 the House was in its forty-seventh sitting — and the last — in Committee on the Bill. At 10 o'clock, in accordance with the Closure resolution, the "guillotine" was to fall and bring the proceedings to an end. Mr Chamberlain rose, at a quarter to the hour, with the evident intention of giving emphasis to the closing scene by a philippic against the Government. He dwelt upon the many changes which Gladstone had made in the Bill in order to win support or disarm opposition. All these surrenders had been accepted by the docile followers of the Government. "The Prime Minister calls 'black', and they say 'it is good'; the Prime Minister calls 'white', and they say 'it is better'," said Chamberlain in his concluding sentences. "It is always the voice of a god. Never since the time of Herod has there been such slavish adulation."

A roar of angry protest against the allusion to Herod rose from the Government benches. "Judas!" cried Mr T. P. O'Connor, and the execrable name of the arch-traitor was taken up and shouted by the excited Nationalists. The Chairman of Committees (Mr Mellor) put the question, and as Members began to leave their places to go to the division lobbies, Mr Logan, a Liberal, crossed the floor and sat down defiantly in the accustomed seat of the Leader of the Opposition, Mr Balfour, which at the moment was vacant. The Unionist Members sitting behind, among whom Mr Hayes Fisher and Mr George Wyndham were conspicuous, resenting this intrusion, seized Mr Logan by the shoulders and pushed him out of the seat.

As a spectator of the scene from the Reporters' Gallery, I noticed, while this incident was proceeding, Mr T. M. Healy rise from his corner seat below the gangway and endeavour to force his way behind the front Opposition bench, with the obvious intention of going to the aid of Mr Logan, but he was stopped by Mr Gibson-Bowles, who was sitting at the corner of the second bench. At the same moment most of the other Nationalist Members, now on their feet, moved towards the gangway. It was uncertain whether they were bent on supporting Mr T. M. Healy by physical force, or were peaceably on their way to the division lobby. Probably they were differently actuated, some being eager for the fray and others intent only on overwhelming their opponents by their votes. At any rate, Colonel Sanderson, the leader of the Irish Unionists, who occupied the corner seat of the third bench above the gangway, was convinced their intentions were hostile, and, striking out with his clenched fist, he dealt Mr Michael Austin, the Nationalist, who happened to be nearest to him, a severe blow on the face, Immediately he was himself struck by Mr Crean, another Nationalist.

All was now confusion and tumult around the gangway dividing the Nationalist from the Unionist benches on the Opposition side. A mist seemed to hang over this quarter of the House — no doubt it was but in the eyes of excited spectators — and through it could be seen swaying figures and angry gestures, as if a general brawl was in progress. The strangers in the crowded public galleries sprang to their feet and leaned forward, eager to see what was the cause of the angry cries and exclamations, and those in the front rows, observing what appeared to be a free fight on the floor, expressed their indignation in hisses. I noticed that Gladstone not only averted his gaze, but with a perturbed expression of face reclined on his side along the Treasury bench, so that the Table might the more effectively hide the horrid business from his view. Happily, it was not so violent a scene as it appeared, or as it was described in some of the newspapers the next morning. One account declared, with a touch of humorous exaggeration, that when order was restored the floor was found to be strewn with scarf-pins and artificial teeth. Those who lost self-control and applied physical violence to each other were few in number. Most of the struggling Members, Nationalist and Unionist, were really peacemakers endeavouring to restrain and calm their more pugnacious colleagues.

The Chairman of Committees, in obedience to the cries of the House, sent for the Speaker. It was universally felt that at such a critical moment the place at the helm must be yielded to that dominant personality. He alone could bring back calm to the passion-tossed assembly; he alone could soothe the ruffled nerves of Members. It was for him also to mete out punishment to the offenders as he thought fit. A minute or two elapsed before Mr Peel appeared. In that short pause the deepest silence prevailed. Members were engrossed in speculating on what had happened and on what the Speaker was likely to do. I am disposed to think that most of them expected to find in Mr Peel a rigid attitude of severe repudiation of their conduct. At last the tall gaunt form of the Speaker, in wig and gown, appeared from behind the Chair, and there arose from all parts of the Chamber a loud shout of greeting in which deep relief was expressed, and angry resentment by each side of the other, as well as devotion to this strong man, and confidence that the evil which had happened would now be set aright.

Michael MacDonagh: The Speaker of the House

***

There are few incidents in this century to match such outbursts. MPs are named from time to time, but it is tamer stuff these days — an occasional rebel chorus of "The Red Flag", a stream of invective in high temper, an unparliamentary word, a refusal by an individual to accept the Speaker's ruling. The incidents are forgotten in a week or two. But for the Speaker, the procedural nightmare is always hovering on the horizon, and MPs are keen as ever they were to exploit the rules of the House to advance their cause. Recently, one of the most notable all-night sittings resulted from a coup set up by Liberal MPs to try to embarrass Labour over the Government's Bill to abolish elections to the Greater London Council and the six English metropolitan councils in preparation for their abolition; the so-called Paving Bill. The best account of a colourful Parliamentary occasion was written by the colourful Godfrey Barker for the *Daily Telegraph*.

AN ALL-NIGHT SITTING

Rarely, ever, not since Alexander the Great routed the Persians in smoke, fire and confusion, has Labour been so shattered and laid low.

Late last night, in the Commons bars and dining-rooms, the inquest into the Great Ambush was still going on — an ambush stretched across 31 hours of anguish, open quarrels and a near-fight between Labour MPs.

It was, to pile Pelion on Ossa, the third longest sitting of the Commons ever — exceeded only by the 1881 Irish Coercion Bill and by the 1951 Finance Bill. Oh My Gladstone and My Asquith long ago!

To see the day when the Liberals took back the Opposition Front Bench and thundered again from the Dispatch Box! (Mr Simon Hughes, actually, so it was more like chuntering.) To see Labour humiliatingly stripped of an emergency debate because its MPs slept too long overnight! And, finest and purest joy for the Conservatives of all, to steamroller through the GLC Paving Bill one day early when Mr Heath was 500 miles away and the other Tory rebels abed!

Somewhere along the line Mr John Biffen, Leader of the House, stands to win the O.M. But we rush on too fast.

On Tuesday, you will dimly recall, Labour MPs showed up in a sea of frothing rage and intimidated Mr Speaker into granting an emergency debate on British Leyland's closure of its Bathgate truck plant. That meant 1,770 jobs lost.

This great gladiators' clash, starring Mr Norman Tebbit vs. Mr Tam Dalyell, was fixed for 3.30 p.m. yesterday. Back to Tuesday afternoon: the House yawned deeply and went into solipsism on the GLC Paving Bill Committee.

In the dead of night, hours later, as amendment after amendment crashed down to majorities of over 100, the Tory and Labour Whips' Offices (alias the usual channels) whispered to each other of packing up for an early night. Labour duly shot off to bed. The Liberals, so often overlooked, were not part of this cosy Horlicks deal. Still in the Chamber after Labour vanished, light dawned on them. They were alone! Only they, the Liberals, were fighting for London day and night! Stuff Ken and the GLC and going to the barricades for Londoners' right to say — Labour when it mattered, had shoved off to sleep!

Mr Simon Hughes, Liberal rates spokesman, and his pals seized their chance. They began to talk, and talk.

Around 6 a.m. Mr "Dave" Nellist (Lab., Coventry S.E.) looked in from haranguing a night-shift picket line in South Wales. His 208 fellow MPs had fled. Militant Nellist was alone on a tide of Liberal oratory. At 7.30 a.m. Mr Hughes almost fell over from exhaustion and moved the closure. But the Government's virility does not allow for Closure Motions moved by Liberals. They voted it down. The House pressed on. Mr Hughes took several notches in his belt, sufflated his windbags and resumed his mighty filibuster. Through the Commons east window, a bright May morning crept up. Around 10.30 a.m. Mr Hughes and Mr Archy Kirkwood (Lib., Roxburgh) occupied the vacant Opposition Front Bench.

Mr Hughes gripped the Dispatch Box as if locked in a close embrace with Mae West. By God, it felt good. Eventually a Labour Whip sneaked in and sat beside them. The Liberal Harries did not budge. Through all this the Treasury Front Bench (Mr Jenkin, Mr Waldegrave, Mr Biffen and Mr John Wakeham, Chief Whip) gazed with interest. As midday drew closer, they began to think; and think. If the House is still sitting at 2.30 p.m. from a previous day, as they well knew, that next day's business falls.

Oh Ho! Did it matter? Stuff Labour's emergency debate on Bathgate; that was losing the Government a day's business and could easily be staged another time.

Much more exciting was the chance to ram through Thursday's business (i.e. today's) on the tail-end of Tuesday's, that business being the third reading of the Paving Bill, replete with eruptions from Messrs Heath, Pym, Gilmour and the Other Cabinet in Exile. Heads went down. Obvious, wasn't it? Around 12.30 p.m. Tories mysteriously began to filibuster. As the minutes dragged on by Labour MPs got angrier. Then they panicked. Fury fell not upon the enemy, but upon the traitors. The Liberals have killed our crisis debate, howled Mr Dick Douglas (Lab. Dunfermline West).

"People have come down from Scotland," raged Mr Dale Campbell-Savours (Lab. Workington). Mr Jack Straw (Lab. Blackburn) hissed at "the stupid and vile tactics of the Liberals".

Not that stupid, of course. The Liberals had enjoyed a macho night posing as the real Opposition. Their idea was to stop circa high noon before Wednesday's business and poor old Bathgate could collapse. Not their fault that the evil Tories were now outwitting Labour. At 1.45 p.m. Mr Nellist, in terminal retch for Bathgate, moved the closure by mistake. Labour Whips seized him from behind and desperately tried to haul him down; but Nellist shook them off. Precious minutes, in which the committee was on the last amendment, were lost in voting. The Government coasted home.

Mr Proctor then merrily invited the chairman to condemn the Labour Whips' "intimidation" of horny-handed Nellist. The Tories killed themselves with laughter. Mr Merlyn Rees and Mr Donald Dewar bitterly savaged the Liberals.

Minutes ticked by to 2.30 p.m. At 2.10 p.m. Mr Straw rose in anguish and asked: "Mr Chairman, is it right that if we do not vote how to report progress, it will be too late?" "Indeed," replied the chair. Whereupon Mr Nellist, a man in another world, asked a Point of Order. Labour MPs fell on him and forcibly laid him low.

Division. Mr Nellist now approached Mr Straw with what, in a heavyweight boxing ring, might have been mistaken for a mortal blow. His face was transfixed by a snarl. His words, one fears, would have outraged deaf and dumb lip-readers. The Closure Motion was lost, hopelessly. The Tories rolled about with as much dignity as could disguise their glee. Labour MPs stormed at each other and, more violently yet, at the Alliance (killing all thought, if you nourished it, of a united Opposition to the Tories). Most painful, most anguishing of all was a final tease from Mr Teddy Taylor (C. Southend): "I doubt if the hon. Gentlemen of the Labour Party are in a fit state to proceed," he mocked them. "They've had too much sleep."

The Tories, as you might well fancy, do not have days like that every day.

Godfrey Barker: Daily Telegraph, *24 May 1984*

***

It is all most confusing at times. Indeed the temptation in the Press Gallery is often to try to find a transport of delight to take you away from the happenings below to a happier world, or perhaps a world where fantasy and the real business of politics can mingle contentedly. Edward Pearce, who is fond of Rudyard Kipling, had just such thoughts during the passage, in 1980, of the Housing Bill and his mind drifted into the jungle. Everyone is there — Norman St John Stevas, the Leader of the House, Michael Jopling and Michael Cocks, the Government and Opposition Chief Whips, the famed troublemakers Bob Cryer and Dennis Skinner on the Labour benches, and their colleagues, the incurable proceduralists Arthur Lewis and Michael English. Speaker Thomas is in the chair.

IN THE JUNGLE

Would you like to hear, oh Best-beloved, how the Order got his Point? Long ago and far away in a bi-cameral legislature near Westminster Bridge all the little animals of the Jungle were angry.

The Stevas-Gazelle sauntered around in a clearing and the opposition beasts hung from the trees, wiggled through the grass and generally threw coconuts at him. For the Stevas-Gazelle has charge of a very special Bill called the Housing Bill, and he has to make it law before the animals and birds of the Jungle fly away to Barbados and Gstaad, Forte Dei Marmi and Wolverhampton South-East. And the beasts were not pleased with the Bill. They wanted to have the Bill amended, if not cut up into little pieces. So the beasts and the birds decided to waste time so that the Bill should not be enacted, oh Best-beloved.

Now just as the snake has venom hidden in his tongue, so the Cryer-creature has great ducts of tedium with which he is able to go on and on and on without pausing. He does not pause for breath, oh Best-beloved, or for thought, or for consideration of the environment. And what is true of the Cryer-creature is true of the Skinneroo, the Arthur Lewisotomus and the Lesser Michael English.

The Stevas-Gazelle announced to the Jungle that as well as the Housing Bill they would have to deal with all manner of extra business in a very short time to make up for their naughtiness in losing Tuesday by a procedural manoeuvre. And then at a certain hour they would have to vote on the Housing Bill. Now when it comes to voting there are more great huntsmen and sepoys and native bearers than there are beasts. So the beasts cried "Outrage" and "Intolerable for our dignity and proper conduct" and "outrage on the procedures of this House" and other foolish customary things.

And the Wise Little Elephant George Thomas, to whom the huntsmen and the beasts all listen, or should do if they are good, said, "Order, order; we can't stop someone speaking just by shouting. That's not the way of this House." Which is a very dubious proposition, oh Best-beloved.

The Stevas-Gazelle announced that he had sent the bearer Jopling and the Great Crested Michael Cocks away to a remote stream in the Jungle known as the Usual Channels to make a civilised agreement, or as some animals call it, a fix: and could we please get on with business now?

At which the beasts all rose in their places waving Order Papers, or clutching the lapels of their waistcoats and crying "Point of Order, Mr Speaker, Point of Order." The Arthur Lewisotomus, who is a very stout and dignified beast, demanded that the Little Elephant suspend him for refusing to sit down in the Little Elephant's presence. And the Little Elephant who knows better than to make a martyr out of an exhibitionist suspended the House instead for ten minutes. But it did no good. For when they returned not only were there more Points of Order and 13 Standing Order No. 9 applications waiting for them: but the Great Foot, who browses beneath the Oratory Tree and who knows where all the secret streams of delay and obfuscation can be found, demanded another suspension.

When the Great Foot said very solemnly and politely: "I fully understand the desire of the House to proceed" the huntsmen were very sad about their Housing Bill. So the Stevas-Gazelle agreed to another suspension and went away to the Usual Channels. When the Stevas-Gazelle returned he brought an in-between sort of beast called a Compromise. The Compromise said, "Beasts of the Jungle, please stop raising Points of Order and in return we will change the Housing Bill just a bit. Which will also please the sahibs in the Great House in Simla."

And beast and huntsman went away thinking that theirs was the most tolerant, sensible Jungle anywhere in the world.

Edward Pearce: Daily Telegraph, *7 August 1980*

***

The first Speaker to become known to the population at large was George Thomas, whose theatrical sense and wit were fortunate qualities for the Commons when, after years of resistance, the invasion of broadcasters was allowed. He retired at the 1983 general election, to be succeeded by Bernard Weatherill, who will, in his turn, go through the traditional and strange little ceremony at the start of each Parliament. George Thomas's re-election in 1979, however, was notable for another reason. Something about the place had changed.

BACK IN THE CHAIR

The hero of yesterday's brief Parliamentary proceedings was supposed to be Mr George Thomas, who was re-elected Speaker. But in a way it was that white-whiskered Heath Robinson character, John Parker, aged 72, Labour MP for Dagenham, and a warning — or inspiration — to all those eager young hopefuls who turned up yesterday for the first time.

Nobody has heard much about Mr Parker since his ministerial career peaked in 1946. He is currently sorting out the wood from the trees as chairman of Labour's back-bench forestry group. But yesterday, as the new Father of the House, he was at the centre of events, chairing the proceedings.

He even made a rare speech, asserting (amid cheers) that the quality of MPs was better than before the war. Mr Parker should know, for he has been around since 1935. And he looks quite well on it all. The triumph of a quiet life in politics. One day, no doubt, it will be Edward Heath.

But first things first. Yesterday's most important task was to check whether the allegations about the new Prime Minister were true.

After all, the whole thing might have been exaggerated or entirely got up by the *Daily Mail*. But yesterday, gazing down upon the Premier, there could be no doubt about it. He is a woman.

Though there had been ample warning, one could hardly fail to be subdued by the sight. This was history in the making. At 2.58, for the first time in 700 years of Parliament, a British Prime Minister publicly rummaged through his handbag. Shortly after 3.00 he — or rather she — made a first prime ministerial speech from the dispatch box, and an elegant, confident little speech it was, too.

Labour won yesterday's election of course, for the very good reason that it was rigged, Mr Thomas being the only candidate. Even without that precaution it would obviously have been a walkover.

Such was the praise lavished upon his personal qualities, generous to the point of hyperbole and some way beyond, that only his strict Methodism and the lack of rosary seemed to stand between him and the papacy.

With Mr Thomas sitting wigless and modest on the Tory back benches, his name was proposed by senior Conservative Sir Derek Walker-Smith, who spoke of the House's "unbounded respect and affection" and quoted Parliamentary giants like Churchill, Bevan and St Paul.

When he had exhausted his stock of superlatives, Labour's Fred Willey had a go. Then Mr Thomas — "the son of a miner from the Rhondda Valley", he recalled with pride — got a fluent word in edgeways.

"The fact that from time to time we are a noisy assembly worries the public at large more than is generally realised in the House," he said. Yesterday the public at large would on this theory have been delighted, though they might have wondered if these were the same people who had been slanging one another for a month.

After Mr Thomas had been dragged to the chair (a show of reluctance is traditional since the days when the Speakership was as dangerous as the chairmanship of the NEB is today) it was the party leaders' turn, starting with Mrs Thatcher.

She described him as "one of the great Speakers" and recalled with gratitude the precedent set by Mr Thomas in his ministerial days, when he had replied to an accusation of "hedging": "Of course I am hedging, and so would the honourable Member be if he was in my position."

Only Mr Callaghan, not evidently at ease in his new seat, injected a touch of irony into his tribute to his old Cardiff ally. Such was the quality of Mr Thomas's preaching, he recalled, that in the American South an audience had been told: "His skin may be white but his soul is as black as ours."

He told Mr Thomas with a hint of bitterness: "We, like all oppositions, will be constructive — they always are. And we shall obey your rulings (pause) whenever we think they are correct." Laughter.

Michael White: The Guardian, *10 May 1979*

10

Entrances and Exits

It is all nothing unless one can go to the very top.
—Anthony Trollope

All political lives, unless they are cut off in mid-stream at a happy juncture, end in failure, because that is the nature of politics and of human affairs.
—Enoch Powell: *Joseph Chamberlain*

"IT was a terrible, thrilling yet delicious experience," Winston Churchill wrote after his maiden speech in February, 1901. It was also a speech which alerted many of his colleagues and his audience to his powers (though the Liberal *Daily News* said, unfortunately as it turned out, "His style . . . is not very literary, and he lacks force"). Notoriously, though, maiden speeches are false harbingers. Stirring orations turn out to be well-rehearsed performances and no more; feeble and nerve-wracked efforts sometimes disguise a talent and a character. But still they are watched because the club has a tradition of welcoming its new recruits in gentlemanly fashion, however much some of the newcomers might resent the ritual of it all. The life of Parliament turns on victory and defeat, election and failure at the polls or in the division lobby, so when someone wins the place takes notice, just as when a member goes out with the turn of the wheel there is a sort of collective muttering — "There, but for the Grace of God . . .". This self-conscious assertion of the community is often at its most striking when the Commons gathers to deliver its eulogies at the death of a leading member. Sometimes such occasions turn mawkish and uncomfortable, but more often they are moving.

First, however, there are the arrivals. One maiden speech has become the touchstone for politicians who want to remind themselves of how first impressions in the Commons can be distorted, and how a sparkling career can emerge unexpectedly from the gloom of an unhappy debut. Benjamin Disraeli rose on 7 December 1837 to speak in a debate on Irish election petitions and was howled down. Whether that was why he made a bad speech no one knows, but it hardly matters now: his grisly experience has passed into the cherished folklore of Westminster. The contemporaneous account in *Parliamentary Debates*, with its mixture of direct and reported speech, gives the sharp flavour of the occasion.

***

ENTER DISRAELI

Mr Disraeli rose and said, that he trusted the House would extend to him that gracious indulgence which was usually allowed to one who solicited its attention for the first time. He had, however, had sufficient experience of the critical spirit which pervaded the House, to know and to feel how much he stood in need of that indulgence — an indulgence of which he would prove himself to be not unworthy, by promising not to abuse it. The hon. and learned Member for Dublin had taunted the hon. Baronet, the Member for North Wiltshire, with having uttered a long, rambling, wandering, jumbling speech. Now, he must say — and he could assure the hon. and learned Gentleman, that he had paid the utmost attention to the remarks which flowed from him — that it seemed to him that the hon. and learned Gentleman had taken a hint from the hon. Baronet in the oration which the hon. and learned Gentleman had just addressed to the House. There was scarcely a single subject connected with Ireland which the hon. and learned Member for Dublin had not introduced into his rhetorical medley. The hon. and learned Member for Dublin had also taunted the hon. and learned Member for Exeter with travelling out of the record of the present debate, while he himself had travelled back 700 years, though the House was engaged in the discussion of events which had taken place within the last few months. The hon. and learned Member had favoured the House with an allusion to poor laws for Ireland. ["No, no."] Perhaps he was wrong; but at all events, there had been an allusion to the Irish Corporation Bill. He did not pretend that he could accurately remember all the topics the the hon. and learned Member had introduced into his speech; but, if no reference had been made by the hon. and learned Gentleman to the subject of Irish poor laws, at least there had been a dissertation upon the measure relating to the municipal corporations of Ireland. Was that subject relative to the debate before the House? . . .

He wished he could induce the House to give him five minutes. It was not much. He stood there tonight not formally, but in some degree virtually, as the Representative of a considerable number of Members of Parliament. [*Laughter.*] Now, why smile? Why envy him? Why not let him enjoy that reflection, if only for one night? Did they forget that band of 158 new Members, that ingenuous and inexperienced band, to whose unsophisticated minds the right hon. the Chancellor of the Exchequer addressed himself early in the Session in those dulcet tones of winning pathos which had proved so effective? He knew that considerable misconception existed in the minds of many of that class of Members on the opposition side of the House in reference to the conduct of her Majesty's Government with respect to elections. He would not taunt the noble Lord opposite with the opinions which were avowed by his immediate followers, but certain views were entertained and certain calculations were made with respect to those elections about the time when the bell of our cathedral announced the death of our monarch. We had all then heard of the projects said to be entertained by the Government, and a little accurate information on the subject would be very acceptable, particularly to the new Members on the opposition side of the House. We had been told that reaction was a discovery that only awoke derision, that the grave of Toryism was dug, and that the funeral obsequies of Toryism might be celebrated without any fear of its resuscitation, that the much vilified Peel Parliament was blown to the winds, when Mr Hudson rushed into the chambers of the Vatican. He did not impute those sanguine views to the noble Lord himself, for he had subsequently favoured the public with a manifesto, from which it would appear that Toryism could not be so easily defeated. It was, however, vaunted that there would be a majority of one hundred, which upon great occasions might be expanded to 125 or 130. That was the question. They wished to know the simple fact whether, with that majority in the distance, they then thought of an alteration in the Grenville Act, and whether it was then supposed that impartial tribunals might be obtained for the trial of election petitions. [*Renewed murmurs.*] If hon. Gentlemen thought this fair, they would submit. He would not do so to others that was all. [*Laughter.*] Nothing was so easy as to laugh. He wished before he sat down to show the House clearly their position. When they remembered, that in spite of the support of the hon. and learned Member for Dublin and his well-disciplined band of patriots, there was a little shyness exhibited by former supporters of her Majesty's Government. When they recollected that the "new loves" and the "old loves" in which so much of passion and recrimination was mixed up between the noble Tityrus of the Treasury bench and the learned Daphne of Liskeard — [*loud laugher*], notwithstanding the *amantium ira* had resulted, as he had always expected, in the *amoris integratio* [*renewed laughter*] — notwithstanding that political duel had been fought, in which more than one shot was interchanged, but in which recourse was had to the secure arbitrament of blank cartridges [*laughter*] — notwithstanding emancipated Ireland and enslaved England, the noble Lord might wave in one hand the keys of St Peter, and in the other—[the shouts that followed drowned the conclusion of the sentence.] "Let them see the philosophical prejudice of man." He would certainly gladly hear a cheer even though it came from the lips of a political opponent. He was not at all surprised at the reception which he had experienced. He had begun several times many things, and he had often succeeded at last. He would sit down now, but the time would come when they would hear him. [The impatience of the House would not allow the hon. Member to finish his speech, and during the greater part of the time the hon. Member was on his legs, he was so much interrupted that it was impossible to hear what the hon. Member said.]

Benjamin Disraeli: Speech, *7 December 1837*

***

How did it feel? Since that ignominious debut Parliamentarians have asked the question. One, Maurice Edelman, tried to give an answer. Edelman, a Labour MP from 1945 until his death in 1975, was maybe the most effective of post-war British novelists in capturing the Westminster atmosphere in fiction, and in his novel *Disraeli in Love* he tried to recreate the hours that followed that speech.

AFTERWARDS

In his mind, he began to compose a letter to his sister. "I made my Maiden Speech last night, rising very late after O'Connell, but at the request of my party and with the full sanction of Sir Robert Peel."

"At the request?" Well, it would hearten Sarah to feel that he had some backing.

"My début was a failure." That, at least, she would soon know from the newspapers, but he would explain it to her. He *hadn't* been incompetent. He *hadn't* broken down. No, the Rads and the Repealers had organized the uproar. They had been determined to shout him down. But Peel had cheered him.

At the Division, Disraeli walked with his head erect into the Lobby, conscious that acquaintances who would otherwise have greeted him, avoided him. Other Members jostled each other in twos or threes, discussing the debate. As he neared the Tellers, the Marquis of Chandos, nicknamed the Farmers' Friend, came up to him, and said,

"Well done, Disraeli. I congratulate you."

Disraeli shook his head. "Failure, I'm afraid," he muttered.

"Ah no, my dear fellow, Peel doesn't think so. Not a bit. I've just spoken to him. Some think you've come a tumble. He says, 'The very reverse. Disraeli will make his way.' Congratulations, my dear fellow."

After Chandos' greeting, a few Members gave him a courteous salute, and the Attorney General, Sir John Campbell, short-sighted, raised his eye-glass to peer at him.

"Ah, Mr Disraeli," he said in a husky voice with its rolling Scottish overtones, "that was a splendid battle you were engaged in. And that image — 'In one hand the keys of St Peter and in the other' — but how was it completed?"

"In the other the cap of liberty, Sir John."

"A good picture."

"I fear your friends wouldn't let me complete it."

Campbell smiled.

"They will," he said. "Have no fear. The mob at the Bar won't always be there."

Disraeli went on to collect his cloak. Outside the Palace Yard, a group of Members were gathering to walk to St James's. He didn't want to join them, and set off alone. He wanted to draw his cloak around him in the December night as if it were a shroud so that he could blot out in the darkness the record of his humiliation. There were humiliations that could turn to triumphs. But this humiliation had been total. Whitehall with its hissing primroses of light should have been his avenue of victory. Instead, it had turned to a *via dolorosa.* As a novelist he had known humiliation at the hands of the critics. As a lover — and he smiled in the darkness — there had been that moment of disaster in his first rendezvous with Henrietta at Upper Grosvenor Street when the world and its beauty had seemed to collapse in sordid failure, only to achieve a transcendant resurgence. But his débacle that night in the Chamber was total. He would have wept, were it not that he had always despised tears.

Behind him, he heard steps, and he turned.

"Good heavens, Ben. You've made me run," Bulwer panted.

"I doubt if I deserve such energetic attention," said Disraeli.

"Indeed you do," said Bulwer. "I want you to dine with me on Saturday. There are one or two excellent people who heard your speech tonight. And one in particular wants to talk to you of its merits."

An east wind was blowing down Whitehall, and Disraeli flicked the corner of his eye that had begun to water.

Maurice Edelman: Disraeli in Love

***

In the last century or so perhaps half a dozen maiden speeches have become permanent reminders of their authors. One is that delivered by Viscountess (Nancy) Astor, who was the first woman to take her seat in the Commons after her election in Plymouth in 1919. In what must have appeared a rash act, she rose to address the Commons for the first time in support of restrictions on the distribution of alcohol.

THE FIRST WOMAN SPEAKS

"I shall not begin by craving the indulgence of the House. I am only too conscious of the indulgence and the courtesy of the House. I know that it was very difficult for some hon. Members to receive the first lady M.P. into the House. [Hon. Members: 'Not at all!'] It was almost as difficult for some of them as it was for the lady M.P. herself to come in. Hon. Members, however, should not be frightened of what Plymouth sends out into the world. After all, I suppose when Drake and Raleigh wanted to set out on their venturesome careers, some cautious person said, 'Do not do it; it has never been tried before. You stay at home, my sons, cruising around in home waters.' I have no doubt that the same thing occurred when the Pilgrim Fathers set out. I have no doubt that there were cautious Christian brethren who did not understand their going into the wide seas to worship God in their own way. But, on the whole, the world is all the better for those venturesome and courageous west country people, and I would like to say that I am quite certain that the women of the whole world will not forget that it was the fighting men of Devon who dared to send the first woman to represent women in the Mother of Parliaments. Now, as the west country people are a courageous lot, it is only right that one of their representatives should show some courage, and I am perfectly aware that it does take a bit of courage to address the House on that vexed question, Drink. However, I dare do it. The hon. Member (Sir J. D. Rees) is more than polite. In fact, I should say that he goes almost a bit too far. However, I will consider his proposal if I can convert him....

I admit that the country is not ripe for, and does not now want, Prohibition. The hon. Member is perfectly right there. I am not pressing for Prohibition. I am far too intelligent for that. Frankly, I say that I believe that men will get nearer the Paradise they seek if they try to get it through a greater inspiration than drink. I hope very much from the bottom of my heart that at some time the people of England will come to Prohibition. I myself believe it will come. I say so frankly. I am not frightened of saying it. I am not afraid at all of working men. I have told it to them for five years, and they know perfectly well what I think. I hope the time will come when the working man will go dry, but we are not yet ready. Do not let hon. Members deceive themselves for one minute. The working man is as good a father as any other man. Show him the figures. Show him what the Liquor Control Board has done for women and children. Tell him the truth. Do not always tell him that his liberty is being taken away, and that the rich man wants to get more work out of him. It is not true, and you know it. I am all for telling the truth, no matter how disagreeable it is. What I find is that if you care enough about people they will listen to the truth. I think the whole world is sick of lies. I believe that you have got to like men or you cannot say 'Boo!' without insulting them....

I know what I am talking about, and you must remember that women have got a vote now and we mean to use it, and use it wisely, not for the benefit of any section of society, but for the benefit of the whole. I want to see what the Government is going to do. As the House knows, I am a great admirer of the Prime Minister, and one of the reasons I have always admired him was the way he faced this vexed question of drink during the War. I know that politicians are a little frightened of the trade, and of this sort of thing, but the Prime Minister was not. He came out and said during the War that 'the State could not afford to let go its hold on the trade, which had beaten them in the past'.

I do not really want to take the joy out of the world, or happiness, or anything that really makes for the betterment of the world; but you know, and I know, that drink really promises everything and gives you nothing. You know it, and the House knows it, and the world is beginning to recognise it. We have no right to think of this question in terms of our appetite, and we have to think of it in something bigger than that. I want you to think of the effect of these restrictions in terms of women and babies. Think of the thousands of children whose fathers even had to put up with more than these vexatious restrictions, who laid down their lives. Think of their fatherless children. Supposing they were your children or my children, would you want them to grow up with the trade flourishing? I do not believe the House would. I do not want you to look on your Lady Member as a fanatic or a lunatic. I am simply trying to speak for hundreds of women and children throughout the country who cannot speak for themselves. I want to tell you that I do know the working man, and I know that, if you do not try to fool him, if you tell him the truth about drink, he would be as willing as anybody else to put up with so-called vexatious restrictions.

Viscountess Astor: Speech, *24February 1920*

***

F. E. Smith, later Lord Birkenhead, became a celebrated wit and source of a hundred epigrams soon after he entered the Commons, but even in his first speech the boldness and independent spirit was evident. He spoke for more than an hour on free trade (he was against it) and showed little desire to treat the Commons with the traditional deference expected of a newcomer. It startled them.

F. E. SMITH

Mr F. E. Smith (Liverpool, Walton) said that in whatever section of the House hon. Members might sit, or however profoundly they might differ from some of the economic views which underlay the remarks of the hon. Member for Blackburn, they would all at least desire to join in a tribute to the energy and ability displayed in the speech he had just delivered. He (Mr Smith) confessed that he had been struck by the admissions which had been made by those hon. Members who had spoken in favour of this Resolution. He wished to ask hon. Members on the Ministerial side at the height of their triumph to consider for a moment what was the sum total of their criticism. The hon. Member for Blackburn had just told the House that the result of sixty years of free trade had been an absolute failure to ameliorate the condition of the working classes. That was a statement with regard to which the Opposition stood on common ground with the hon. Member. Where, however, they parted company with him was not on the unreasonableness of his criticisms as to the necessity of ameliorating the condition of the working classes, but when he proceeded to say that they could deal with these thirteen million people on the verge of starvation by a revision of railway rates, by unexplained dealing with mine owners, or by loose, mischievous, and predatory proposals affecting those who happened to own land. He would entreat hon. Members to make quite sure that they had cleared their minds of cant upon this question when they heard vague and general proposals put forward at the expense of large incomes,without any precise explanation as to the principle upon which those incomes were to be appropriated or tapped for the service of those who had them not. . . .

Since this House of Commons met they had heard a great deal about the war. He would suggest to hon. Gentlemen, as a humble admirer of their methods, that if they wished for targets in that matter they ought not to aim at the Opposition Benches, but at right hon. Gentlemen who sat on the Front Government Bench. Hon. Gentlemen opposite should remember that the present Secretary of State for War had said that the Boers waged the war not only with the object of maintaining their independence, but also to undermine our authority in South Africa, and the present Attorney General had said that the war could be shown to be as just as it was inevitable, and was defensible on the grounds of freedom. The circumstances of which they complained were anterior to the war. While the only panacea which hon. Gentlemen opposite could suggest was the employment of broken-down artisans to plant trees and construct dams against the encroachment of the sea, the Unionist Party need not be discouraged by their reverses at the polls. They would say of the golden goddess who presided over the polls as Dryden said of Fortune in general—

> "I can enjoy her, while she's kind;
> But when she dances in the wind,
> And shakes her wings, and will not stay,
> I puff the prostitute away."

Was the verdict unqualified having regard to the aggregate number of votes polled on behalf of the Liberal Members? The votes polled at the last election for Liberal, Labour, and Nationalist candidates were 3,300,000, while those polled for tariff reform candidates and other gentlemen sitting around him were 2,500,0000. He gathered that it was suggested that his figures were wrong. [Cries of "Yes".] They very probably were. He got them from the *Liberal Magazine*. He did not know where the Minister of Education was responsible for them before he gave up the hecatomb line of business for the Christian toleration and charity department. He ventured to suggest to hon. Gentlemen opposite that the figures he had quoted, so far as they were accurate, were not altogether discouraging to those who for the first time in the nation's history challenged the verdict of the country on the issue of tariff reform. What would hon. Gentlemen who represented Ireland say if it were suggested that they were Cobdenites? Would one of them get up to say that Cobdenism had brought prosperity or success to Ireland, or to guarantee that a representative Irish Parliament would not introduce a general tariff on manufactured articles? The jury who gave this unqualified verdict were unaccountably silent. The spectacle of the Cobdenite hen cackling over a protectionist duckling of her own hatching in Ireland would add a partially compensating element of humour even to the prospect of Home Rule. He had heard the majority on the other side of the House described as the pure fruit of the Cobdenite tree. He should say they were begotten by Chinese slavery out of passive resistance. He read a short time ago that the Free Church Council claimed among its members as many as 200 of hon. Gentlemen opposite. [Ministerial cries of "Oh!"] He said that the Free Church council gave thanks publicly for the fact that Providence had inspired the electors with the desire and the discrimination to vote on the right side. He did not in the least mind being cheated at cards; but he found it a trifle nauseating if his opponent then proceeded to ascribe his success to the favour of the Most High. What the future had in store for right hon. and hon. Gentleman opposite he did not know. He, however, heard that the Government proposed to deny to the Colonial Conference of 1907 free discussion on the subject which the House was now debating, so as to prevent the statement of unpalatable truths. He knew that he was the representative of an insignifcant numerical minority in this House, but he ventured to warn the Government that the people of this country would never forget or forgive a Party which, in the heyday of their triumph, denied to the infant Parliament of the Empire one jot or tittle of that ancient liberty of speech which their predecessors in that House had vindicated for themselves at the point of the sword.

F. E. Smith: Speech, *12 March 1906*

***

In recent years the general decline in the art of rhetoric — and a simultaneous ebbing away of interest in it — has meant that fewer maiden speeches are memorable, or perhaps are remembered at all. One exception still leaps out of the pages of *Hansard* — Bernadette Devlin's attack on Harold Wilson's policy on Northern Ireland on the very day of her arrival in the Commons in 1969 after winning the Mid-Ulster by-election as an Independent. Her assault on the Unionists ("there are always those of us who can see no difference between the Paisleyite faction and the O'Neill faction, except that the unfortunate Paisleyite faction do not have hyphenated surnames") was a gem of invective, and after the MP, then only 22, had startled the House with her fierce oratory Jeremy Thorpe, the Liberal leader, rose to follow her and described her speech as an example of political courage.

BERNADETTE DEVLIN

"I understand that in making my maiden speech on the day of my arrival in Parliament and in making it on a controversial issue I flaunt the unwritten traditions of the House, but I think that the situation of my people merits the flaunting of such traditions.

I remind the hon. Member for Londonderry (Mr Chichester-Clark) that I, too, was in the Bogside area on the night that he was there. As the hon. Gentleman rightly said, there never was born an Englishman who understands the Irish people. Thus a man who is alien to the ordinary working Irish people cannot understand them, and I therefore respectfully suggest that the hon. Gentleman has no understanding of my people, because Catholics and Protestants are the ordinary people, the oppressed people from whom I come and whom I represent. I stand here as the youngest woman in Parliament, in the same tradition as the first woman ever to be elected to this Parliament, Constance Markievicz, who was elected on behalf of the Irish people.

This debate comes much too late for the people of Ireland, since it concerns itself particularly with the action in Derry last weekend. I will do my best to dwell on the action in Derry last weekend. However, it is impossible to consider the activity of one weekend in a city such as Derry without considering the reasons why these things happen. . . .

I was in the Bogside on the same evening as the hon. Member for Londonderry. I assure you, Mr Speaker — and I make no apology for the fact — that I was not strutting around with my hands behind my back examining the area and saying 'tut-tut' every time a policeman had his head scratched. I was going around building barricades because I knew that it was not safe for the police to come in.

I saw with my own eyes 1,000 policemen come in military formation into an oppressed, and socially and economically depressed area — in formation of six abreast, joining up to form 12 abreast like wild Indians, screaming their heads off to terrorise the inhabitants of that area so that they could beat them off the streets and into their houses.

I also accept that policemen are human and that if someone throws a stone at a man and injures him, whether he be in uniform or out of uniform, if he is human he is likely to lift another stone and, either in self-defence or in sheer anger, hurl it back. Therefore when people on either side lose control, this kind of fighting breaks out.

An unfortunate policeman with whom I came into contact did not know who was in charge in a particular area. I wanted to get children out of the area and I asked the policeman who was in charge. He said, 'I don't know who is running this lot.' I well understand this kind of situation at individual level, but when a police force are acting under orders — presumably from the top, and the top invariably is the Unionist Party — and form themselves into military formation with the deliberate intention of terrorising the inhabitants of an area, I can have no sympathy for them as a body. So I organised the civilians in that area to make sure that they wasted not one solitary stone in anger. [*Laughter.*]

Hon. Members may find this amusing and in the comfortable surroundings of this honourable House it may seem amusing, but at two o'clock in the morning in the Bogside there was something horrifying about the fact that someone such as I, who believes in non-violence, had to settle for the least violent method, which was to build barricades and to say to the police, 'We can threaten you'.

The hon. Member for Londonderry said that the situation has got out of hand under the 'so-called civil rights people'. The one thing which saved Derry from possibly going up in flames was the fact that they had John Hume, Member of Parliament for Foyle, Eamonn McCann, and Ivan Cooper, Member of Parliament for Mid-Derry, there. They went to the Bogside and said, 'Fair enough; the police have occupied your area, not in the interests of law and order but for revenge, not by the police themselves but because the Unionist Party have lost a few square yards of Derry and people have put up a sign on the wall saying "Free Derry".' The Unionist Party was wounded because nothing can be morally or spiritually free under a Unionist Government. They were determined that there should be no second Free Derry. That is why the police invaded that area. The people had the confidence of those living in that area to cause a mass evacuation and to leave it to the police alone, and then to say, 'We are marching back in and you have two hours to get out'. The police got out.

The situation with which we are faced in Northern Ireland is one in which I feel I can no longer say to the people 'Don't worry about it. Westminster is looking after you'. Westminster cannot condone the existence of this situation. It has on its benches Members of that party who by deliberate policy keep down the ordinary people. The fact that I sit on the Labour benches and am likely to make myself unpopular with everyone on these benches — [Hon. Members: 'No.'] Any Socialist Government worth its guts would have got rid of them long ago. . . .

Possibly the most extreme solution, since there can be no justice while there is a Unionist Party, because while there is a Unionist Party they will by their gerrymandering control Northern Ireland and be the Government of Northern Ireland, is to consider the possibility of abolishing Stormont and ruling from Westminster. Then we should have the ironical situation in which the people who once shouted 'Home Rule is Rome Rule' were screaming their heads off for home rule, so dare anyone take Stormont away? They would have to ship every Government Member out of the country for his own safety — because only the 'rank' defends, such as the Prime Minister and the Minister of Agriculture.

Another solution which the Government may decide to adopt is to do nothing but serve notice on the Unionist Government that they will impose economic sanctions on them if true reforms are not carried out. The interesting point is that the Unionist Government cannot carry out reforms. If they introduce the human rights Bill and outlaw sectarianism and discrimination, what will the party which is based on, and survives on discrimination, do? By introducing the human rights Bill, it signs its own death warrant. Therefore, the Government can impose economic sanctions but the Unionist Party will not yield. I assure you, Mr Speaker, that one cannot impose economic sanctions on the dead."

Bernadette Devlin: Speech, *22 April 1969*

***

There are different kinds of entrances, and one of the most extraordinary was the arrival of Charles Bradlaugh, elected for Northampton in 1880, who professed atheism and was therefore deemed incompetent by some MPs to take his seat. Bradlaugh insisted on affirming his loyalty and refused to take the religious oath. As a result it was not until January, 1886, after he had been elected three times, that he took his seat, the House having relented in the face of the radical's campaign (and public opinion). Henry W. Lucy watched from the reporters' gallery to see, as he put it, "the Bradlaugh cloud burst" for the first time.

BRADLAUGH AT THE BAR

The Speaker took the chair at four o'clock, the crowded appearance of the House, unusual at this hour, appearing to indicate expectation of a moving event. There was not long to wait before the anticipation was realised. The Speaker, in accordance with the usual formula, invited members desiring to take the oath to come forward. Thereupon Mr Bradlaugh, who had been standing by the Bar, advanced. As he moved in the direction of the table there were heard some cries of horror from the Opposition side. One or two members rose and began to address the Speaker. Sir Henry Wolff, standing well out on the floor of the House, as if he were prepared as a last resource physically to contest the passage of Mr Bradlaugh, shouted "I object!" From the other side Mr Dillwyn rose to order, the two members confronting each other across the floor of the House. The storm was stilled by the voice of the Speaker explaining that the House was in the ordinary course engaged in administering the oath of allegiance, and if any member had anything to say, now was the time to speak. Thus authorised, Sir Henry Wolff, amid stormy cheers from the Opposition, said, "I oppose the administration of the oath to the hon. Member for Northampton."

In the meantime, Mr Bradlaugh had been standing at the table at the corner of which Sir Erskine May met him in the usual form, holding the printed form of the oath in his hand ready to administer it. The Speaker called upon the hon. Member for Northampton to "withdraw for the present", which he was about to do, when Mr Dillwyn succeeded in making his point of order. This was to ask whether a member could interpose when another member offered himself to take the oath. The Speaker answered, in guarded language, that he knew of no precedent for a member offering to take the oath having been met by the interposition of another member. At the same time, if Sir Henry Wolff had any observation to offer, the Speaker would consider it his duty not to interpose. Thereupon Mr Bradlaugh withdrew, having made no remark since he crossed the Bar.

Sir Henry Wolff, who on rising again was interrupted by cries of "Move, move", and encouraged by cheers from the Opposition, disclaimed any intention of making the matter a party question. He raised the objection simply on the ground that Mr Bradlaugh was an atheist, and that by the Common Law of England an atheist was not competent to take an oath. If that were not sufficient, he objected to him as the author of a pamphlet, entitled "The Impeachment of the House of Brunswick". Both these arraignments were loudly cheered by the opposition; but there was general laughter when Sir Henry, arguing that this was a particular case differing from others that had been cited, observed that when claims to be relieved from the necessity of taking the oath had previously been urged, they were put in by men "who had a general belief in some divinity or other". He concluded by moving a resolution to the effect that Mr Bradlaugh be not allowed to take the oath. This was seconded by Mr R. N. Fowler, who implored the House not to admit an atheist within its walls.

Henry W. Lucy: A Diary of Two Parliaments

They come and they go, and Lucy recorded meticulously each moment he perceived as having a special significance. In 1880, he watched the end of the ninth Parliament of Queen Victoria's reign, and noted that it marked the end, too, of a golden period in the careers of Gladstone and Disraeli, who had dominated all its six years, though (as he well knew) there was much more to come.

THE END OF A PARLIAMENT

On Monday night, by an unpremeditated coincidence, an event happened in Parliament to which the newspapers have not called attention, though history will doubtless not find it unworthy of notice. On that night Gladstone in one House, and Beaconsfield in the other, for the last time addressed the Parliament which has proved such a memorable turning-point in the career of both. Gladstone spoke first, having taken upon himself the duty of demolishing the latest financial scheme of his former pupil. He carried with him a sign, the significance of which is familiar to those accustomed to his House of Commons habits. He was most carefully dressed, his hair — alas! woefully scanty — was brushed with much solicitude, and in his buttonhole he wore a white rose. All this, more particularly the flower, meant that Gladstone intended to make an important speech. Ordinarily he is most careless in his attire, and averages the trouble he says he gives to his hatter by drawing very little on the resources of his tailor. But when he proposes to make a great speech in the House of Commons he always submits himself to the control of others, puts on his very best clothes and passively stands whilst a flower is pinned in his buttonhole.

The portent of Monday night was not misleading. He did not say much on the general question of the Budget. But for the Probate Duty Bill, which adds to the already sufficient tax on frugality, increasing the duty on small estates while dealing tenderly with the wealth of millionaires, he had no words too strong, no condemnation too severe. He thundered at the Chancellor of the Exchequer across the table, and whilst the Opposition loudly cheered, the Ministerialists sat sullen and silent, incapable of answering the argument, even by their favourite scheme of counter-cheering.

This dumbfoundering of the Ministerialists was of itself a remarkable success. The Ministerial case must be bad indeed if gentlemen who sit on the back benches cannot be prevailed on to cheer for it. Gladstone himself disclaimed all hope of more substantial success. He had, he said, done his duty when he had made the real bearing of the case clear to the country, and had entered his protest against the Bill. But as it turned out, he underrated the power of his own eloquence and the solvent force of truth. His speech was made on Monday, and on the following morning he left for Midlothian. On Tuesday the Bill was further discussed in its later stages. Today (Wednesday), at the last moment, when it had passed through Committee, and was before the House in its penultimate stage, Stafford Northcote quietly announced his submission to Gladstone's views, and moved amendments which practically met them to the extent that he abandoned that portion of the Bill which increased the Probate duty on small estates up to £2,000 in value.

Mounted on his favourite horse, Spirited Foreign Policy, the Premier in the other House caused it to prance and curvet to the beaming delight of Cranbrook and the undisguised admiration of the messengers at the open doorway. He had an excellent foil for his wit in Stratheden and Campbell, a peer whose oratorical manner, if reproduced by an actor in comedy, would be denounced as an exaggeration insulting to the intelligence of the pit. The Premier made some good fun out of the eccentric custodian of British foreign policy, which was serenely relished by the august assembly. But it was when he came to the dark passages pointing to the mysterious conspiracy against England, which in spite of our continued triumph of the past six years, stalks through the capitals of Europe, it was then that the Prime Minister was at his best. Then did his voice reach its most sonorous tones, then was his brow contracted with mingled resolve and indignation, then was his right arm waved aloft as if cheering on a united England to a final assault, then did Cranbrook's smile yield to a look more suitable to the solemnity of the occasion, and then did the messengers crowding at the door tremble with unnamed horror, and, their emotions strained too highly for speech, nudge each other in interchange of opinion that here truly was a great man.

The physical energy with which this election speech was delivered was certainly very remarkable for a man in his seventy-fourth year. There is, however, unmistakable evidence of pumping up in the Premier's latest oratorical feats. The vigour is spasmodic, the strength artificial, and the listener has a feeling that at any moment a spring may break, a screw grow loose, and the whole machinery come to a sudden stop.

Gladstone's *tours de force* are perfectly natural. When after one of his great speeches he resumes his seat, he is, and often proves himself to be, ready to start again. With the Premier, the excitement of the moment over and the appointed task achieved, he falls into a state of prostration painful to witness. His eyes seem to lose all expression, his cheeks fall in, and his face takes on a ghastly hue. Physically he is at least ten years older than Gladstone. He, nevertheless, retains something of the dandy air of Vivian Grey. His hair is a marvel for a man of seventy-four. Just before he left the Commons this triumph of art was permitted to show a few grey threads, a circumstance at the time accepted as confirming the current rumour that he was about to retire from office. But when he went to the Lords this graceful concession to the approach of old age was abandoned, and now, whilst noble lords many years his juniors sit about him bald and grey, Lord Beaconsfield shakes ambrosial locks, alike untamed and untinted by age.

Henry W. Lucy: A Diary of Two Parliaments

***

Naturally, it is the departure of a Prime Minister which usually has a special poignancy or, at least, an extra element of drama. In recent times Harold Wilson's exit was the most surprising, conceived as a deliberately titillating manoeuvre by one who had been a dominating influence in the Commons since he became leader of the Labour Party in 1963, but was about to slide from view more quickly than his friends could have believed or his enemies predicted. On Tuesday, 16 March 1976, he told his Cabinet he had informed the Queen he was resigning as Prime Minister. That afternoon he faced the Commons.

WILSON'S EXIT

Mr Wilson had so timed things that his first Commons appearance since the sudden announcement that he was relinquishing all earthly power was for this twice-weekly answering of questions to the Prime Minister. And he timed his entry into a heaving crowded Chamber to within a minute of 3.15 p.m., the hour at which he was due to take the boards.

Question time, rather than the British economy under his stewardship, or high diplomacy under his guidance, is what had always provided him with his greatest triumphs. It had been for Mr Wilson what La Scala was for Callas or (if you find that one a little too ethereal) what downtown Chicago was for Capone.

The House was nearly full a quarter of an hour before he was expected. Even the Peers' Gallery was crowded. That normally means war, or sexual scandal! No one had yet recovered from the shock of the Downing Street announcement of three and a half hours earlier. True to form, Mr Wilson the Great News Editor had made known his departure by means of a Shock Bombshell Sensation. Mrs Thatcher waited on the Tory front bench, flanked by Mr Whitelaw, deputy Opposition Leader, and Mr Prior, shadow Employment Secretary. Mr Heath, who nowadays keeps his distance from that class of person, brooded below the gangway — with Mr Wilson perhaps not his ideal choice of party leader who should stand down.

Each of the real or imagined contenders for the Wilsonian succession was greeted with Tory ho-hos, and nudge-nudges. Mr Roy Jenkins, Home Secretary, strolled in at 3.10. In the leadership election, he is expected to sweep Belgravia and the offices of *The Times*. Securing comparable support from the Labour Party may be more difficult for him. Anyway, he sat next to Mr Mellish, the Chief Whip, and they chatted. All the potential contestants were opting frantically for casualness. Mr Crosland, hands in pockets, walked in past the benches where the Tribunites lurk. He smiled in their direction. They will form a cohesive voting bloc. He may have had it in mind to explain there and then that when in the past, he had often privately described the average left-winger as mad, he meant mad in the inspired manner of, say, Beethoven.

Mr Crosland got his share of Tory irony. So did the next arrival — grey, sepulchral! Mr Edward Short. A candidate? Surely not! It's impossible! One's worst enemy's stable should contain such a dark horse! Finally, an enormous round of ho-hos for Mr James Callaghan — who sees himself, at nigh on 64, as the candidate of the New Generation. Mr Callaghan squeezed himself on to the crowded bench — almost squashing Mr Crosland (Aha! Symbolic!). Mr Healey, the Chancellor, did not sit in a prominent position. Perhaps he was pondering that had he known (when he said such rude things about all those Tribune voters last week) what he knew now about Mr Wilson's future. . . .

The conspiratorial chatter and all that Tory irony were drowning the Junior Employment Ministers, who were supposed to be answering routine questions. "Order! Order!" shouted the Speaker. "I don't know what's wrong with the House today."

Alas, the poignant moment of Mr Wilson's arrival coincided with a Dispatch Box answer from an earnest, highly unemotional Minister of State, Mr Booth — an artist capable of removing the pathos from the closing moments of *La Bohème*. But Mr Wilson got his cheer — though only Mr Mellish, and a few of the most slavish of Government narks, waved their order papers.

First Mr Wilson answered a routine inquiry about when an interim Royal Commission report was due. But because of the special circumstances of this Question Time the Speaker allowed questioners to stray from the point. Thus Mrs Thatcher conveyed to the Prime Minister some conventional good wishes. But you had to be fleet of ear to catch them. For, to her credit, she did not submerge us in the brand of House of Commons humbug usual on these occasions. Instead, she rasped something about hoping Mr Wilson would enjoy a happy retirement, and went on to demand that his successor call a general election.

Mr Wilson thanked her for her good wishes. But lest he lead anyone to think that she was prone to that sort of thing by nature, he quickly pointed out that "on occasions such as this, nice kind words such as hers have been used". But he added: "I totally reject what she said in the second part of her remarks. I am not sure she is all that keen on it [an election] either," at which there was a bellow of Labour laughter.

The acid, in place of celebratory champagne, continued to flow between the two leaders. Mr Wilson warned Mrs Thatcher against "a certain degree of hubris about recent by-elections". It seemed that he had taken the trouble to look up by-election swings against previous governments at this stage during previous parliaments — thus showing that, at a time when the pound was sinking fast and his public expenditure policy was in doubt, our boy had made sure he had got his research priorities right. The swings were much smaller now, he explained.

Mrs Thatcher rose again and sweetly asked: "Would he try three weeks on Thursday? We would be ready."

Frank Johnson: Daily Telegraph, *17 March 1976*

***

Wilson's successor, James Callaghan, made his own memorable exit after the confidence debate on March 28, 1979 ("The House has given its verdict . . ."). There followed the entrance of Margaret Thatcher.

A PRIME MINISTER'S DOODLE

Mrs Thatcher took her first question time yesterday. There were also important speeches on the economy from Sir Geoffrey Howe and Mr Denis Healey. But as objects for serious political analysis none of them could rival the day's main talking point: the Prime Minister's doodle.

Mrs Thatcher is believed to be the first big doodler to reach the top in British politics since Mr Attlee. Yesterday's effort, apparently inspired by Mr Healey's gripping analysis of Sir Geoffrey's problems, was an important insight into her thought.

Rival schools of doodling, Freudian, neo-Keynesian, abstract Impressionist, are bound to disagree. But those who observed the doodle from its humble beginning on the top of a clean sheet of paper (the *Morning Star* was particularly well placed to impose a Marxist interpretation) were in no doubt that it was constructed round the monogram MHR.

The letters being printed first in a small box, then in a large one, and ultimately subsumed in the finished work.

As Mrs Thatcher's many biographers will immediately notice, the letters do not lack significance, being the maiden initials of Margaret Hilda Roberts.

Whatever Mrs Thatcher was building on her early roots (a psychiatrist writes) the final product was neat and elaborate.

Opinion in the press gallery was divided about whether it looked like (a) a turbine design, (b) a Dalek, (c) Mr Healey or (d) something unpleasant to make us all work harder.

So much for important matters. Mrs Thatcher's question time was pretty good for a first-timer, though — this being before the doodling outbreak. Its self-confidence revealed one or two slightly jarring egocentric touches.

The session was marked by Labour ex-Ministers trying out their rusty talents for writing their own material and by varying degrees of toadiness from never-say-die Tory hopefuls, who are apparently unaware that the U.S. embassy job is now filled.

"Why don't you grovel a bit more?" cried Labour ex-grovellers at the Birmingham Tory, Hal Miller. Mr Callaghan made only one mild inquiry about Rhodesia, as did Mr Steel.

Mrs Thatcher seemed quite keen to recognise Bishop Muzorewa, but she gave nothing much away and sailed calmly through, unruffled even when Frank McElhone (ex-Scottish Office) raised her old friend, free school milk, and St Francis of Assisi (the patron saint of this Parliament).

"I am not known for my objectives or proposals being unclear," she told Mr Miller on the union question. She indulged herself a little more in reply to the Tory Michael Brotherton, the legendary Man from Louth, whose world view makes the maddest Ayatollah sound like a Manifesto Grouper.

For some murky motive (he cannot be an office-seeker?), Mr Brotherton made the oily suggestion that his leader should abolish the Equal Opportunities Commission because her "presence at the Dispatch Box is living proof that it is unnecessary".

"Not today," she said, "though I agree with my honourable friend that I did not exactly need it."

Mr Healey's idea of equal opportunities is for him to have equal opportunity to tell whoppers and persecute Sir Geoffrey in or out of office.

He began with a few subtle jokes, which earned him admiring cries of "Cheap", before embarking on a predictable explanation of the magnificent inheritance he had left Sir Geoffrey and the mess Sir Geoffrey had already made of it through his "irresponsible election promises".

Alas for Sir Geoffrey, the aphrodisiac of power does not seem to have worked, not yet anyway. He was courteous, mild and mournful as ever. "A dismal inheritance," he said. "Jolly lucky," said Jim. He had not promised "an economic miracle", Sir Geoffrey insisted. "Oh yes you did," they bellowed.

Michael White: The Guardian, *16 May 1979*

***

Sometimes, perhaps once in a session, a figure disappears who has risen above the throng, and it calls for a special show of affection. Norman

Shrapnel was in the gallery for the tributes to Nye Bevan, simultaneously a tenacious rebel and someone without whom the institution would never be the same, having lost a pillar.

THE DEATH OF BEVAN

"I regret to have to inform the House," the Speaker told the Commons when it met yesterday, "of the death of the Right Honourable Aneurin Bevan, the member for Ebbw Vale."

It is a frequent sort of announcement, usually applying to some devoted back-bencher of whom the public has scarcely heard. Its very formality, its acknowledgement that all men are equal at this point in their career, its traditional air of bringing the news to us as though for the first time, made it almost the most poignant moment of all this mourning day. The silence was like a groan.

The House was mourning Nye Bevan, but in one sense it was also mourning itself. Something more has died than a great political figure and a well-loved man. An entire Parliamentary era ruled by the golden tongue and the flamboyant personality has now put out its last light.

Its last active light that is to say. For the greatest of them is still with us and he was in his place yesterday. As dearest enemy and for so long target-in-chief of the ever-battling Mr Bevan, Sir Winston Churchill was perhaps the closest of all. He no longer, however, shares with us the rich and grumbling world of his memories. Now he sat huddled in his corner by the gangway, an outpost of grief.

Bevan's last gift to the Commons, as it turned out, was a posthumous one. Fine speaker that he had been, he was now the cause of fine speaking in others. The tributes paid to his memory by Mr Macmillan and Mr Gaitskell, followed by others from Mr Clement Davies and Mr James Griffiths — fellow-Welshmen both — added up to a vivid portrait that Bevan himself would have been proud to recognise. One could pay no higher tribute to a tribute than that.

Fine speaking in this context meant emotionally honest speaking, and the Prime Minister set the tone in a frank, affectionate appraisal that moved at least one Labour member to unashamed tears. "He was a genuine man," he said. "There was nothing fake or false about him."

And here quite naturally to his hand were whole sets of those paradoxes that Mr Macmillan so loves, all embodied in this dead man under whose lash, as he now almost proudly confessed, he had himself smarted. Revolutionary, but a patriot; ebullient, yet deeply serious; a man who moved in a wide circle, yet kept his simplicity; a politician — and this sounded the most paradoxical of all — who never played at politics.

So the Prime Minister went on about his old antagonist of the Back and Front Benches with a lively sadness that struck exactly the right note in mourning such a man. It was in saying that he expressed, in his personality and his career, some of the deepest feelings of humble people throughout the land that Mr Macmillan came to the heart of the matter.

Both he and Mr Gaitskell emphasised a side of Bevan that has not been made much of by the obituary writers. He was a cultivated man. (Lord Alexander of Hillsborough went still further in the Lords and called him, in no derogatory sense, an intellectual.) Nobody denied that he was a difficult man.

Mr Gaitskell, indeed, was outspoken on this theme. A fire had gone out, he said — "a fire which we sometimes found too hot, by which we were sometimes scorched, a fire which flamed and flickered unpredictably, but a fire which warmed us, cheered us, and stimulated us, a fire which affected the atmosphere of our lives here and which illuminated all our proceedings".

He did not flinch from recalling how very much at odds he and Bevan were for several years after 1951, and how strained were their personal relations — an unhappy period, he called it, followed by a loyal and fruitful partnership.

Another part of this speech that particularly gripped the attention was about their Russian visit last summer. Bevan was in great form, in spite of, as Mr Gaitskell told us, "the shadow of his approaching illness". He was utterly frank with the Russians and laughed at what he called their bourgeois puritanism.

So the last portrait was built up, stroke by stroke. Staunch, gay, courageous, dominant, Mr Gaitskell called him. Upright, downright, forthright, Mr Clement Davies added. In every mining village, Mr Griffiths softly put in, they would be saying to each other, "Our Nye is gone."

The tributes over, the House virtually emptied itself as though, just then, it had no heart for routine business. But Sir Winston sat on a little, alone with his memories. The remarkable thing was that so much that had been so truly said about Aneurin Bevan will have to be said again, one day, about him.

Norman Shrapnel, The Guardian, *8 July 1960*

***

The tributes to Bevan's powers as a speaker, a polemicist and a persuader touched on one of the Commons' favourite traditions, the oratory of the Welsh. It has a history in the place, and though its exponents are invariably described as "windbags" by their political opponents, it is still enjoyed. Neil Kinnock grew up in the tradition of that emotional speaking style, and used it effectively to help his successful campaign for the Labour Party leadership in 1983. Shortly after that victory he made his entrance in the Commons as Leader of the Opposition. His first major speech, appropriately enough for an admirer of Bevan, was on the National Health Service, created by his boyhood hero.

THE NHS

"Concern about the NHS is not limited to the Labour Party, either inside or outside the House. I know that there is concern on the Government Benches. I read the papers and I listen and hear. I hear the complaints of the hedgers who have been ditched. These include the right hon. Members for Cambridgeshire, South-East (Mr Pym), for Chelmsford (Mr St John-Stevas), for Chesham and Amersham (Sir I. Gilmour), and now the right hon. Member for Guildford (Mr Howell) has joined the honourable ranks of those who are continually offering their encoded messages and warnings to the Government about the way in which they are proceeding.

There are new figures on the scene. We now hear from the right hon. Member for Shropshire, North (Mr Biffen), the Leader of the House, and the right hon. Member for Worcester (Mr Walker), the Secretary of State for Energy. When issues about the welfare state and unemployment are raised, the right hon. Member for Waveney (Mr Prior), the Secretary of State for Northern Ireland, seems to be in a permanent state of suspended resignation. I understand that when the onset of the cuts following the election became obvious, the Secretary of State for Social Services made it clear that he disagreed with them. We see him now on television justifying the cuts and wagging his finger. The right hon. Gentleman seems to be in a permanent state of animated suspension. His protestations that there are no cuts will not wash with us.

As I have said, concern about the NHS is not limited to either side of the House or to the House generally; it extends beyond this place. More importantly, it is to be seen with greater intensity and is expressed with greater frequency by all the organisations that represent the health professions, including the Royal College of Nursing, the Royal College of Physicians, the Royal College of Surgeons, the Family Planning Association, the National Association of Health Authorities, Age Concern and all the trade unions. The list continues, and includes the Junior Hospital Doctors Committee of the British Medical Association and the BMA itself.

Recently, the secretary of the BMA said:

'Many authorities have been compelled to have recourse to measures such as transferring moneys from their capital accounts in an attempt to meet the cuts without making immediate reductions in services to patients, and this may well have long-term serious effects on the Service. It is already clear that if the cuts are carried forward into next year there will be serious consequences for patients.'

That was said not by a Labour Party spokesman, but by an organisation that is generally not terribly generous or close to the views of the Labour Party. However, it is united with us, as are many others, in unremitting antagonism to the way in which the Government are deliberately subordinating themselves to an utterly unrealistic economic and public expenditure policy, thereby seriously eroding the NHS, Britain's proudest possession.

The Secretary of State, who hears from the organisations that I have mentioned, describes them as vested interests. That is how he described them in his Conservative Party conference speech. Yes, they are vested interests, but their interests are vested in patient care, healing and recovery. Those are the vested interests to which I should think the Secretary of State would want to listen. They have a vested interest not only of professionalism — the highest in the world — but of decency and altruism. The right hon. Gentleman should listen to those people.

Of course, the Secretary of State protests that he is not after those vested interests. He says that the cuts are after 'the administrative tail'. If his protests are valid, the people who should feel most reassured are the surgeons, physicians, nurses, auxiliaries — all those who demonstrably are not in any 'tail' in the Health Service. They are what he calls the front-line personnel — the doctors and the nurses. However, those people are alarmed. They are not reassured by the Secretary of State's protests, or the protests of the Prime Minister, that the National Health Service is safe only in the hands of the Conservative Party. Those practitioners are not reassured, because they are losing jobs, and they see the deteriorating services and the lengthening waiting lists. Day by day they are up against the realities of the consequences of cuts. Our motion has been tabled because of the testimony that we have received from those people of the contempt with which the Government are treating the National Health Service.

When I put that view the Secretary of State shakes his head and says that what I say is exaggerated. He points to what he calls 'the NHS facts that give the lie to Mr Kinnock'. The right hon. Gentleman said so in the *Sunday Express* last Sunday. He may seek to give the lie to me, but that does not fool me. What bothers me is the way in which the lie that he wants to give is accepted by so many people in the country. . . .

Of course the NHS is not perfect, and we cannot say that we want to preside over waste. Of course we want to reduce any such waste and to achieve greater efficiency, but the fact remains that we are asking for more from the best in the world. The Government's policies show that they do not regard the opportunities for new and better care, new technology, care for old people and the saving of more children's lives as opportunities for investment in compassion, modern technology and efficiency, but as a burden upon public expenditure. That is their best attitude. Their other attitude is the recognition of pain as an opportunity for commercial exploitation.

Far from being a burden on public expenditure, the facilities and opportunities that modern medicine affords mean that the grave issues of life and death — not on a grandiose scale of war and peace but in the intimate matters of which child shall hear, which old person shall not be cold and which 55-year-old renal failure patient shall live and which shall die — are on the doorstep of modern governments. Such issues cannot be evaded, as the Government are trying to do.

The Government should greet with joy — with rejoicing, may I say — the opportunity that they now have to invest in liberating people from the fear and insecurity of unnecessary pain, and its prolongation, which go with the waiting lists, the health cuts and the sackings of qualified staff. According to the British Medical Association, 3,500 doctors are now unemployed. That is an unmitigated crime against the British people.

Are the Government not prepared to learn that the British Health Service is not some attractive but expendable bauble that they can allow to decay? The Health Service is above partisan politics. It is cherished and will be fought for by people of all political views. The Government should understand that the British people's affection for the NHS does not arise out of sentimentality. The public's affection is born out of its usefulness, dependability and utility. That is why they will fight to save it.

The NHS cannot be dismembered or dismantled by British Prime Ministers or foreign economists, because it is not theirs to dispose of. It belongs to the British people. They will strive to retain their proud possession because they depend upon, need and use it. They know that in defending it they are defending themselves. They are defending a service that is compassionate in its concept, efficient in its administration and effective in the alleviation of suffering. It is a service which now needs full-hearted and full-funded support to improve upon the superb level of patient care that it provides.

I beg the Government, not merely on behalf of the Opposition but on behalf of millions of people beyond, to reverse their policy towards the NHS and to invest in the combat with pain, the conquest of disease and the provision of facilities for the British people. If they do that, they will earn our gratitude, whatever political difficulty it might give us. There is something which lies beyond any disagreement that we can have in the House. It must be the extent of service for and the practical commitment to the welfare of all British people — every last one of them."

Neil Kinnock: Speech, *27 October 1983*

***

They come and they go . . . and as farewell speeches, the traditional explanation of a resignation from the backbenches by a departing Minister has always had a special appeal to MPs,and a capacity to create drama. Francis Pym's was different, because he had not resigned but had been dismissed summarily by Mrs Thatcher on the weekend she formed her second administration. The former Foreign Secretary, hurt at his departure, spoke soon afterwards in the Queen's Speech debate and made an exceptionally powerful speech, in which he expressed publicly the fears he had been voicing at the Cabinet table for four years.

BACKBENCHER AGAIN

"For the first time in 21 years, apart from a few months in 1975, I speak in the House without either the responsibility or the opportunity of Government office or party position. Like everyone celebrating 21 years, I am thinking of the future and not the past.

During the past two or three weeks, as hon. Members may well imagine, I have persistently been asked to comment on my loss of office. I have resisted the temptation to do so until now because this House is the proper place to express such views. The press and television have a vital role to play in our national political debate, but the centre of that debate is here.

It was an honour to serve as Secretary of State for Foreign and Commonwealth Affairs. I had hoped for the opportunity to continue serving the country and the Government in that capacity. Indeed, I expected to do so, but instead I was abruptly dismissed. As some of my right hon. and hon. Friends and others know, that is an acutely hurtful experience. It is all the more so in the light of press speculation which, if not deliberately inspired, was remarkably well informed. In my case, it was as much the manner of the event as the event itself which bruised me. I say this to the House today so that my silence should not be mistaken for indifference. By expressing my feelings this once, there is no more to be said about it. I shall not allow what has happened to colour my approach to the future.

It is the future that matters. I should like to say three things today. The first concerns the interpretation to be placed on the general election. We now stand at the dawn of a new Parliament, which is the right moment to reflect on the meaning of the event that has returned us all here — before it is consigned to the recesses of our memories. It is extremely important at the outset of every Parliament to interpret very carefully the election that has brought it into being. The verdict of the British people is seldom as simple as the sheer numbering of the seats might suggest. That is expecially true of this general election.

For the past 60 years two great political parties have held the stage of British politics. At this election, in different ways and to vastly differing extents, a warning has been served to each. There are some hon. Members, but more particularly people outside, who claim that the disastrous performance of the Labour Party was due to a manifesto that was not Left-wing enough. If the Labour Party listens to those people when deciding its future it will be listening to the same siren voices that have lured it on to the rocks of its present abject defeat. An objective person examining the results of the election must surely conclude that the country wants and needs as an alternative Government a moderate, left of centre party with a clear leadership and clear policies that belong to the future, not the past.

The electorate has made it abundantly plain that if the Labour Party fails during this Parliament to become such a party again, it will turn elsewhere for that requirement. What is more, I profoundly believe that that change can occur — if that is what the electorate wants — without recourse to electoral reform. Our system has never yet failed to respond appropriately to the popular will and it will not fail to do so in the future. . . .

The warning that the electorate has served to my party is of an utterly different scale and nature but it must still be understood and heeded. In the euphoria of victory, we should not forget that the Conservative Party polled fewer votes than in 1979, despite the weakness of the main opposition and despite the political inheritance of the Falklands conflict. It would be churlish indeed not to acknowledge that the victor of the campaign has been the Prime Minister. It was a great victory for her. In that case, the warning is to her as well. I believe that the message of the people to the Prime Minister is this: 'We admire your leadership, we admire your determination, we admire your sense of national pride. Will you now please prove to us that you really can use these formidable talents to serve all the people of this country — not only those who can stand on their own two feet but also those who cannot?'

That is why the challenge to the Government is the challenge to nurture and sustain the unity of our nation. The key to meeting that challenge is how the Government cope with what is by far the overwhelming problem on the nation's mind — unemployment.

The past four years have seen an enormous improvement in our economic competitiveness and the Government are entitled to take a lot of credit for that. And yet for every gain there is a price to be paid. In this case, the price has been the highest level of unemployment for 50 years. That is not the Government's fault. The Government have not caused unemployment, but part of the current level of unemployment is the price that the nation has paid for our greater economic competitiveness. The fact is that many people in Britain have made a sacrifice for a principle that they do not yet understand. The only way in which the principle will be understood and accepted is if we can now demonstrate to the nation that the sacrifice was not in vain.

I am inevitably reminded in this context of the Falklands war. In that instance, the principle for which we fought was understood throughout the nation and all round the world. On that point I am, I think, well qualified to speak. The sacrifice that was made then was not made in vain and the reward for it lay in victory.

The reward for economic sacrifice lies in victory of a different sort. It lies in the victory of hope over frustration. It lies in the prospect of a better life to come. It lies, ultimately, in the tangible fulfilment of that better life. The task of this Government is to give substance to that hope and to create the means for its fulfilment.

If we assert, as we justifiably do, that unemployment is not the Government's fault, we must, equally, acknowledge that neither is it the fault of the unemployed. We must understand their feeling of disillusion and be responsive to it. We must see to it that this country never has to make the choice between being divided but rich, or united but poor. It is our duty to ensure that such a choice never has to be made. . . .

The need to resolve those problems in a way that unites the country is one message of the election. However, there is also another message, which brings me to the last point that I wish to make today. It is the clear view of the overwhelming majority in this country that we need, as a nation, to be strong enough to defend ourselves. But there is equally no doubt that people are still deeply and understandably concerned by the present arms race. They wish to see a strategy based on the twin pillars of firmness and dialogue, and not one based on firmness alone. It seemed to me that over the years the dialogue had become a bit thin. I believed it important to start to talk more to the Soviet Union. I was doing that, and I hope that my right hon. and learned successor will continue the process.

We need to show the Russians that a more constructive relationship could be available. We need to put over to them our point of view and our aims and try to discern theirs. By talking we do not compromise or diminish our own ideals: indeed, we can make our position even more clear. And, even more important, we need to avoid the very real danger of misreading each other's intentions. None of these things is possible unless we talk to each other. I can see nothing to lose in closer contacts, and we stand to gain an understanding that can help all of us. It is something that we need to do, and something that the nation expects us to do.

Today there is a sea of new faces in this House, most of them on the Conservative benches, many of them representing constituencies that have been Labour strongholds for generations. I have no doubt that they are all aware that they have been elected to think for and to fight for all the people in those constituencies. I ask them to remember the historical role of the Conservative Party in this respect. At its best, the Conservative

Party has always been broad in its view, national in its interest, tolerant in its outlook, constructive in its debate, and unifying in its aim. This is the party that I have always served, and that I shall continue to serve in whatever capacity I can."

Francis Pym: Speech, *29 June 1983*

***

The thrill of an arrival or of an abrupt departure is at the heart of the political game. Trollope sensed it, though to his regret he did not experience it at first hand, and Phineas Finn had a fictional political life familiar to so many practitioners of the art — starting with the delicious fear of a maiden speech, rising to prominence, and ending in failure.

A BEGINNING AND AN END

Phineas took his seat in the House with a consciousness of much inward trepidation of heart on that night of the ballot debate. After leaving Lord Chiltern he went down to his club and dined alone. Three or four men came and spoke to him; but he could not talk to them at his ease, nor did he quite know what they were saying to him. He was going to do something which he longed to achieve, but the very idea of which, now that it was so near to him, was a terror to him. To be in the House and not to speak would, to his thinking, be a disgraceful failure. Indeed, he could not continue to keep his seat unless he spoke. He had been put there that he might speak. He would speak. Of course he would speak. Had he not already been conspicuous almost as a boy orator? And yet, at this moment he did not know whether he was eating mutton or beef, or who was standing opposite to him and talking to him, so much was he in dread of the ordeal which he had prepared for himself. As he went down to the House after dinner, he almost made up his mind that it would be a good thing to leave London by one of the night mail trains. He felt himself to be stiff and stilted as he walked, and that his clothes were uneasy to him. When he turned into Westminster Hall he regretted more keenly than ever he had done that he had seceded from the keeping of Mr Low. He could, he thought, have spoken very well in court, and would there have learned that self-confidence which now failed him so terribly. It was, however, too late to think of that. He could only go in and take his seat.

He went in and took his seat, and the chamber seemed to him to be mysteriously large, as though benches were crowded over benches, and galleries over galleries. He had been long enough in the House to have lost the original awe inspired by the Speaker and the clerks of the House, by the row of Ministers, and by the unequalled importance of the place. On ordinary occasions he could saunter in and out, and whisper at his ease to a neighbour. But on this occasion he went direct to the bench on which he ordinarily sat, and began at once to rehearse to himself his speech. He had in truth been doing this all day, in spite of the effort that he had made to rid himself of all memory of the occasion. He had been collecting the heads of his speech while Mr Low had been talking to him, and refreshing his quotations in the presence of Lord Chiltern and the dumb-bells. He had taxed his memory and his intellect with various tasks, which, as he feared, would not adjust themselves one with another. He had learned the headings of his speech — so that one heading might follow the other, and nothing be forgotten. And he had learned verbatim the words which he intended to utter under each heading — with a hope that if any one compact part should be destroyed or injured in its compactness by treachery of memory, or by the course of the debate, each other compact part might be there in its entirety, ready for use — or at least so many of the compact parts as treachery of memory and the accidents of the debate might leave to him; so that his speech might be like a vessel, watertight in its various compartments, that would float by the buoyancy of its stern and bow, even though the hold should be waterlogged. But this use of his composed words, even though he should be able to carry it through, would not complete his work — for it would be his duty to answer in some sort those who had gone before him, and in order to do this he must be able to insert, without any prearrangement of words or ideas, little intercalatory parts between those compact masses of argument with which he had been occupying himself for many laborious hours. As he looked round upon the House and perceived everything was dim before him, that all his original awe of the House had returned, and with it a present quaking fear that made him feel the pulsations of his own heart, he became painfully aware that the task he had prepared for himself was too great. . .

The day of the debate had come, and Phineas Finn was still sitting in his room at the Colonial Office. But his resignation had been sent in and accepted, and he was simply awaiting the coming of his successor. About noon his successor came, and he had the gratification of resigning his armchair to Mr Bonteen. It is generally understood that gentlemen leaving offices give up either seals or a portfolio. Phineas had been in possession of no seal and no portfolio; but there was in the room which he occupied a special armchair, and this with much regret he surrendered to the use and comfort of Mr Bonteen. There was a glance of triumph in his enemy's eyes, and an exultation in the tone of his enemy's voice, which were very bitter to him. "So you are really going?" said Mr Bonteen. "Well; I dare say it is all very proper. I don't quite understand the thing myself, but I have no doubt you are right." "It isn't easy to understand; is it?" said Phineas, trying to laugh. But Mr Bonteen did not feel the intended satire, and poor Phineas found it useless to attempt to punish the man he hated. He left him as quickly as he could, and went to say a few words of farewell to his late chief.

"Goodbye, Finn," said Lord Cantrip. "It is a great trouble to me that we should have to part in this way."

"And to me also, my lord. I wish it could have been avoided."

"You should not have gone to Ireland with so dangerous a man as Mr Monk. But it is too late to think of that now."

"The milk is spilt; is it not?"

"But these terrible rendings asunder never last very long," said Lord Cantrip, "unless a man changes his opinions altogether. How many quarrels and how many reconciliations we have lived to see! I remember when Gresham went out of office, because he could not sit in the same room with Mr Mildmay, and yet they became the fastest of political friends. There was a time when Plinlimmon and the Duke could not stable their horses together at all; and don't you remember when Palliser was obliged to give up his hopes of office because he had some bee in his bonnet?" I think, however, that the bee in Mr Palliser's bonnet to which Lord Cantrip was alluding made its buzzing audible on some subject that was not exactly political. "We shall have you back again before long, I don't doubt. Men who can really do their work are too rare to be left long in the comfort of the benches below the gangway." This was very kindly said, and Phineas was flattered and comforted. He could not, however, make Lord Cantrip understand the whole truth. For him the dream of a life of politics was over for ever. He had tried it, and had succeeded beyond his utmost hopes; but, in spite of his success, the ground had crumbled to pieces beneath his feet, and he knew that he could never recover the niche in the world's gallery which he was now leaving.

That same afternoon he met Mr Gresham in one of the passages leading to the House, and the Prime Minister put his arm through that of our hero as they walked together into the lobby. "I am sorry that we are losing you," said Mr Gresham.

"You may be sure that I am sorry to be so lost," said Phineas.

Anthony Trollope: Phineas Finn

Epilogue

"My dear fellow," said Holmes, as we sat on either side of the fire in his lodgings at Baker Street, "life is infinitely stranger than anything which the mind of man could invent. We would not dare to conceive the things which are really mere commonplaces of existence. If we could fly out of that window hand in hand, hover over this great city, gently remove the roofs, and peep in at the queer things which are going on, the strange coincidences, the plannings, the cross-purposes, the wonderful chain of events, working through generations, and leading to the most *outré* results, it would make all fiction with its conventionalities and foreseen conclusions most stale and unprofitable."

—Arthur Conan Doyle: *A Case of Identity*

A WHIFF of old times still clings to Westminster. The place can't shake off a sense of the past, of a world of gaslit streets, melodramatic politics, perhaps a special kind of theatricality — the imagined excitements of a lost world of colour and character which becomes, in the end, romance. So looking for that atmosphere it's natural enough to think of the scene at 221b Baker Street, where Holmes and Watson sit expectant at the fire, listening for the footstep of the anxious client on the stair. Alan Watkins, a columnist successively with the *Sunday Express* (as Crossbencher), *The Spectator*, the *New Statesman* and now *The Observer*, has long been a political voyeur with the urge to freshen the contemporary political world with that air of melodrama. It is 1968. At Westminster the Parliamentary Labour Party is in turmoil, as usual, and Harold Wilson is nervous of threats to his leadership from Cabinet plotters, as usual. A figure resembling Gerald Kaufman, ever the faithful retainer, scurries off to serve his leader. In Whitehall, George Brown, the Foreign Secretary, prepares for a party. A hansom rattles off to Baker Street. Politics, skulduggery and fantasy are about to come together again.

A FINAL PROBLEM SOLVED

It was a fine evening in mid-March, and the rain beat an incessant tattoo upon the windows of our sitting-room. My friend Sherlock Holmes and I sat beside a roaring fire made up of old boots, back numbers of Hansard, discarded colour supplements and statements by the Prime Minister.

"Ah, Watson," said he, "times are very dull, to be sure. I have looked through the entire press and find nothing of interest, with the exception of a letter in today's *Times* which leads me to believe that the Parliamentary Labour Party is quite insane. The students continue to be restless, I see." "I observe," said I, "that Mr Worsthorne has come out in their support."

"The paradox was only to be expected," replied Holmes. "The signs were there for all to read. But I will not bore you with my deductions. No, my dear chap, I see nothing for us in this student business." So saying, my friend went over to the sideboard and prepared to inject himself with a concentrated solution of the speeches of Mr Edward Heath. This was a drug to which Holmes would occasionally resort in quiet times, guaranteed as it was to produce several days of complete oblivion.

"Wait, Holmes," I cried, for I hated to see my old friend in one of his despairing moods. "Is there no mystery in the resignation of Sir Con O'Neill?" "Alas I fear not," said he. "The fellow appears to have explained his position adequately enough, although I grant you there may be more than meets the eye in the actions of Mr Brown."

Just then there was a tap at the door, and a messenger entered bearing a heavy cream envelope. Dismissing the messenger with a sharp kick, Holmes tore open the envelope and settled down to read. "Ha," he exclaimed, "our services appear to be required. What do you make of that?" I began to read. "A gentleman of the utmost probity," went the note, "will shortly be calling upon you to discuss a matter of national importance. Your discretion must be absolute." The note was unsigned.

"There are few clues there," said I, baffled. "On the contrary," replied Holmes, "it appears to me that we are shortly to be plunged into the world of politics." "How on earth do you make that out, Holmes?" said I. "From the fact," replied my friend, "that the note is written on House of Commons headed paper. It is really very simple. But I venture to think that our curiosity will not remain unsatisfied much longer. For here, unless I am very mistaken, is the gentleman himself."

As he spoke, there was a knock at the door and our visitor was shown in by the landlady. A second fellow in a mackintosh, accompanied by two Alsatian dogs, stood on the landing outside. Our guest entered diffidently. He was of middle height, with spectacles, and a bald head. I judged him to be in his mid-thirties and of sedentary habits. He bore the indefinable stamp of a man who, in his younger days, had knocked about the rough world of Fleet Street.

"Oh Mr Holmes," said he, "thank God I find you in. We are at our wits' end to know what to do, and you are our veritable last hope." "Pray compose yourself, my dear Sir, and be seated," replied Holmes. "Tell me your story, and I will see what can be done." "And this gentleman?"

"He is my friend and colleague, and to be trusted absolutely." "Well,

Sir, it is like this," said our visitor. "The gentleman by whom I am employed is distressed at the constant attacks made upon the Prime Minister in the national press. He is still more distressed at the rumours of plots to oust the Prime Minister from his position. Being a patriotic and public-spirited gentleman, he is determined to get to the bottom of these stories, particularly the latter. We have tried everybody — private investigators, the Whips' office, Lord Wigg — and you are the last man who can help us."

"Sir, if I am to help you, you must conceal nothing from me," said Holmes sternly, absent-mindedly knocking out his pipe on our visitor's head. "Who's your principal in this matter?" Our strange visitor stiffened. "I confess, Sir," he replied, "that I do not greatly care for your tone of voice. My principles, despite the jibes you may read from time to time, are as good as yours. Similarly my master is a God-fearing gentleman who has nothing but the best interests of this dear country at heart. He has been sorely maligned of late." Holmes laughed heartily, dislodging a bust of the Queen and causing a twinge of pain in my shrapnel-wound from the Afghan campaign. "Pray do not distress yourself, Sir," said he. "Your principles do not professionally concern me. I was merely inquiring on whose behalf you were acting." "That I cannot tell you." "But I think I know," said Holmes. "Your principal is none other than the Prime Minister of England."

"Why, Holmes," I cried out in astonishment, "it is impossible. How did you know?" "From the fact," replied my friend, "that our distinguished visitor is frequently pictured in the press and on television, walking two paces behind the Prime Minister on his numerous travels. I wonder you had not noticed. But it is of no consequence. Well, Sir," he went on to our guest, "I will see what I can do." "Thank you a million times over," responded our visitor. "I promise you will not find the Prime Minister ungrateful. Should an ambassadorship fall vacant, should Mr Freeman decide to leave Washington . . ." "One of the surviving members of the red-headed league," murmured Holmes. "But I must respectfully decline. My only reward is my work." And, with this, our visitor left.

"Well, this is a pretty problem and no mistake," mused Holmes. "I suggest that you, Watson, should make a tour of the various ministries, disguised as a member of the press. The accredited political correspondents are, as I understand the position, well known. It will therefore be necessary for you to pose as an itinerant member of the *Sunday Times* 'Insight' team. The editor, Mr Harold Evans, is a public-spirited fellow who is known to me. However, your clothes will need attention. I recommend a button-down shirt and trousers supported by a belt. Fortunately moustaches are in fashion. But your manner must, at all costs, be enthusiastic and brisk. And take your life-preserver, for we are dealing with some desperate characters." "And what will you do,

Holmes?" said I. "My dear fellow," he replied, "I shall merely sit here and think."

The next day found me at the office of Mrs Barbara Castle at the Ministry of Transport. Alas, even I am not at liberty to disclose fully what passed between us. Suffice it to say that her conversation almost entirely concerned a complicated Bill whose details I could but dimly apprehend. She appeared uninterested in the rest of the Government's policy. As for the Prime Minister, she confessed herself unable to support all his actions, but maintained he was her dearest colleague and friend. Mr Crossman made similar replies, and I further gathered that Mr Jenkins was now one of the Prime Minister's closest allies. Throughout my travels on that weary day I did not, it is true, discover any notable enthusiasm for the Prime Minister, but nor did I discover any evidence of conspiracy. Later that evening I reported my findings to Holmes.

"It is just as I thought," he said. "You have done well, Watson." "What do you mean, Holmes?" said I. "The plot is that there is no plot," he replied. With this, he pointed to a headline in the evening newspaper: "Left rallies to Wilson after new 'plot' stories". "Does this mean, Holmes," I inquired angrily, "that we have been used?" "Who are we to judge?" replied my friend with a shrug. "Let us stroll down to Mr Brown's party at the Foreign Office, to which I have been invited. Covent Garden palls, and I am told the Foreign Secretary has been in good voice lately. At least the traditions of the English music-hall are not wholly extinct."

Alan Watkins: New Statesman, *15 March 1968*

Index

Entries in bold type indicate the author of an extract or, in the case of a speech, the speaker. Names are listed as they appear in the text: subsequent ennoblement, for example, is treated as an anachronism and omitted from the index.

INDEX